Little Turkey in Great Britain

TRANSNATIONAL PRESS LONDON

Little Turkey in Great Britain

Ibrahim Sirkeci, Tuncay Bilecen, Yakup Çoştu, Saniye Dedeoğlu, M. Rauf Kesici, B. Dilara Şeker, Fethiye Tilbe, K. Onur Unutulmaz

TRANSNATIONAL PRESS LONDON
2016

LITTLE TURKEY IN GREAT BRITAIN

Ibrahim Sirkeci, Tuncay Bilecen, Yakup Çoştu, Saniye Dedeoğlu, Mehmet Rauf Kesici, Betül Dilara Şeker, Fethiye Tilbe, Kadir Onur Unutulmaz

First Published in 2016 by TRANSNATIONAL PRESS LONDON in the Ukinted Kingdom, 12 Ridgeway Gardens, London, N6 5XR, UK. www.tplondon.com

Paperback

ISBN: 978-1-910781-37-1

Cover Design: Nihal Yazgan

Contents

Acknowledgements

Several chapters in this book have drawn upon various independent research projects which are carried our individually and/or as a group. Some of the studies are supported by generous grants from institutions and external bodies. Therefore, we are grateful to a series of organisations for their support. These include: "Positional Determinants of the immigrants from Turkey in the Labour Market in London" project supported by TUBITAK 2219 Program; "Understanding the acculturation patterns and adaptation processes of migrants in Turkey" project supported by TUBITAK 2236 Program.

We would like to thank the reviewers, committee members and participants of Turkish Migration Conferences 2014 in London and 2015 in Prague where majority of the studies mentioned here were presented and we have benefited from the feedback received. We thank our colleagues at respective universities who helped and supported our research and writing up of this book. We also thank many individuals, researchers, research assistants and more importantly respondents who kindly answered our –sometimes, very cumbersome and demanding- questions. We thank Emine Akman, Ezgi Kızıltan, Thomas Long, Burcu Oskay, Mustafa Ökmen, Buğra Özer, Therese Svensson, Güven Şeker and Ali Taşyurdu for their assistance and support at various stages of research which this book is drawing upon.

Finally, we also thank our families for their continuous support and love despite our occasional absence from various chores at home.

About the authors

Dr Tuncay Bilecen is Assistant Professor at Kandıra Vocational School of Kocaeli University, where he also completed his undergraduate and graduate education. At Master's level, he has studied post-Balkan War Migration Movements. Dr Bilecen completed his PhD research on Birikim journal at Sakarya University, Department of Public Administration. In 2013, he was a visiting researcher at Westminster University, London with a research scholarship from YÖK (Council of Higher Education), conducting a field research on the political participation of Turkish migrants. In 2014-2015, with a scholarship from TÜBİTAK (The scientific and Technological Research Council of Turkey) he carried out further research on political participation of migrants from Turkey in London as a visiting researcher at Regent's University's Centre for Transnational Studies. The author is also investigating political participation, urban rights and democratic theory. He is member of the Editorial Board for *Göç Dergisi*.

Dr Yakup Çoştu is Associate Professor in Sociology of Religion Department at Hitit University, Çorum, Turkey. He is a graduate of Ondokuz Mayıs University (BA, MA, PhD). Dr Çoştu has conducted research in the UK (2007-2008 at SOAS, London University and 2012 at London Metropolitan University) and Germany (2012 at Osnabrück University). He has published several books, book chapters and articles in national/international peer reviewed journals as well as being a frequent participant to international conferences at home and abroad. He is the editor of Hitit University Journal of Social Sciences Institute (HÜSBED).

Dr Saniye Dedeoglu is an Associate Professor in the department of Labour Economics and Industrial Relations at the University of Mugla, Turkey and has been a Marie Curie Research Fellow at Warwick University, UK. She gained her PhD degree in 2005 from the School of Oriental and African Studies (University of London) based on her research examining women's garment work in Istanbul. She is the author *Migrants, Work and Social Integration: Women's Labour in the Turkish Ethnic Economy*, Palgrave (2014) and *Women Workers in Turkey: Global Industrial Production in Istanbul*, I.B. Tauris (2008-2012) and the co-editor *Gender and Society in Turkey: The Impact of Neoliberal Policies, Political Islam and EU Accession*, I.B. Tauris (2012). Her research interests include women's industrial work, labour migration, and Turkish ethnic economy in Europe.

Dr Mehmet Rauf Kesici was Associate Professor of Labour Markets at Kocaeli University, Turkey. He was dismissed in September 2016 as a result of his signature on the petition for peace titled, "we will not be a party to this crime". His past studies include projects funded by The Scientific and Technological Research Council of Turkey and Council of Higher Education. He has published widely on the labour market, migration, unemployment, employment policy and poverty while conducting research in Turkey and the UK. He has been a member of Scientific Review Board of several peer-reviewed journals including *Çalışma Toplum* and *Göç Dergisi*. He has published several journal articles, book chapters and a book (*Emek Piyasaları*, 2013, Dipnot Yayını).

Prof Ibrahim Sirkeci is Professor of Transnational Studies and Marketing and the Director of the Regent's Centre for Transnational Studies (RCTS) at Regent's University London (UK). Sirkeci holds a PhD in Geography from the University of Sheffield (UK) and a BA in Political Science and Public Administration from Bilkent University (Turkey). Prior to joining Regent's University London in 2005, Sirkeci had worked at the University of Bristol. His main areas of expertise are human mobility, Transnational Marketing and consumers, minorities, labour markets, remittances, and integration. He is the editor of several journals including *Migration Letters* and *Transnational Marketing Journal*. His books include *Transnational Marketing and Transnational Consumers* (Springer, 2013), *Migration and Remittances during the Global Financial Crisis and Beyond* (World Bank, 2012 with J. Cohen and D. Ratha), and *Cultures of Migration, the global nature of contemporary mobility* (University of Texas Press, 2011 with J. Cohen). He is the chair of *The Migration Conference* series since 2012.

Dr Betül Dilara Şeker was Assistant Professor of Psychology and Head of Department for Psychology at Celal Bayar University, Manisa, Turkey. She is a graduate of Ege University where she has completed her PhD in Social Psychology. Before joining Manisa Celal Bayar University in 2012, Dr Şeker has worked at Van Yüzüncü Yıl University. She has moved to academia after a spell as a teacher working at Ministry of Education. She has carried out research in London while she was a post-doctoral visiting researcher at Regent's Centre for Transnational Studies at Regent's University in 2013. Her recent research mainly focuses on acculturation, and migrant integration.

Dr Fethiye Tilbe works at Department of Labour Economics, Namik Kemal University, Tekirdag, Turkey. She was a visiting research fellow at Regent's Centre for Transnational Studies, Regent's University London at the time this study was carried out. Tilbe earned her PhD in Labour Economics from Marmara University, Istanbul. She has carried out field research among immigrant communities in London in 2014 – 2015. Her research on irregular migrant remittances in London was funded by a grant from Turkish Scientific Research Council (TUBITAK). Her recent research focuses on remittances and irregular migration.

Dr Kadir Onur Unutulmaz received his doctorate from the University of Oxford in Social and Cultural Anthropology in 2014. His doctoral research focused on the Turkish-speaking communities in London. He received a Master's Degree from Oxford in Migration Studies in 2009 and another Master's Degree in International Relations in 2007 from Koç University in Istanbul. Unutulmaz also holds two undergraduate degrees, both received in 2005 from Boğaziçi University in Istanbul, in Political Science & International Relations and Sociology. Dr. Unutulmaz currently working as a full-time member of faculty at the Faculty of Political Sciences, at the Social Sciences University of Ankara. He is currently involved in several projects concerning mostly Syrian refugees, including one EU Horizon 2020 project on adult education policies towards refugees in Turkey and an IOM project with the Directorate General of Migration Management on supporting Turkey to create a Strategic Document and Action Plan on its emerging integration policy.

Introduction

Turkey saw mass labour migrations in the 1960s and 1970s, refugee migrations in the 1980s, asylum seeker flows through the 1990s, and irregular migration flows over decades from the late 1980s onwards. Migration to the UK was part of these larger population flows from Turkey. In all five distinct periods of Turkish emigration, there were some destined to the UK: 1) Unskilled and skilled workers's migration dominated the first period from 1961 to mid-1970s; 2) Family reunifications from the late 1970s onwards; 3) Refugees and asylum seekers along with contract workers to Arab countries from the late 1970s onwards; 4) Irregular migration to Western Europe in the late 1990s and 2000s; and 5) Contemporary migration from Turkey which is more varied in composition and mechanisms since the 2000s. The last two periods are also marked with the emergence of a Turkish culture of migration which ensures steady outflows but also attracts inflows from the countries where sizeable Turkish populations are present (Sirkeci, Şeker, Çağlar, 2015).

Nevertheless, migration from Turkey to the British Isles do not fit to this story line perfectly but there is still a long history producing a sizeable diaspora population and enclaves of people with origins in Turkey that have emerged in the last four to five decades. Earlier groups that arrived were Cypriots fleeing the troubled island in the Eastern Mediterranean whilst many Turks and Kurds of the mainland were not even considering the UK as a destination in the 1960s and 1970s. Migration flows from mainland Turkey to the UK have been influenced by the three key political events in Turkey. The 1980 military coup in Turkey brought a subsequent wave of Turkish movers to the UK. Prior to the 1980 military coup, a sizeable group of Alevis had arrived as refugees following the Maraş massacre in the late 1970s. The third wave of movers from Turkey was the Kurds who arrived mostly as asylum seekers mainly from south-eastern Turkey in response to the protracted armed conflict between Turkish troops and the PKK which also involved forced displacement of local populations by the State in southeastern Turkey. Though UK's Turkish diaspora community is not as large as some other ethnic groups such as Indians, it is similarly fragmented through ethnic, religious and political differences.

In line with the propositions of the conflict model of human mobility, Turks, Kurds, Arabs, Cypriots, Laz, Circassians, Zazas, Alevis, Sunnis, and others fled Turkey to avoid conflicts, to overcome difficulties and barriers, and to escape from disagreements, tensions, dislikes over the last six decades. Each and every group as well as every individual within those groups has a unique story of conflicting interests and disagreements with what was at offer back in Turkey. Some of these are latent tensions quietly left behind whereas some others are explicit and gross conflicts which cannot be ignored and preferred not to be ignored. The latter has been brought and cultivated in 'diaspora'. Kurdish and Alevi identities are prominent issues among these brought over conflicts. This book's title emerged out of another such discussion of whether to call some communities as 'Turks in Britain' or 'British Turks'. It feels more like a half-way house between the two. The tensions between the Turks and Kurds as well as Alevis and Sunnis are as alive in the UK as they are back in Turkey and are so many shades of these tensions on a spectrum so colourful. These distinct groups that may look identical to a foreign eye have their own communities, institutions and ways in which they integrate with the mainstream and other minority populations in Britain. In any sphere of life, one may spot several nearly identical, competitive initiatives. Several think tanks reflecting the crack lines of politics in Turkey, several mosques representing different interpretations common in certain parts of Turkey, even academic groupings divided along certain political lines set in stone long ago back in Turkey.

It is important for us to clarify our definition of the population we examine here. Choice of a name is always problematic but for migrants from Turkey and Turkish Cyprus, the term 'Turkish speaking community' is commonly used. It is meant to refer to three major ethnic communities, i.e. Turkish-Cypriots, Turks, and Kurds from Turkey as well as some other minor groups such as Bulgarian or German citizens with Turkish ethnic origins. There are various analytical reasons to justify referring to these very diverse groups of people as a 'Turkish speaking community' which is widely used as an operational definition (e.g. Aksoy, 2006; Atay, 2010; Issa, 2005; Lytra & Baraç, 2009; King et al., 2008; Küçükcan, 1999; Mehmet Ali, 2001; Strüder, 2003; Unutulmaz, 2014; Wright & Kurtoglu-Hooton, 2006). Turkish is not the mother tongue for many of the individuals who are referred to in this book, however it is spoken and understood by a vast majority of them. There are Kurds speaking Kurdish and Zazaki as well as many individuals from second and third generations who express themselves in English better than any other language. Nevertheless, the focus of our study is all these groups who are either migrants from Turkey (including Turkish controlled part of Cyprus) or their descendants. These groups share a geographical and more importantly political, cultural and socio-economic space in London and elsewhere in the UK. Thus, they are engaged with one another, if not totally integrated. There is no intention to suggest or imply a cultural or otherwise homogeneity.

2

Turkish migration, like any other migration stream, has also been coloured by various conflicts. Population movements from mainland Turkey and Turkish part of Cyprus are outcomes of major conflicts at the macro level as well as not so openly expressed conflicts at micro level. While the mass movement of Kurds and Alevis from Anatolia are linked to open confrontations and violent clashes particularly in the 1980s and 1990s, Turkish Cypriots have fled the Mediterranean island in response to the protracted conflict between Turkey, Greece, Greek Cypriots and Turkish Cypriots since the 1950s. As presented in chapter four, detailed accounts of a new wave of movers benefiting from the Ankara Agreement of 1963 show that individual narratives refer to rather subtle conflicts, clashes of interests, dissatisfactions, disagreements and difficulties among their motives for migration.

This book is about these contemporary movers originating from Turkey, their movement trajectories, experiences, practices, and integration in Britain. Eight researchers from different disciplinary backgrounds and methodological schools came together to do the groundwork for students of this emerging subfield of migration studies. Turkey is now at the forefront of accommodating large-scale inward mobility mostly due to the crises in Syria and Iraq. This also brings some attention to Turkey's own diasporic populations as well as Turkey's migration history.

Unlike large Turkish communities found in countries like Germany, the Netherlands, Austria, and Switzerland; Turks, Kurds and Turkish Cypriots are relatively small minority groups in the United Kingdom. Despite some unsubstantiated claims by several NGOs, thinktanks and some 'careless' academics, the number of movers originated from Turkey and Turkish section of Cyprus and their descendants born in the UK are estimated to be somewhere between 180,000 and 250,000 (Sirkeci & Esipova, 2013). We believe anything beyond this range are unsubstantiated claims, which, unfortunately, are very common. The number of arrivals, asylum seekers, settlements, naturalisations, and some demographic trends are presented in this book. Nevertheless, this relatively small population has been part and parcel of a British-Turkish culture of migration. That is to say that now a two-way migration corridor is established between the two countries and increasing exposure to what is "Turkish" have made Turkey a potential destination for British to visit more often and settle in thousands. Perhaps not comparable to the size of Turkish population in Britain but a significant number of British citizens have already settled in Turkey, particularly in southwest coastal areas.

The events unfolded in Turkey since 2011, Gezi protests, 17-25 December operations, general and presidential elections, restarting conflicts between the state and PKK (Kurdistan Workers' Party), the failed military coup on 15 July 2016 and the purge that followed have provided more fuel to the fire. Thus, one should expect more immigration from Turkey to Britain in the near future. These flows may include some asylum seeking movers but given the established culture of migration between the two countries, all types of movers arriving in various channels are more likely. While the purge pushes more intellectuals and academics arriving, Ankara Agreement and education opportunities are likely to be exploited more often by Turkish citizens who seek security.

Starting with the migration of Cypriot Turks in the 1940s, growing with Turkish immigrants from Turkey in the 1970s, and also the Kurdish immigrants from Turkey in the 1990s, nowadays Britain has a sizeable population composed of Cypriot Turks, Turks and Kurds from Turkey (Ladbury, 1977; Robins & Aksoy, 2001; Mehmet Ali, 2001; Issa, 2005). These immigrant communities have a heterogeneous composition owing to differences in their life styles, experiences, ideas, feelings, hopes and expectations. Therefore, these immigrants have been observed living in the different ethnic, ideological, cultural and religious communities for decades.

Content of this book

In this book, we have attempted to provide a comprehensive account of social, economic, cultural, religious, and demographic aspects of the population in London who originally came from Turkey and Turkish part of Cyprus. In chapter one, we present the facts about the size, spatial characteristics and some other features of this particular population.

In chapter two, we are outlining the main patterns of ethnic and religious identity, mother tongue, preferred languages used on a day to day basis, as well as employment and education as indicators of integration. There are significant differences between Turkish and Kurdish segments as well as men and women regarding various aspects of identity and integration.

Chapter three discusses findings from our study on political participation in London. It is clear that political interests and participation levels differ between Turkish Cypriots, Turks and Kurds partly determined by the contemporary political agenda, political baggages brought in from Turkey, and migration history.

Ankara Agreement has a special place in Turkish movers in London as when the other "doors" for immigration faded this special agreement signed in 1973 (and became binding for the UK in 1963, when the country joined the European Economic Community) emerged as another formal channel to move to the UK. We dissect the moves and challenges faced by these particular movers in chapter four.

Chapters five and six focus on labour market and employment experiences of movers from Turkey with a particular focus on London where majority resides. The role of ethnic economy and women's -often hidden- contribution is discussed in these chapters.

Chapter seven begins with a snapshot of remittances by Turkish movers in the UK before moving onto outlining the ways and mechanisms used and invented at the face of cost and security challenges when sending usually small – and sometimes large- sums of money to Turkey.

Chapter eight offers an inventory of religious organisations formed in the UK by movers from Turkey. The diversity of religious convictions is obvious while the main purposes of these organisations univocally include the desire to preserve the heritage cultures. Some organisations are seemingly more politicised than others.

In chapter nine, we move away from what is "political" but still serious as we look into football and its magic power in bringing adversary groups together literally on the same pitch. We look into ways in which identity is negotiated and renegotiated through ethnic community football leagues established and organised by Turkish speaking communities for over four decades.

This book is an attempt to offer a comprehensive understanding of multiple facets of diaspora communities of Turkish origin in the UK. We have covered certain aspects better than others and surely there are features and issues left out. Nevertheless, we do hope our effort will be perceived as a first step to better understanding this particular group of movers and will be of use in understanding others in other contexts and countries.

Sirkeci, Bilecen, Çoştu, Dedeoğlu, Kesici, Şeker, Tilbe, Unutulmaz

Chapter 1. The Numbers about Turks, Kurds and Turkish Cypriots

The number of Turks, Kurds and Turkish Cypriots in the UK is interestingly controversial. Many in the community believe that there are about half a million Turks in the UK if not more. Some even go further arguing only Turkish Cypriots are that many or Alevis are in several hundred thousands. We believe the "half a million Turks" figure is coming from a vague and careless comment quoted in a parliamentary commission hearing. We also understand the sentiments among the community leaders and members who simply want to make an impression to claim perhaps political significance. Nevertheless, none of these figures is based on hard evidence and they lack credibility. Therefore, it is important to clarify what we know and what we do not know about the size, composition and spread of this particular population.

Population statistics and statistics on international migration are always a little contested however in most European countries we have relatively good statistics compared to many other parts of the world. Population statistics in the UK are largely based on the last population census which took place in 2011. We present here the statistics publicly available from the Office of National Statistics, government departments, and from international organisations.

Emigration from Turkey

Turkish Ministry of Foreign Affairs claim that more than 5 million Turkish citizens are living outside Turkey, around 4 million of whom reside in Western Europe, 300,000 in Northern America, 200,000 in the Middle East and 150,000 in Australia[1]. Although this number is relatively low in comparison to the total number of Turkey's population (6%), it is significantly large compared to some smaller European Union member countries. According to Turkish official statistics (YTB, 2011), the overwhelming majority of Turkish migrants and family members live in Germany ([1,527,118][2] - 2,500,000), France (541,000), the Netherlands (384,000), Belgium (160,000), Switzerland (120,000), Austria (112,000), and the United Kingdom (180,000-250,000) (Sirkeci & Esipova, 2013), and smaller populations in Denmark (Yazgan, 2010; Yazgan, 2012) and Sweden (Baser, 2014) excluding the former Turkish citizens who were

---

[1] See for details, http://www.mfa.gov.tr/the-expatriate-turkish-citizens.en.mfa (Date Accessed: 25.01.2015). United Nations reports about 2,545,214 Turkish born outside Turkey by around year 2000 (http://data.un.org/ Accessed: 25:01.2015).

[2] Turkish population in Germany by 31 Dec. 2014 according to Statistiches Bundesamt (2015).

naturalized in these countries. Turkish Ministry of Labour and Social Security statistics[3] reveal that an important portion of Turkish migrant workers and their families have so far acquired the citizenship of their host countries. Majority of these populations are built around communities who arrived in the 1960s and 1970s. The dominant feature of population flows has changed over time. For example, family-related population movements (reunification and marriage) are different in terms of legal mechanisms but they are part and parcel of the overall mobility. After the energy crisis in the 1970s, the volume of family migration had risen mostly due to restrictions in other migration categories. Asylum seeker and refugee flows have dominated a period from the 1980s till 2000s when other migration channels were tightened. Total number of asylum applications by Turkish citizens in industrialised countries between 1980 and 2011 were 1,033,000 (Sirkeci and Esipova, 2013:3). Although the volume of asylum seekers from Turkey sharply decreased over the last decade, as of July 2014, the total number of refugees originating from Turkey was 65,900.[4] The number of asylum applications lodged by Turkish citizens between 2010 and 2016, though, has reached 41,224 and there has been an upsurge in the aftermath of the 15 July failed military coup and the purges followed according to the UNHCR. The number of asylum applications by Turkish citizens filed in industrialised countries rose three times in July-August 2016 compared to previous year. Corresponding number of applications lodged in Germany have increased six fold.

Variations of mover categories in countries can also be seen in response to national legislations. For example, in the UK, due to further restrictions on immigration, many Turkish citizens arrive with visas based on Ankara Agreement[5] which provides special advantages while limiting settlement

---

[3] Between 1972 and 2009, the number of Turkish citizens who obtained German citizenship is 777,904. Between 1946 and 2008, that number for Dutch citizenship is 259,958. Between 1985 and 2008, Turkish citizens who chose Belgian citizenship amounts to 130,374. Austrian citizenship between 1999 and 2009 is 88,597. Between 1991 and 2008, the number of Turkish citizens who obtained French citizenship is 71,323. The number of Turkish citizens in these countries as of 31 December 2010 are respectively; Germany 1,629,480, Netherlands 372,728, Belgium 39,419, Austria 110,678, and France 459,611. (Calisma ve Sosyal Guvenlik Bakanligi, http://www.csgb.gov.tr/ csgbPortal/ diyih.portal?page=yv&id=1) (Date Accessed: 26.01.2015). The number between 1980 and 2011 for British citizenship is 78,296 and the number of Turkish born people in England and Wales increased from 52,396 in 2001 to 91,115 in 2011 according to the UK Census (Sirkeci & Esipova, 2013:6).

[4] 2015 UNHCR country operations profile – Turkey, http://www.unhcr.org/ pages/49e48e0fa7f.html, (Date Accessed: 31.01.2015).

[5] The Ankara Agreement, aka the Ankara Association Agreement or in full the "Agreement Creating an Association between the Republic of Turkey and the European

options. Besides, up to 3 million Turkish movers who had previously returned to Turkey should be taken into account while speaking of Turkish migration and integration.

Contract-workers arrived in Turkish migration history with sizeable moves to Arab countries and former Soviet Union countries in the 1970s and the total numbers reached nearly 150,000. These flows are relatively small in the rich variety of current migration flows from Turkey. Similarly, a significant number of Turkish students study abroad and some stays while some returns. The total number of Turkish students abroad grew from 37,000 in 2007 to 53,000 in 2012 (OECD, 2014).

Overall, we can confidently claim that there is now an established Turkish culture of migration, which is particularly strong in between Turkey and several destination countries including Austria, Germany, Netherlands, Switzerland, Sweden, the UK, and France. In the 25 years since 1987, on average annually about 85,000 Turks moved in to the OECD countries while, over 45,000 moved out (OECD, 2014). The number of Turks moving to OECD countries, per annum, declined to around 60,000 in the decade to 2013. These steady moves created strong diaspora populations including over 1,969,979 Turkish citizens and 1,720,892 Turks naturalized in their countries of residence within the OECD area by the end of 2012 (OECD, 2014). Due to changing economic balance between Turkey and destination countries and established culture of migration, some popular destination countries have become source countries as we saw a sizeable number of Turks moving [back] to Turkey (Sirkeci & Zeyneloglu, 2014). It is becoming more of a pattern of mutual flows between Europe and Turkey, whereas Turkey emerges as a key destination for those in relatively deprived parts of the world.

Migrants' remittances between the two countries are partly covered in this volume. They constitute a significant part of Turkish migration studies. Over the decades, these small sums of money sent by Turkish movers have contributed to Turkey's economy remarkably in the last fifty years, helping to cover the balance of trade deficits, but more importantly enhancing the household finances at micro level.

As a destination, Turkey had to fast track as sudden arrival of around 3 million Syrian and Iraqi refugees as of October 2016[6] have shifted the paradigm. Steady slow growth of European immigration along side

---

Economic Community", was signed in 1963 between Turkey and what is then European Economic Community (EEC). The agreement was signed as a step towards full accession and included special provisions which give Turkish nationals working in EEC and now in EU countries certain rights.

    [6] UNHCR: https://data.unhcr.org/syrianrefugees/country.php?id=224; and DGMM: www.goc.gov.tr.

controlling efforts on irregular migration were the basis for the new legal framework. Syrian and Iraqi arrivals turned all attention to conflicts and integration. Thus ambition to become a full member of the European Union (EU) cannot be the only guiding criteria for Turkish migration policy. Soon Turkey will possibly need to revisit both the newly adopted *Law on Foreigners and International Protection* (April 4, 2013) and the readmission agreement with the EU governing the treatment of unauthorized migrants originating from or transiting through Turkey. Another important change came as Turkish citizens who live abroad are allowed to vote locally where they are resident with the 2014 local and presidential elections. This is a sign for Turkey's intensifying relations with its diaspora populations and further transnationalisation of Turkish politics.

Turkish, Kurdish and Turkish Cypriot movers in Britain

Migration from Turkey to Britain has followed a different path than to migration to Germany where a rather structured and 'controlled' mobility was in place. Migration of Turkish Cypriots should be treated separately in these flows. Turkish-Cypriots' migration to the UK dates back to the interwar period when Cyprus was a Crown Colony. Migration from mainland Turkey was mainly destined to Germany and other neighbouring countries such as the Netherlands, Austria and Switzerland. Thus, until the late 1980s, very few from Turkey arrived in Britain despite a bilateral social security agreement was signed between the two countries on 9 September 1959 and implemented from 1961[7]. Nevertheless, the UK has never been a favoured destination for guest workers and the numbers remained relatively low.

Earlier Turkish movers who arrived in the UK were from Cyprus which was facilitated by the colonial ties between the two countries, mainly responding to the labour needs in the 1930s. Turkish Cypriots, who migrated to the UK in the early 1960s due to internal strife in Cyprus, worked in jobs in textiles industry (Küçükcan, 2006, p.247; King, 2008, p.426).

In the 1970s, the Maraş Massacre, military interventions of 1971 and 1980 were among the catalogue of political conflicts pushing movers from Turkey to the UK and elsewhere. Later in the 1980s and 1990s, thousands of Kurdish asylum seekers arrived in the UK (Sirkeci & Esipova, 2013).

---

[7] Despite common belief and some less than careful academic accounts, there is no bilateral labour exchange/migration agreement between Turkey and the United Kingdom. The 1959 Agreement is a Social Security Agreement which was published in Turkish Official Gazette on 21 December 1960 (number 10686) and implemented from 1 June 1961.

With reference to the conflict model of migration (Sirkeci, 2009), many Kurds as well as other minorities[8] in Turkey joined the ranks of emigrants although only some of them filed asylum applications in industrialised countries. We would expect the vast majority of 1.03 million asylum applications filed by Turkish citizens in three decades after the 1980 coup (Sirkeci & Esipova, 2013) were by the Kurds and other minorities, including a sizeable group of left wing political affiliates.

Overall, we expect political, ethnic and religious minorities from Turkey are to be overrepresented among emigrants. This holds true for the UK too. The UK has begun requiring entry visas from Turkish citizens on 23 June 1989 which, unsurprisingly, has influenced the mechanisms of migration. Initially much larger numbers reported to have applied for asylum and irregular migration increased dramatically in the following period. Similarly, after the historic case of Tum and Dari vs the UK paved the way for a new category of Turkish immigrants that might be called "Ankara Agreement movers" since 2004.

Those born in Turkey

The Turkish and Kurdish immigrants who arrived in the 1990s have mostly settled in the northern boroughs of London, namely Enfield, Hackney, Haringey and Islington. According to the 2011 UK population census, the total number of residents born in Turkey was 93,916 (Table 1.1). Very small numbers about those who were born in Northern Cyprus (i.e. Turkish Cypriots) were reported in the 2011 Census: Only 3,026 residents in England and 11 in Wales while 2,497 of them were located in London.[9] This overall figure supports the argument that despite all hearsay and unfounded claims common in the migrant community as well as some parts of academia, the total population of Turkish, Kurdish and Cypriot Turks including their later generations in the UK should not be beyond 200-250 thousand band (Sirkeci & Açık, 2015, p.144).

As can be seen from Table 1.1, immigrant population born in Turkey does constitute only a fraction of population in each of the countries and never beyond a sixth of a percentage point. While England is clearly home to over 95% of the Turkish born, London, the British capital unsurprisingly accommodates nearly 64% of them. When London's neighbouring counties such as Essex, Hertfordshire, Sussex in the South East England included only about a fourth of Turkish-born, overall the population seems dispersed around the country. Particularly the Kurds are dispersed and present more outside London compared to the Turks who are

---

[8] See Mahmutoglu (2015) for Assyrians in the media.
[9] Source table: QS213EW - Country of birth (expanded) from the ONS.

predominantly in London. Sizeable communities of 500 or more also exist in larger cities outside London such as Manchester, Glasgow, and Sheffield. During the late 1990s and in 2000s, many asylum seekers from Turkey were sent to remote parts of the UK as a result of the then asylum dispersal policy. Many of those moved to London and surrounding areas later but many others settled in these areas they were sent. Nationwide spread of Turkish and Kurdish run take away shops (mostly serving *döner kebab*) and relevant supply chains might have also contributed to the dispersal of population born in Turkey to an extent. At the most recent British Kebab Awards ceremony, it was mentioned that there are over 20,000 kebab shops/restaurants in the UK, although the UK Companies House registers list only about 2100 businesses with "Kebab" in their names (Sirkeci, 2016).

Table 1.1. Population born in Turkey by countries of the United Kingdom, 2011.

	Born in Turkey	% of Turkish born in total	% of Turkish born among foreign born	% of Turkish born among non-EU foreign born	% of foreign born in total
UK Total	93,916	0.15	1.17	1.88	12.65
Great Britain	93,539	0.15	1.19	1.89	12.83
England	89,484	0.17	1.22	1.92	13.84
Wales	1,631	0.05	0.97	1.73	5.48
Scotland	2,424	0.05	0.66	1.23	6.97
N. Ireland	377	0.02	0.32	1.13	6.58

Source: 2011 UK Census (ONS, 2013)

Nevertheless, like nearly all other immigrant minorities, those born in Turkey as well as overall Turkish and Kurdish speaking communities in the UK are mostly settled in London although there are some differences between ethnic groups in terms of geographical dispersal as mentioned above. A few Scottish islands are the only places where virtually no Turkish born resident reported in the 2011 Census. 53% of Londoner Turks and Kurds live in inner London boroughs. 23% of the Turkey born Londoners are resident in Enfield, a north London borough where foreign-born constitute 35% of the population. One of the largest immigrant groups in this particular borough, 4.5% of the total population and 25% of foreign born are originally from Turkey. As we have discussed in another chapter, this is also one of very few places where Turkish and Kurdish populations are tensely engaged with local and national politics.

Table 1.2. Resident population born in Turkey by areas and boroughs of London, 2011.

	Born in Turkey	% of Turkish born in total	% of Turkish born among foreign born	% of Turkish born among non-EU foreign born	% of foreign born in total
London	59,596	0.73	1.99	2.98	36.68
Inner London	31,717	0.98	2.32	3.61	42.21
Outer London	27,879	0.56	1.71	2.48	33.07
Top 10 London Boroughs					
Enfield	13,968	4.47	12.74	25.17	35.08
Haringey	10,096	3.96	8.88	17.92	44.60
Hackney	8,982	3.65	9.33	15.42	39.08
Islington	3,777	1.83	5.17	9.23	35.43
Waltham Forest	3,279	1.27	3.29	5.42	38.65
Barnet	1,952	0.55	1.41	2.23	38.86
Croydon	1,382	0.38	1.29	1.69	29.58
Lewisham	1,294	0.47	1.39	2.03	33.74
Southwark	1,123	0.39	0.99	1.41	39.43
Westminster	1,056	0.48	0.90	1.43	53.32

Source: 2011 UK Census (ONS, 2013)

Spatial concentration and isolation also matter. Immigrants tend to concentrate in certain areas characterized by migration history, economic attractiveness, and many other factors depending on country and time. For example, Turks in Germany concentrate in a few cities (Kastoryano, 2002), while over 64%[10] of Turkish and Kurdish live in London according to the 2011 UK Census (ONS, 2015). "Little Istanbul" in Berlin (Kaya, 2000, p.11), "Istanbul in 200 meters" in Cologne (Sirkeci, 2003, p.68) are examples of enclaves connecting with Turkey but also creating transnational living spaces through enclaves which economically enable migrants. It is also part of a historic phenomenon of ethnic segregation and unemployment (Friedrichs, 1998). Yet, similar to many other immigrant

---

[10] Once the Turkish Cypriots are excluded, this figure is 43% for the Kurds and 70% for the Turks from Turkey resident in the UK.

minority groups in Europe, they face difficulties in the labour market (Sirkeci & Açık, 2015).

Being home to about 109,000 Turkish, Kurdish and Turkish Cypriot, London is perhaps the only UK city where one can find a strong presence of Turkish, Kurdish and Cypriot enclaves with economic and socio-cultural institutions. This is evident in numerous community organisations across North London, several community festivals such as Newruz, Turkish Film Festival, Kurdish Film Festival and so on. Many streets in North London such as Green Lanes in Haringey, and others in Hackney, Enfield, Tottenham, and Edmonton are full of Turkish shops, restaurants, cafes, jewellery shops, associations, and other enterprises mostly serving to the local communities. These areas have also developed some sort of a touristic appeal over the years attracting people from other parts of London as well as visitors from out of town.

Like those early comers, majority of the Kurdish and/or Alevi immigrants who arrived in the UK by the early 1990s through irregular migration also settled in London's northern and eastern boroughs, once home to an active textile industry.

We presented numbers in above tables of only those people who were born in Turkey but currently live in the UK according to the 2011 UK Census. When second and third generations are also included, these figures are expected to go higher. However, it is worth to look at the size of the population born in Turkey as reported by the two previous censuses in 1991 and 2001, respectively, to avoid any exaggeration regarding the total number of Turkish born and their descendants in the UK. According to the 1991 UK Census, in England and Wales, there were about 26,000 individuals born in Turkey. This number grew to 52,893 in the 2001 Census and of those 39,128 were resident in London. As mentioned above in each inter-censal period (i.e. 1991 to 2001 and 2001 to 2011), Turkish born population has nearly doubled. This is a remarkable increase, which also coincided with high levels of asylum seeker flows from Turkey on both sides of the Millennium.

Those who says I am Turkish, Kurdish and Turkish Cypriot

In the 2011 UK census, one novelty was the inclusion of open ended (write in) questions about ethnicity. This allows us to gage with the data and understand the size and dispersal of Turkish and Kurdish speaking populations in the UK. Those who wrote Turkish, Turkish Cypriot and Kurdish as their ethnicity are summarised in Table 1.3.

The total number of people who associate with ethnic groups from Turkey was 169,771 which represent 1.6% of the total minority ethnic groups in the UK. Possibly some of the Kurdish were from Iraqi Kurdistan as Iraq is not indicated separately in the Census. However, there could be also some others who were reported within the "Cypriot" category. 59.9% of the Turkey-linked population was identified as Turkish, whereas 28.8% Kurdish and 11.2% Turkish Cypriot. 98% were located in urban areas while 67.4% were based in London.

Table 1.3 shows a much larger number indicating a significant growth in later generations. Comparing with the numbers in Table 1.2, for instance, the population of those who define themselves as Turkish, Kurdish and Turkish Cypriot in London is nearly double those who were born in Turkey. Assuming many of the Kurds arrived as asylum seekers and were subject to dispersal policies, it is understandable that they were spread over the country more than Turks and Turkish Cypriots. About 40 percent of Kurds live in London compared to over 70 percent of Turks and Turkish Cypriots.

Table 1.3. Self-identified ethnic groups in the UK, 2011.

	Total Non-British	Kurdish	Turkish	Turkish Cypriot	Turkish Kurdish Turkish Cypriot Total
East	857,365	2,315	6,313	1,175	9,803
East Midlands	659,504	3,108	2,890	106	6,104
London	4,482,570	20,988	71,301	16,609	108,898
North East	164,636	1,221	983	14	2,218
Yorkshire & Hum.	749,740	5,723	2,999	63	8,785
West Midlands	1,162,541	6,121	2,384	227	8,732
Wales	206,810	1,106	1,406	38	2,550
South West	430,622	1,141	2,822	93	4,056
South East	1,270,587	2,446	7,267	656	10,369
NA	907,285	4,808	3,356	92	8,256
TOTAL Eng. & W.	10,891,660	48,977	101,721	19,073	169,771

Source: Census 2011, https://www.nomisweb.co.uk/census/2011/ CT0010/ view/ 2092957703.

How do they arrive in British Isles?
The earliest arrivals from the Turkish community in the UK were Cypriots along with an odd number of individuals, diplomats, and students from mainland Turkey.

In the 1990s and 2000s, asylum seekers and irregular migrants have dominated the flows from Turkey. More recently, asylum seeker flows have drastically decreased but overall number of arrivals in various forms seemingly continued. These included people moving in as irregular migrants, family members, au-pairs, and students. As the rules of admission are tightened and border controls became tougher, the Ankara Agreement appeared as a solution to some Turkish citizens. Some of those who already arrived on student or au pair visas as well as others who wanted to leave Turkey have overstayed and/or applied to become entrepreneurs referring to the provisions of Ankara Agreement. It is important to recognize here that for many, if not all, there have always been multiple causes to migrate and yet they have been officially classified into a few categories for administrative purposes.

Table 1.4 documents the number of asylum seekers, number of acquisitions of British citizenship, number of permanent residency grants and admissions to the UK. Referring back to the 2011 Census results, about 93,000 Turkish-born individuals which is around 20 percent of UK residents born in Turkey have migrated as asylum seekers.

One should bear in mind that these cumulative numbers given in Table 1.4 also include those who have returned to Turkey or moved onwards to other countries. A significant number of Turkish citizens arrived in the UK as partners (husbands and wives) and some British born partners of those acquired Turkish citizenship. Therefore, it is difficult to accurately estimate the number of Turks who returned to Turkey. However, the increasing number of visitors (or person trips) indicate more frequent exchange and eventually contribute to the creation and maintenance of a culture of migration between the two countries. Number of Turkish visitors to the UK per annum exceeded 200,000 and British visitor numbers to Turkey exceeded 2 million in the 2010s and stayed around 2.5 million level on average until the bombings and failed coup attempt in 2016. Many Turkish or Kurdish origin immigrants in the UK visit Turkey once or more every year and the British residents in Turkey do the same. Again it is known that some of these British residents in Turkey have acquired Turkish citizenship and they may also show up in the admission statistics. Hence one should be cautious in reading these statistics.

Nearly 92,000 Turkish citizens have been naturalised in the UK between 1980 and 2016 (Tables 1.4. and 1.5.). More than half of those acquiring British citizenship were naturalised on the grounds of lawful residency for 5 years or more while the remaining citizenship acquisitions were by the spouses and dependent children (Table 1.5.). It must be noted, as shown in the last column, that Turkish citizens represent a small percentage of all citizenship acquisitions registered in the UK.

Table 1.4. Number of Turkish citizens by ways of entering the UK

Year	Asylum applications	Naturalisations	Grants of settlement	Admissions
1980	21	120		
1981	0	175		
1982	38	215		
1983	43	210		
1984	61	340		
1985	27	390		
1986	86	350		
1987	121	485		
1988	337	365		
1989	2,415	445		
1990	1,590	559		
1991	2,110	988		
1992	1,865	541		
1993	1,480	710		
1994	2,045	689		
1995	1,820	706		
1996	1,420	931		
1997	1,445	1,118	4,235	
1998	2,015	2,154	2,360	
1999	2,850	2,913	5,225	
2000	3,925	4,875	5,220	127,000
2001	3,693	4,037	3,310	
2002	3,494	8,040	2,920	
2003	2,992	4,916	4,365	
2004	1,588	4,860	6,060	124,000
2005	951	6,767	5,331	140,000
2006	567	5,583	3,039	160,000
2007	256	4,709	2,547	147,000
2008	232	4,641	3,671	172,000
2009	216	7,207	3,452	178,000
2010	176	4,630	5,580	191,000
2011	181	3,627	3,681	212,000
2012	200	4,726	2,376	205,000
2013	267	4,184	3,519	219,000
2014	296	1,843	2,396	218,000
2015	254	1,609	2,354	226,000
2016*	147	1,322		
Total	41,224	91,980	71,641	

*Source: Home Office Immigration Statistics, ONS (25 August 2016); Sirkeci & Esipova, 2013; UNHCR data base. * First seven months only.*

Only about less than 3 percent of Turkish citizens who applied for permanent residency in the UK were refused. Two thirds of those granted settlement permit were dependants while workers and businesspersons representing only about 12 percent. However, as we discuss in chapter four, the growing number of businesspersons obtaining permanent residency after the mid-2000s can be linked to the number of Turkish citizens arriving on the terms of Ankara Agreement as they are also eligible to settle after four years. It is also noteworthy that over 10 percent of settlement grants were issued to refugees from Turkey (Table 1.6). This equates to nearly all asylum applications filed in the same period (Table 1.4).

Table 1.5. Grounds for citizenship acquisitions by Turkish citizens in the UK, 2004-2015.

	Naturalisation grounds					
Year	Residence (5 years+)	Marriage	Dependent children	Other	Total	% of all acquisitions
2004	2,566	1,200	1,082	12	4,860	3.3
2005	3,641	1,172	1,942	12	6,767	4.2
2006	2,881	941	1,752	9	5,583	3.6
2007	2,577	1,019	1,109	4	4,709	2.9
2008	2,455	959	1,221	6	4,641	3.6
2009	3,575	1,992	1,633	7	7,207	3.5
2010	2,187	1,611	824	8	4,630	2.4
2011	1,699	1,341	582	5	3,627	2.0
2012	2,711	1,395	613	7	4,726	2.4
2013	2,233	1,458	485	8	4,184	2.0
2014	973	587	277	6	1,843	1.5
2015	945	441	214	9	1,609	1.4
Total	28,443	14,116	11,734	93	54,386	2.8

Source: Home Office Immigration Statistics, ONS (25 August 2016).

According to the Home Office records, 5,844 Turkish citizens were removed from the UK and about 3,099 were refused admission between January 2004 and August 2015. Nevertheless, presence of Turks particularly in London is often very visible not because of a large diaspora community as claimed by many but due to a relatively large traffic of visitors. Increasingly more visitors from Turkey are on record according to border statistics (Table 1.7). These constituted about 95 percent of the total number of Turkish citizens admitted to the UK in 2014. About 80 percent of the remaining 10,000 visitors were students.

Table 1.6. Settlement grants issued to Turkish citizens in the UK, 2004-2015

			Settlement categories			
Year	Workers	Business persons	Refugees and asylum related	Dependants	Other	Total
2004	109	2	1,505	4,244	200	6,060
2005	169	1	1,536	3,473	152	5,331
2006	67	2	445	2,360	165	3,039
2007	105	28	137	1,830	447	2,547
2008	148	258	11	2,629	625	3,671
2009	208	35	3	2,627	579	3,452
2010	204	451	77	2,960	1,888	5,580
2011	171	460	295	2,284	471	3,681
2012	187	287	149	1,662	91	2,376
2013	192	917	216	2,065	129	3,519
2014	156	870	79	1,105	186	2,396
2015	144	1,184	64	771	191	2,354
Total	1,860	4,495	4,517	28,010	5,124	44,006

Source: Home Office Immigration Statistics, ONS (25 August 2016).

Table 1.7. Admissions of Turkish citizens in the UK, 2004-2015

		Admission categories				
Year	Work	Study	Family	Visitors*	Total	visitors as %
2000	1,760	8,100	790	112,200	127,000	88.4%
2004	1,240	4,710	1,280	116,000	124,000	93.5%
2005	1,630	7,470	1,210	129,000	140,000	92.1%
2006	1,980	9,480	1,750	147,000	160,000	91.9%
2007	1,830	8,670	1,340	135,000	147,000	91.8%
2008	1,790	11,000	1,260	158,000	172,000	91.9%
2009	1,150	12,000	985	164,000	178,000	92.1%
2010	1,230	12,600	1,040	176,000	191,000	92.1%
2011	1,060	14,400	765	196,000	212,000	92.5%
2012	1,200	11,200	740	192,000	205,000	93.7%
2013	1,670	13,600	630	203,000	219,000	92.7%
2014	1,550	9,940	515	206,000	218,000	94.5%
2015	1,720	7,570	420	216,000	226,000	95.6%

Source: Home Office Immigration Statistics, ONS (25 August 2016).
* Including those who are returning after temporary absence abroad.

How to interpret all these numbers?

As mentioned at the beginning of this chapter, we are very much aware of the tendencies to exaggerate the numbers. Often when such figures from census or official resources are presented, some members of the community may not be happy about it. Nevertheless, these official registers and censuses offer us the largest and possibly most representative figures to work with. "Illegal migrants" or irregulars are often mentioned when official figures are questioned. However, even when these included the numbers will not be altered substantially. Despite all the efforts of consecutive UK governments to reduce the number of immigrants in the country, we are still in the opinion that they did not take it to the level of manipulating census results. At the same time, one should bear in mind that the UK, and particularly London is home to tens of different diaspora populations from all over the world. Indians, Irish, Pakistanis, Bangladeshis, Polish, South Africans, French, and Germans are among the largest to name a few. Immigrants from Turkey usually do not show up in the top 20 of the largest minority groups in the UK. If one takes the claims mentioned in the opening of this chapter seriously and apply it, pro-rata, to all those other groups (i.e. those officially larger than Turks or Kurds), the population of the UK would go over 100 million while London would have a population of 20 million instead of 8 million. Although sometimes in Central London we feel overwhelmed with the crowding, that much undercounting or underestimation is extremely unlikely.

Hence, the statistics presented in this chapter are derived from the most up to date and reliable data available to us at the time of writing this book. This is of course not to say that there can not be differences between receiving country statistics and those of the countries of origin. Neither can we claim that these numbers are perfectly accurate. Migration is one very dynamic population feature and the numbers are likely to change relatively quickly. Another issue closely affecting the accuracy of migration statistics is the changing legislations, regulations and the ways in which people are counted and categorised.

Now, nevertheless, we will move to outline and discuss the specifics of the Turkish, Kurdish and Turkish Cypriot populations in Britain and particularly in London, where they are dominantly concentrated.

Chapter 2. Identity and integration

Ethnic identity is a dynamic construct which can change over time, space and context and must therefore be considered with reference to its formation and variation (Phinney & Ong, 2007). Identity formation and variation is part of the acculturation process which does affect ethnic identity formation and relates to the identification with the culture of origin and with the new society (Dimitrova et al., 2013).

Emphasizing parents' cultural socialisation and transmission, parents' familiarity with the ethnic group, values, attitudes and pride are part and parcel of the identity formation (Ferrari et al., 2015). Ethnic identity is also seen as context-specific (Cleveland, & Chang, 2009). Strong ethnic identity may have led to increased committment to the group and internalization of ethnic practices. However, if the interest is limited and identification is weak, then a lower commitment, or involvement is likely (Abu-Rayya & Abu-Rayya, 2009; Ting-Toomey et al., 2000). Ethnicity and religion are often intertwined in identification process (Maliepaard, & Phalet, 2012). Religion can be an effective concept for social identity and it may be associated with ethnic identity too (Martinovic & Verkuyten, 2012). Religious groups can also provide support for individuals while religious beliefs and values may have a bearing on the ways in which individuals design their lives (Dumont, 2003). Thus a number of studies identified religion as a key component of the lives of Muslim immigrants in Western Europe (Yağmur & Van de Vijver, 2012; Modood et al., 1997; Phalet and Güngör, 2004; Güngör et al., 2011; Verkuyten & Martinovic, 2012; Verkuyten & Yıldız, 2007).

Those who study immigrants from Turkey are familiar with a common controversy. Is it Turkish migration, Kurdish migration or Turkish Cypriot migration? It is difficult to find a term which pleases everybody and be comprehensive and politically correct as these identities are variable depending on the references (Yazgan, 2016:292). We have presented official statistics and census results showing the identity preferences among those who are originally from Turkey in the previous chapter. The 2011 Census is the most authoritative source of data in this regard because there were three clear 'write-in' questions asking for nationality (question number 15), ethnic group (question number 16) and main language (question number 18). The results show that those from Turkey are most likely to have answered these questions by entering Turkish, Kurdish, Turkish Cypriot, Turkish Kurdish, and Cypriot along with possible selections of English, Scottish, Welsh, and British. However, in our studies, some respondents also self-identified as "Alevi" or "Muslim" as their ethnic identity. These groups share many common characteristics and it is obvious to the naked eye that among these groups Turkish is the main language of exchange. From a geographical and administrative perspective, it is possible to classify all as 'Turkish' denoting they are all coming from Turkey as an administrative territory. Nevertheless, we stayed in the boundaries of self-description and presented our findings and framed our discussions using Turkish, Kurdish and Turkish Cypriots where and when necessary.

In 2013 and 2014, we have carried out a questionnaire survey supplemented with a small scale qualitative interviews of semi-structured kind among these populations mostly located in North London. The survey was conducted through both face-to-face interviews with respondents recruited through snowball sampling technique and an online survey distributed via emails and social media platforms. The final sample included 624 individuals. The results presented in this chapter are produced by SPSS. Our results are similar to the results of the 2011 Census in terms of language and ethnicity distribution. This is very comforting in terms of reflecting the general characteristics of the Turkey born population in the UK although we cannot claim representation and generalize these results.

Ethnicity and language

Self identified ethnic identities of the participants revealed that 48.2% of the participants are Kurdish, 44.2% of them are Turkish and 5.1% of them are Cypriot. However, 2.6% of the participants did not specify their ethnic identity. These numbers are not far from the census statistics we have presented in previous chapter, but we are aware of the underrepresentation of Turkish Cypriots in our sample. This is possibly due to the selection issue by snowball sampling and the locations we have targeted in recruiting our respondents.

Language is often used as a proxy in studies of ethnic groups, although there are serious concerns raised about this choice of construct (see for example, Zeyneloglu, Sirkeci, Civelek, 2016). Minorities often switch to the mainstream language with or without any political pressures. This makes language a very weak tool to identify ethnic groups. Our findings support these criticisms. 37.9% of Kurdish male respondents and 47.4% of Kurdish female participants, for example, have reported Turkish as their mother tongue (Table 2.1.). For Turkish respondents, on the other hand, about 99 specified Turkish as mother tongue.

We have also crosstabulated the ethnicities of partners to identify intermarriages (Table 2.2.). The Kurds have the lowest inter-ethnic marriage rates in our sample. This is in contrast with the patterns in Turkey (e.g. Sirkeci, 2000). However, as Kurds constitute the majority group within Turkish diaspora in the UK and given the possible impact of the conflict between Kurdish and Turkish forces in Turkey, the intermarriages may be lower. Another factor can be the larger pool of mates available in the UK. In addition, in order to examine the relationship between the participants' ethnic identity and their partner's ethnic identity a Chi-square test was used and results represented in Table 2.3. Results revealed a significant association between the participants' reported ethnic identities and their partners' ethnic identities, $\chi2(6) = 539,452$, $p < .00$.

Table 2.1. Ethnic group by gender and mother tongue

Ethnic group	Mother tongue	Male (N = 414)		Female (N = 210)	
		Frequency	Percentage	Frequency	Percentage
Cypriot	Turkish	14	87.5	15	93.8
	Kurdish	-	-	-	-
	Mixed	2	12.5	1	6.3
Kurdish	Turkish	78	37.9	45	47.4
	Kurdish	125	60.7	43	45.3
	Mixed	3	1.5	6	6.3
Turkish	Turkish	183	98.9	89	98.9
	Kurdish	-	-	-	-
	Mixed	2	1.1	1	1.1

Table 2.2. Ethnic group by partner's ethnic group

		Partner's ethnic group				Total
		Cypriot	Kurdish	Turkish	Others	
Cypriot	Count	23	0	2	0	25
	%	92.0	0.0	8.0	0.0	100
Kurdish	Count	1	185	21	4	211
	%	0.5	87.7	10.0	1.9	100
Turkish	Count	2	20	129	9	160
	%	1.3	12.5	80.6	5.6	100
Total	Count	26	205	152	13	396
	%	6.6	51.8	38.4	3.3	100

We have asked respondents how strongly attached they feel themselves to their ethnic group and to what extent they consider ethnic identity as part of their personality. Using a 7-point likert scale, we have found that on average, both Kurdish and Turkish Cypriot females place more importance to their ethnic identities compared to males while overall average scores were around 5 or higher. Among Turkish though, males were praising their ethnicity slightly more than females. While both Turkish and Kurdish males attributing similar significance to their ethnicity as part of their personality and feeling equally attached to their ethnic group, Turkish Cypriots, overall, scored relatively lower on attachment to their ethnic group compared to their scores on ethnicity being important for their identity.

While clear ethnic lines are drawn by ethnic group members, the most frequently used daily language was Turkish (44.1%) followed by Kurdish (21.4%) among our participants. Besides, 8.4% of the participants specified the most frequently used language. Female and male participants' daily language preferences are examined separately in Table 2.3. English was preferred the daily language by 10.2% of the male participants. This correlates with the fact that men spend more time outside home. Significantly higher percentage of mixed language use among women can be related to frequent use of Kurdish and Turkish at home as well as the inevitably dominant use of English when it comes to official business and life outside homes.

Table 2.3. Most frequently used language by gender

	Male (N = 414)		Female (N = 210)	
Language	Frequency	Percentage	Frequency	Percentage
Turkish	160	38.9	112	54.4
Kurdish	125	30.4	7	3.4
English	42	10.2	12	5.8
Mixed	84	20.5	74	32.5

However, within our sample 46% male and 54% female, mother tongue of 69% was Turkish and 27% Kurdish while about 1% with mixed languages also including English and Zazaki (Figure 2.1). However, when it comes to the most frequently used language, Turkish goes down to 44% and Kurdish to 22% because about a quarter of Turkish speakers are bilingual (with English and other languages).

However, 5.8% of the female participants preferred English as the daily language. In addition to frequent language, we measured English language competency in understanding, reading, writing and speaking on a five-point scale. When average scores are compared, males have overall higher mean scores than females in understanding and speaking. These differences between the male and female participants might be originated from various social contexts (Cleveland & Chang, 2009) of the male immigrants such as working environment and frequent interaction with host society. Also, it is important to mention that, immigrants' preference to use host language as daily language contributes to their adaptation.

Figure 2.1. Mother tongue by gender and age among immigrants from Turkey

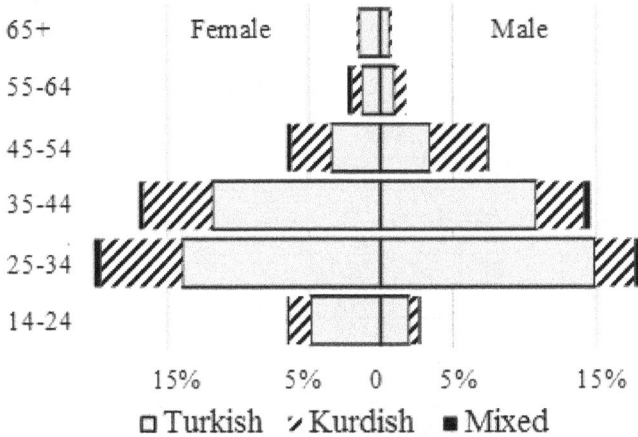

Religion and identity

In terms of the size of religious belief groups among the movers from Turkey in London, the largest one was Sunnis (44%) followed by Alevis (41%) and those with no religion (15%, including agnostics and atheists) (Table 2.4). Majority of respondents stated that they feel strong belonging to their religion. This was slightly stronger among females compared to males and stronger among Kurdish compared to Turkish. We have observed a similar pattern indicating stronger ethnic group belonging among the Kurds compared to Turks.

The largest group of the participants were Sunnis (35.3%) closely followed by Alevis (29.2%). However, given the peculiar selective nature of migration from Turkey to the UK, i.e. predominantly comprising opponents of the regime and minorities, the largest segment was that of Agnostics, Atheists and people with no religion (42.6% among males and 20.4% among females) (Table 2.5). This can be also partly encouraged by the liberal environment of freedom of expression in the UK, where non-religious population segment is larger than religious one. We have also applied a likert scale module on strength of religious belonging and found that majority of respondents felt strong belonging to their religion which was slightly stronger among females than males.

Scores on 7-point likert scale for religious identity and belonging were slightly lower than those for ethnic identity. Religious identity was perceived as more important among Turkish respondents than their

Kurdish counterparts. Religious belonging was stronger among Turkish Cypriot females, Turkish males and Kurdish females than others.

Table 2.4. Religious identity by gender and age

Age	Male (%)			Female (%)			Total
	Sunni	Alevi	No-religion	Sunni	Alevi	No-religion	N
14-24	47.1	29.4	23.5	48.8	39.0	12.2	58
25-34	58.0	26.8	15.2	35.5	49.2	15.3	236
35-44	43.3	37.8	18.9	45.2	47.1	7.7	194
45-54	41.3	43.5	15.2	30.8	48.7	20.5	85
55-64	25.0	58.3	16.7	35.7	42.9	21.4	26
65+	60.0	20.0	20.0	70.0	30.0	0.0	15
Total	49.0	34.0	17.0	41.0	46.0	13.0	
N	137	97	48	135	154	43	614

Table 2.5. Religious status by gender

Relious status	Male (N = 414)		Female (N = 210)	
	Frequency	Percentage	Frequency	Percentage
No-religion	77	18.6	17	8.1
Agnostik	84	20.3	15	7.1
Alevi	102	24.7	80	38.1
Ateist	11	2.7	11	5.2
Sunni	135	32.7	85	40.5
Christian	1	0.2	2	1.0
Other	2	0.5	17	8.1

Employment and economic activity

Legal status is an important aspect in economic (and labour market) integration for immigrants. 70% of our respondents acquired British citizenship and 65% were dual citizens (Table 2.6). This was no surprise as 67% of respondents have been resident in the UK for 10 years or more. The mean value for the years since first arrival in the UK is 14.16 (SD = 9,604). Such long duration of stay in the UK supports the idea that living longer in host society facilitates the adaptation process. This is a pattern in line with the official statistics of naturalisations as presented in the previous chapter (See also Table 1.4.). When it comes to migration status, majority of participants had British or dual citizenship (65%) and 17,8% had resident permit (Table 2.6).

38.5% of the participants were dual British and Turkish citizens, whereas 31.7% had only UK citizenship and 28.3% had only Turkish citizenship (Table 2.7). Dual citizenship was much more likely among women than men. This could be due to the fact that Turkish citizenship also imposes compulsory military service on males aged 18 and over.

Hence many Turkish and Kurdish men may have been opting to quit Turkish citizenship to avoid this compulsory service.

Table 2.6. Migration status by gender

Migration Status	Male (N = 414)		Female (N = 210)	
	Frequency	%	Frequency	%
British / Dual	274	66.7	128	61.8
Permanent residency	39	9.5	16	7.7
Resident permit (Student or work)	72	17.5	38	18,4
Asylum-Refugee	24	5.8	22	10.6
EU citizen	1	0.2	2	1.0
Other	1	0.2	1	0.5

Table 2.7. Citizenships of participants by gender

Citizenship	Male (N = 414)		Female (N = 210)	
	Frequency	%	Frequency	%
Turkish	124	30.2	51	24.6
British	157	38.2	39	18.8
Dual citizen	125	30.4	113	54.6
Other country	5	1.2	4	1.9

Employment and economic activity is probably the most frequently studied aspect of migration partly because of data availability. In our survey, multiple and mixed migration motivations were evident partly proving that widely used dichotomy of economic migrants versus refugees is misleading. 35% of our respondents said they moved for family followed by education (25%), economic reasons (20%) and political reasons (20%) (Table 2.8).

We can say that this balance of migration motivations was reflected in educational attainment levels. About 40% of respondents had university degrees or higher. There were gender and ethnic differences in this regard as those with degrees or higher were more common among males than females and similarly those with degrees were more common among Turkish than Kurdish. One may relate this to the migration patterns as we expect vast majority of 41,224 asylum seekers arrived in the UK since the 1980 military coup in Turkey to be of Kurdish origin. Asylum migration patterns often show that families move together or remaining family members join after a while whereas when there is no such political involvement migration is selective by marital status and skills. Hence, we have seen, for example, never married individuals were more common among the Turks compared to Kurds. Migration of ethnic Turks is also more likely to be more selective by skill levels as well as studying is being a more common migration motivation.

Table 2.8. Reason for immigration to UK by gender

	Male (N = 414)		Female (N = 210)	
	Frequency	%	Frequency	%
Education	171	42.2	50	25.5
Family	51	12.6	49	25.0
Marriage	13	3.2	32	16.3
New life	11	2.7	5	2.6
Political	75	18.5	36	18.4
Economic	84	20.7	24	12.2

Analysis of employment status showed these ethnic differences starkly (Table 2.9). About 80% of full time students were Turkish. Shares of salaried employment and/or self-employed were similar between the Turks and Kurds (57% and 53% respectively), however, those who cannot work due to health related reasons were nearly four times more common among the Kurds. Majority of females and over 40% of males were not in employment or education. The majority of the both male (46.8%) and female participants (38.8%) reported that they have salaried jobs. One of the prominent differences between male and female participants is the not job seeker option which is the secondly preferred option of the female participants (34.3%). According to our respondents, this was also partly because there were no suitable jobs.

Disadvantages and discrimination in the labour market faced by immigrant minorities is well documented in the literature on minorities in the UK (Khattab et al., 2010 and 2011; Sirkeci & Acik, 2013; Saunders, 2015). About 26% of Turkish and 21% of Kurdish males reported that they have been discriminated against due to their ethnicity in seeking jobs. Corresponding figures were about 15% among females in both ethnic groups. Nevertheless, these disadvantages can also be related to language competency.

We measured self-reported language competency in understanding, reading, listening and writing on a five-point scale. When average scores are compared, males have overall higher mean scores than females. 40% of Turkish males compared to 15% of Kurdish have mean scores of 4 to 5 (very good) in English language competency. Corresponding scores for females are 26% and 20% for respective groups. These ethnic differences can be due to different backgrounds for Turks and Kurds as the latter group have arrived mostly as asylum seekers while the former are likely to have higher human and social capital prior to migration.

Table 2.9. Employment status by gender

Employment status	Male (N = 414)		Female (N = 210)	
	Frequency	%	Frequency	%
Salaried employee	193	46.8	78	38.8
Self-employed	57	13.8	20	10.0
Unemployed - job seeker	17	4.1	19	9.5
not job seeker	41	10.0	69	34.3
Full time student	12	2.9	11	5.5
Retired	75	18.2	1	.5
Health issues	12	2.9	1	.5
On social benefits	5	1.2	2	1.0

We found differences at income levels too. This is partly due to the level of integration, duration of stay in the UK, as well as strength of human capital. Turkish immigrants have relatively higher income levels than Kurdish immigrants. The majority of the participants are the most frequently salaried employees (44.2%). In addition, 17.9% of the participants specified that they do not seek a job and 12.6% of them have their own business.

Perception of discrimination and disadvantages would result in frustration and possibly encourage return intentions. Therefore, we have asked our respondents whether they are considering returning to Turkey, again using a five-point likert scale. Turkish females were less likely to consider returning to Turkey (50%) than males (59%). Return was a less likely option for Kurds but similarly higher among males (48%) than females (41%). This gender difference is an important lead for further studies but given the traditional characteristics of Turkish and Kurdish society where women are often treated infavourably, lower return intentions among women than men should not be surprising.

Education, marital status, migration status and citizenship

Regarding education, 68% of the participants have been educated in Turkey, 27% in the UK and 5% in other countries. 75% of the male and 55% of the female participants have been educated in Turkey. According to education levels of the participants who have been educated in Turkey, 55% of the participants are primary and high-school graduates. 19% of the participants did not have any education at all. On the other hand, 23% of the male and 34% of the female participants were educated in the UK. 75% of the participants who have been educated in the UK have bachelor's and master's degrees.

We can say the patterns of migration motivations (Table 2.8 above) was in a way reflected in educational attainment levels. About 40% of respondents have university degrees or higher. There were gender and ethnic differences in this regard as those with degrees or higher were more common among males than females and similarly those with degrees were more common among Turkish than Kurdish.

Table 2.10. Marital status by gender and age, %

	Males (N = 414)					Females (N = 210)				
	18-24	25-34	35-44	45-54	55 +	18-24	25-34	35-44	45-54	55 +
Single	94	47	13	-	-	85	54	2	3	4
Maried	6	47	74	81	65	11	41	80	78	65
Divorced/Separated	-	3	9	15	35	-	3	12	12	13
Widow	-	1	1	2	-	-	1	2	4	17
Living together	-	2	3	2	-	4	1	4	-	-
N	31	161	136	60	17	27	72	57	27	23

In our field research, there were a total of 624 participants, 66% of whom were males and 34% were females. As represented in Table 2.10, the majority of participants aged 18 to 24 were single. Understandably, married people constitute the vast majority of both males and females in later age groups. In the last age group, 55+, widows and divorcees/separated among females are significantly higher than their male counterparts. Although within a life course perspective, we expect such an increasing pattern as people age but one third of both males and females being either divorced, separated or widowed is significantly large even though the sample is small (i.e. 40 people in this age group).

In this chapter we presented the ethnic and religious characteristics common among the Turkish population in the UK and London in particular while also indicating some basic measures of integration. Strong belonging and affiliation with ethnic and religious identity combined with certain language use patterns may not be considered as ideal for integration processes. However, these should be considered as a multitude of environmental factors influences the process of integration. While belonging over gender, ethnicity and religion shape the formation of social identity, these are also part and parcel of survival strategies in ethnic enclaves. Demographic patterns among our respondents were more or less comparable to immigrant populations and to general population to an extent. For example, majority were Kurdish and males and marriage rates increase as the group gets older. Similarly divorce rates are higher among older age groups. The rarity of intermarriage between Turkish and Kurdish groups were interesting but not so surprising given the ethno-political contest continue between these groups in parallel to the conflict in Turkey. Following what literature suggests, Kurdish as medium of communication is loosing its grip as the most frequently reported daily used language was Turkish despite our majority Kurdish sample.

English competence was found to be higher among males than females. This is mostly to do with typical life arrangements where women often focus on domestic chores while men work outside. Such stereotypical gender differences were evident in terms of dual citizenship and migration motives too. Another important aspect of the integration process is political participation. In the next chapter, we discuss findings of our study on political participation in London.

Sirkeci, Bilecen, Çoştu, Dedeoğlu, Kesici, Şeker, Tilbe, Unutulmaz

Chapter 3. Political participation in London

Movers from Turkey have their own internal variations in terms of political ideas and attitudes. The migrants' period of arrival in the UK; the reasons for their arrival; ethnic, sectarian and class affiliations; gender; as well as the districts they used to inhabit back in Turkey all effect this variation. This chapter will examine how these forms of diversity affect the level of interest and participation of migrants from Turkey (including Turkish and Kurdish immigrants) and Turkish Cypriot migrants in the politics of the UK and Turkey.

In the period when this study was carried out, the news agenda was dominated by national elections in Turkey and the UK, as well as presidential elections in the Turkish Republic of Northern Cyprus (TRNC). Therefore, all the interviews were carried out at a time of intense political debate. However, as we will discuss under the heading of "Political Participation," this study does not consider the concept of political participation only in terms of the level of participation in the elections. Instead, it takes up a wider perspective by discussing such parameters as attention to political events; involvement in associations that carry out political activities and participation in political activities; the building of direct or indirect relationships with politicians; participation in political events (rallies, demonstrations, marches, petitions, etc.); donations made for political purposes; and other similar factors.

The interviews accounted for gender balance throughout the study. However, women within the community from Turkey, especially, have the highest level of inactivity among migrant groups, with a proportion of 62.53% inactive; this results in the invisibility of a large proportion of women in public space (Demireva, 2011: 643). In other words, the women who are visible in the public sphere are already more politically active compared to other women.[1] Thus, one limitation of this study is that the level of women's participation found here is above the normal standards for these communities.

In developing this chapter, we used data from a survey based on semi-structured interviews. A random sample of 60 individuals were interviewed during a field research carried out in London between September 1, 2014 and August 31, 2015. While selecting the sample,

---

[1] Dedeoğlu (2014) discusses the invisible labour of women migrants from Turkey in the ethnic economy in London. According to Dedeoğlu, women's invisible labour has a significant contribution to the development and success of Turkey's ethic economy in London. Even if women are not actually registered workers, they work as unpaid labour or a cheap labour force at the restaurants, cafes, and off-licence (*bakkal*) businesses run by the community from Turkey.

special attention was paid to obtaining a consistent distribution of class, sectarian and ethnic positions, as well as age and gender. In this respect, fieldwork involved visits to locations (associations based on geographical origin, community centres, religious centres, cultural centres, municipalities, newspapers, restaurants, cafes, etc.)[2] where migrants from Turkey socialise and work. The sample was secured through observations and established connections made in these locations.

Individual interviews were conducted in different locations in London from December 6, 2014 to April 23, 2015. Interviews lasted between 30 and 80 minutes. Interviews were tape recorded but the names of the respondents were removed from the transcripts. Instead, each interviewee was assigned a number from 1 to 60.

Interview questions were grouped into four main headings. In the first part, the objective was to outline demographic characteristics of the interviewees. The second part included questions about their migration stories. These included questions about the reasons for migration, the date and mode of migration, the existence or absence of social networks, and the individual's residency status. In the third part, questions were asked about migrants' relationships with each other and with members of other communities. This module of questions was to examine how class, ethnicity, and sectarian factors were having an effect on migrants' social relations. In the fourth and the last part, questions were designed to understand the migrants' interests in and engagement with politics in both Turkey and the UK. We have also asked about the trust in the politics in Turkey and in the UK. Along side the interviews, we have also used data from the election results for the UK's May 7, 2015 general elections and Turkey's June 7, 2015[3] general elections.

---

[2] Day-Mer (Turkish and Kurdish Community Centre), Gik-Der (*Göçmen İşçiler Kültür Derneği*, or Migrant Workers' Cultural Association), *Derman* ("for the wellbeing of Turkish and Kurdish Communities"), *Tohum Kültür Merkezi* (Tohum Cultural Centre), *İmece* Women's Centre, Türk Eğitim Birliği (Turkish Education Group), Kurdish Community Centre, *Halkevi*, *Emek Araştırmaları Vakfı* (Easdale Foundation for Labour Research), *Güney Londra Kıbrıs Türk Derneği* (South London Turkish Cypriot Association), Hackney Cypriot Association, Turkish Cypriot Community Association, Cypriot Women Project, Turkish Youth of London, *Pekünlüler Derneği* (Pekünlüler Association), *Dersimliler Derneği* (Dersimliler Association), *Tilkililer Derneği* (Tilkililer Association), *Elbistanlılar Derneği* (Elbistanlılar Association), *Pazarcıklılar Derneği* (Pazarcıklılar Association), *Anadolu Kültür Merkezi* (Anatolian Cultural Centre), *Süleymaniye Camii* (Suleymaniye Mosque), *Aziziye Camii* (Aziziye Mosque), *Mevlana Camii* (Mevlana Mosque), *Diyanet Camii* (Divanet Mosque), *Cemevi*, Einfeld Municipality, *Londra Olay Gazetesi* (London Olay Newspaper), *Londra Gazetesi* (London Newspaper).

[3] For the national elections held in Turkey on June 7, 2015, Turkish citizens living in London voted on June 30 and 31 at election centres in London and Edinburgh.

Socio-demographic profiles

In our sample, 20 participants self-identified themselves as Kurdish[4] of whom, 11 were males and 9 were females. 9 interviewees declared their native language to be Kurdish, 6 as Turkish, 4 as Zazaki and 1 as English. 6 respondents were single and 14 married. 2 of the interviewees did not have any education at all, while 4 had a primary school education, 1 was a secondary school graduate, 6 were high school graduates, 6 were university graduates, and 1 had a master's degree. Average age of these 20 interviewees was about 41.

21 participants self-identified themselves as Turkish[5] including 11 men and 10 women, all of whom reported Turkish as their native language. 9 were single and 12 married. 4 of them had primary school education, 1 was a secondary school graduate, 7 were high school graduates, 3 were university graduates, and 3 had master's degrees. 2 interviewees were students at a highschool and at a university respectively whereas 1 interviewee chose not to disclose this information. The mean age of these 21 interviewees was about 39.

19 of the participants self-identified themselves as Turkish Cypriots.[6] Among these 10 men and 9 women, 13 stated Turkish to be their native language whereas 5 stating English, and 1 reporting both Turkish and English as native languages. 12 of the interviewees were single and 7 married. 2 respondents were primary school graduates, 1 was a secondary school graduate, whereas 5 were high school graduates, 8 university graduates, and 2 had master's degrees. 1 of the interviewees was a PhD student. The mean age of the interviewees was about 47.

Political participation of Turks, Kurds, and Turkish Cypriots

We examine two aspects of immigrants' political participation; first, migrants' interest and involvement in politics in the country of settlement; and second, their interest and involvement in the politics of the country of origin.

In a wider sense, political participation refers to all citizenship activities that aim to participate in the existing political system or to create a change in the system. Traditionally, political participation most significantly involves participation in elections. Dahl (2001) discusses political participation under four main headings: "interest," "caring," "information," and "action" for public and political activities. Milbrath's classification also sets a hierarchical order relating to the level of political

---

[4] One of the interviewees among these 20 interviewees answered the question of identity as Alevi. Another one also expressed that he/she is a Zaza Kurd.

[5] One of the 20 interviewees is Bosniak and one is Circassion.

[6] It is significant to note that some interviewees answered this question as British.

participation, beginning from those who are indifferent. Besides indifferent individuals, Milbrath also defines various activity types including spectator activities, transition (interval) activities, and contentious (militant) activities. According to this classification, party membership, giving inspiration, discussion, and participation in elections are spectator activities; participation in rallies and meetings, making donations, or having connections with official authorities are considered as part of transition activities; and behaviours such as becoming a candidate or participating directly in political campaigns constitute contentious activities (Tatar, 2003: 334).

Personal and demographic factors, such as age, gender, level of educational attainment, income level, marital status, health status, and interest in politics all effect the individual's political participation (Voicu and Comşa, 2014: 1577).

Recent studies show that migrant communities from Turkey in Europe have a high level of socialisation and political participation (Jacobs and Phalet, 2007: 145; Dirk and Tillie, 2004; Fennema and Tillie, 2010). Political participation is discussed in relation to certain parameters such as the extent of involvement of the movers from Turkey in the politics of the country of residence; their engagement with non-governmental organisations and in relation to the concept of social capital and, trust in political institutions, usually in comparison to other mover communities. Here we are looking into the variation within the community of movers from Turkey.

First we examine migrants' party memberships in their countries of settlement and origin, their active participation in election campaigns, and their voting behaviours. On March 22, 2008, the Law 5749 ("Law On Fundamental Principles of the Elections and the Law on the Amendment of the Register of Electors") was passed in Turkey to allow Turkish citizens living abroad to vote, from their countries of settlement, in the national and presidential elections held in Turkey (Resmi Gazete, 2008).[7]

In terms of voting behaviour, we found that Turkish Cypriots were most flexible, or less loyal to political parties they vote or engage with compared to Turks and Kurds. The political party programme, promises of the party, and attitudes towards Cyprus politics have an effect on the movers' attitude towards that party. This was clear in one interviewee's response to the question "Are you a member of any party?":

Not now. I was a member of both Labour and the Conservatives in the past. In forming my political opinion, I care for the political

---

[7] The citizens of the TRNC do not have this right concerning elections in their country of origin.

interests of Turkish Cypriots. Before I joined the Labour Party I did not see any interest for the Turkish Cypriots; I saw the opposite. After a while, a friend of mine from the municipality of Enfield asked me to attend the Conservatives' events. I usually attended their meetings, with the aim of making Turkish Cypriots' voices heard. (...) The Liberals and Conservatives are closer to us than Labour... (Interviewee 3, 61 years old, male)

One interviewee, saying that he changed the party he voted for in every election depending on the program of the party, criticised movers from Turkey who consistently support the same parties:

In four years, I voted for four different parties. In Turkey, they support political parties like football teams. (Interviewee 33, 61 years old, male).

Another Cypriot interviewee said that he changes the political party he votes for depending on their political programs and party activities:

No, it [the party] has changed. I first voted for the Conservatives, and then I voted for Labour. I later voted for the Liberal Democrats. But I gave them my vote by looking at their party programs and activities. (Interviewee 31, 46 years old, male).

Compared to Turks and Kurds, Turkish Cypriots seem more indifferent to political issues. Many Cypriots indicated that they did not believe that their vote would change anything.

I didn't vote for a long time. I didn't. It was a conscious choice. So we can't get anywhere with elections. (Interviewee 20, 58 years old, male).

Choosing not to vote depends on me. It won't change anything. Another political party can come to power and nothing changes. Politics is always the same politics. Foreign policy, economy, foreign affairs—they're all the same. (Interviewee 23, 39 years old, male).

Interviewee 35 said that he did not trust the political system in the UK and that he does not vote because he cannot find any party that reflects his opinions:

I don't trust the parties. I don't believe that current politics would support my opinions. I don't think that anything would change if I vote. At least I'm trying to stay away from this system. (Interviewee 35, 22 years old, male).

One possible reason for being relatively indifferent to politics among Turkish Cypriots is the fact that they arrived in the UK much earlier than the Kurds and Turks and they have become acculturated in British political system. Thus they believe nothing can change easily in the British political system and they might be relatively satisfied with their lives. Additionally, Kurds' and Turks' participation in non-governmental organisations is higher than Turkish Cypriots. This may be a symptom of as well as a reason for their disinterest in politics overall.

Immigrants with language deficiencies often experience isolation, rejection, and powerlessness (Alexander et al., 2007: 784; Tanyas, 2012: 705; Şeker, 2015: 20). Duration of stay in the host country reduces that risk but after nearly half a century since the first arrivals of Turkish and Kurdish communities in the UK, one of the factors that negatively affect political participation is the limited language skills. Interviewee 4, who moved in 2000 but 'could not fully learn English', underlined this as a reason for his resignation from politics in the UK:

I don't deal with these things here. As I said, I know little English. My wife's English is good, and she votes for whatever party she wants. I already encourage her, too. (Interviewee 4, 38 years old, male).

This was also clear for some Turkish women who stay away from politics due to their limited English skills which does not improve also because they are often confined to the private sphere and have limited presence in public.

Children and home—we always deal with these things. That's why we have no idea about anything. All my acquaintances deal with cleaning, the house, cooking... Their husbands would not allow them (...) My husband says that's good, and then I vote for that party. I don't know which one is better (...) So due to the fact that we don't have political knowledge, you just have to do what your husband says to do, since we do think that our husbands have a right. (Interviewee 10, 31 years old, female).

One other reason for lack of participation in politics is the fact that many Turkish movers living in London often work long hours in the service sector. In Jensen's terms (2008: 81), immigrants often cannot find time to participate in political activities due to their work obligations. Interviewee 27 expressed that he stopped actively participating in the Labour Party after entering the kebab business:

20 years ago, I was a member of the Labour Party. Then I quitted (...) For us, for "kebabçıs," there's not much free time left. This is the reason why I quitted. (Interviewee 27, 55 years old, male).

Migrants from Turkey living in North and East London mostly support the Labour Party that they believe have moderate policies towards immigrants. However, we have observed very low levels of political party membership and party support among the Turks in London.

Usually, I would vote for the Labour party like everyone else. Now, [in 2014] for five years, the right wing is in power and they constantly constrain immigrants. When you look at it, the other [party] is more moderate. They're closer to you, and they give you more opportunities. (Interviewee 44, 30 years old, male).

Nevertheless, even if they support right wing parties in Turkey, these movers still have a tendency to vote for the Labour Party in the UK. We have seen, for example, Islamist AKP (Justice and Development Party) supporters voting for Labour while also it was clear in the May 7, 2015 UK elections, Labour Party candidates won in places where Turks reside in large numbers (BBC, 2015).

Kurdish movers in London have overall higher political participation rates than Turkish ones although both groups' voting preferences are similar (Bilecen & Araz, 2015a). Their higher participation is possibly partly because of the fact that the Kurdish question is an ongoing political struggle and always on the agenda. Therefore, Kurds are more inclined to participate in political activities such as demonstrations, meetings as well as becoming members in civil society organisations and lobbying. This is also to do with the conflicts in Middle East over Kurdish towns and regions in Syria like Kobane-Rojava, events in Suruç following a deadly terrorist attack, and general elections in Turkey at the time of our field research.

In the general elections of June 7, 2015 in Turkey, the HDP (the pro-Kurdish party) gained 14,594 votes out of 24,606 casted in London, accounting for 59.3% of the total votes in the UK. It thus won the highest percentage of votes casted outside Turkey (YSK, 2015).[8]

---

[8] The national elections held on June 7, 2015 were at the top of the agenda of movers from Turkey in London. Debates were heightened with developments in Kobane around that time. A few months before the elections, debates were increasingly about whether the HDP would pass the national election threshold (10%). In this process, the community running HDP activities set up registration desks in various locations across London to encourage migrants to vote. Volunteers carried out neighbourhood activities. The associations organized campaigns for their members to vote. Even though the republican

Photo: 2015 General Election Voting Centre at Olympia, London

During the fieldwork, we observed that Kurds were especially interested in politics around the Kurdish question in Turkey and in the Middle East in general. For instance, interviewee 7 answered the question of whether he is a member of any political party as follows:

No, I'm not a member, but I am a true supporter of the resistance for the freedom of Kurdistan. I'm a Kurd. Today, the heart of the world beats in Kurdistan. Kurds are struggling for all humanity. Kurds are the ones who will represent the future and build democratic socialism. (Interviewee 7, 63 years old, male).

Another interviewee said that he followed Kurdish politics and voted for the party suggested by the PKK.

In general, the politics of the Kurdish party gets my attention. Our party says this, and we go there, whether it's a UK party or whatever. We'll do whatever our party tells us to do. The PKK is our military. (Interviewee 41, 50 years old, male).

CHP and governing AKP also formed various organizations, none of these parties were as active as the HDP in London. In the course of the two days of voting, the community in North London was mobilized to go to the election centre in Olympia, in South London. The coaches were organized from Daymer, Halkevi, Cemevi, and the Kurdish Community Centre, while in front of the metro station, volunteers with their HDP placards waited to direct people to the voting centres.

Civil society participation

Social networks, connections play a significant role in the political participation of ethnic and religious minorities (Giugni *et al.*, 2014). Through the non-governmental organisations they established, migrants continue to produce their political identities based on 'values' including sharing a common geographical origin, ethnicity, set of religious beliefs, and ideological stance. Following Putnam's (1993) suggestion that a high level of participation in non-governmental organisations leads to high level of political participation, many studies attribute importance to migrant's engagement with non-governmental organisations and the frequency of their involvement in such associations' activities, as an indication of their level of political participation.

Some recent studies on immigrants' political participation in Europe also focused on the role of non-governmental organisations and social capital (Giugni et al., 2014; Long et al. 2014; Fennema and Tillie, 2010). Hundreds of such immigrant organisations in London aim to strengthen social, cultural, and political ties among movers. They also serve to consolidate the boundaries of group identity. Since migration from Turkey to the UK has historically not developed as migration of workers but that of politically motivated groups including left wing Turks, Alevis and Kurds fleeing conflict and persecution, movers' political stances seemingly determined the character of organisations/associations they set up.

These associations are commonly referred to as 'institutions' [*kurumlar* in Turkish] among the Turkish and Kurdish movers in London. These organisations served as intermediaries and offered substantial support for movers, particularly in their early periods after arrival. They have not only offered help with the paper work and language classes, but also offered a venue, and a space for socialisation. Many of these associations in North London represent one or the other fractions of Turkey's socialist tradition or in smaller numbers perhaps, they reflect some religious divisions in Turkey.

It was clear that depending on the changing nature of population flows from Turkey and the changes in admission rules, members of these associations fluctuate as well as the number of their visitors. Nevertheless, it was clear that movers tend to distance themselves from these organisations once they settle in the UK. Movers, understandably integrate and the need for the support offered by these organisations decline over time while also having less time for social activities. A respondent we interviewed at *Emek Araştırmaları Vakfı* (Easdale Foundation for Labour Research) stated that:

In the early years, we gave a lot of help to those coming here for political reasons. We tried to solve their issues with institutions. Now these immigrants head the other way when they see us. Migrants' relations with political associations are similar. When they first arrived, they were like fish out of water, so they embraced political associations that would solve their issues. They worked for those who gave them asylum. But when they settled into their lives, they no longer had any need for these associations. Most of them became deeply occupied with the problems of life. They had no time to devote to these activities. Only the 'militant' ones remain at these associations. Others don't come through these associations, because they think that they'll ask for money.

We have observed lower participation levels in civil society activities among Turkish Cypriots compared to two other groups. One possible explanation is that compared to Turks and Kurds, Turkish Cypriots are geographically dispersed around London and across the country; so there are hardly any areas of concentration. A key reason is also the higher level of integration among Turkish Cypriots who were the first group to arrive in the UK from the 1950s onwards. Thus they are more involved in mainstream organisations. This is also evident in declining membership by those who are not first generation movers. The Cyprus Turkish Association of South London, the Democracy Association, the Hackney Cypriot Association, the Turkish Cypriot Community Association, and the Cypriot Women's Project are important associations for this group.

Membership in these associations and participation levels appear to be determined by: 1) Movers who benefited from an association in the initial periods following arrival or during the official asylum seeking process continue to engage in the activities of the same association(s). 2) Geographic origins are still effective in social relations among movers from Turkey. For example, there are many associations representing geographic origin of movers from various districts of *Maraş* province. These associations play a key role in the creation of an ethnic economy as well as for social solidarity. 3) Political and legal solidarity offered by organisations for movers attract membership. 4) Institutions engaging in religious activities and services are also attractive and active. The *Cemevi* is one of the largest organisations in London and well attended by the Alevi community. This organisation does not just offer religious services but also serves as a citizens advice bureau helping members with bureaucratic problems, while also offering translation and facilitation services, extra curricular training and support classes. Apart from this, several mosques, such as the *Aziziye* Mosque, the *Süleymaniye* Mosque, and the *Mevlana* Mosque, serve as major support organisations and socialisation places for Sunni movers along with religious services (see the later chapter on these religious organisations).

Overall, we have observed that a higher number of Kurdish movers participate more actively in association activities compared to Turkish and Turkish Cypriots. This is again partly due to a heavy and bitter agenda around the conflicts in the Middle East affecting Kurds directly. Nearly every day, Kurdish organisations have an event related to these subjects aiming to affect the public opinion in the UK.

Photo: A march by Alevi Federation in Green Lanes, Haringey, 2015

The physical space and bonding offered in these organisations are important for maintaining identity as well as socialising and other services (Holgate et al., 2012: 606). For example, interviewee 43, a restaurant manager, described what he does at the Kurdish Community Centre as follows:

If there's a meeting, I wait; I attend the meetings. I join the chats. Or I just wait and take in the air there. It's like the air of my hometown... If I don't see anyone there, I still sit there for half an hour. (Interviewee 43, 40 years old, male).

Making donations

Donations are considered to be an indication of political participation (Austin & Tjernström, 2003). Therefore, we have explored the movers' attitude towards donations to these migrant associations. Turkish Cypriots, particularly younger ones, have less interest in the politics of Cyprus, and therefore are more likely to donate to charities instead of political associations.

Interviewee 52, a Cypriot, said that she preferred to donate to charitable organizations, since she thinks that the donations she might make for political purposes would not reach the right place.

I've never made a donation. I have made other donations, but never in a political sense. I didn't donate to charities for political activities; I'm not doing this [donating] based on that idea (...) I do so because I don't have confidence about where the donation will go if I donate for political purposes. It seems to me that my income would be wasted. But I give to the homeless, although I don't directly donate to the homeless. I either donate clothes or I work as a volunteer for them... because they immediately see that contribution. But if you donate money directly, they can make a profit at the office, so, no. (Interviewee 52, 36 years old, female).

Older Turkish Cypriot interviewees who are committed to Cyprus politics tend to make monetary donations directly to political parties. For example, interviewee 51 made such donations for years:

They set 10,000 pounds as the goal from London. 10,000 pounds will be collected in London. I would give 2,000 pounds, but each year. There is this party, the Socialist Liberation Party. I would support that, too. I would support all of the existing left wing parties. (Interviewee 51, 67 years old, male).

It was more common that movers from Turkey would make monetary donations to 1) those institutions carrying out activities for religious purposes and 2) those Socialist and Kurdish movements. They seem to be selective about their choices of the causes, too:

Yes, I do it for political purposes, often for migrants coming from Syria to Turkey (...) Like I did for the ones from Somalia, Afghanistan... I donate to the ones from Muslim countries, whoever is in need. (Interviewee 36, 53 years old, female.)

Of course (...) to the utmost of my power. There are orphans I donate to, or people in times of need. (Interviewee 37, 37 years old, female).

Subscription fees for political magazines and newspapers, as well as concert and event tickets bought from various organizations, might all be considered as forms of donation. From time to time, NGOs working for the Turkish community in London meet their expenses using these kinds of monetary contributions.

After we started it [they own a café] here, leftists brought books and magazines. We have been giving them just money, that's all... Kurds... The ones from the People's House (...) (Interviewee 15, 48 years old, female)

My husband, I don't know... in the past, he used to donate to the People's House. But after we got married, he didn't ever donate. When they go to houses and ask for money, you feel a [sense of] obligation and you give money, but it never happened after our marriage. (Interviewee 10, 31 years old, female).

Some donations might function as means to maintain the balance and to keep the community alive without any religious or political discrimination:

So far, I've never become a member of any Turkish association except the mosque. When they needed something, we did the doors and windows. We help all the Cemevis and village associations (...) So far, we haven't discriminated on the basis of whether it's a Cemevi or a mosque. The Turks and this community keep us alive (Interviewee 18, 49 years old, male.).

In particular, entrepreneurs with relatively larger businesses tend to be cautious and balanced about their donations so that they appear neutral to political, ethnic and religious divisions in the community of movers from Turkey. A Kurdish respondent, who owns two restaurants in North London, was a good example:

I sponsor. I sponsor all, not just one, not only the Cemevi. You know that the community is very influential in this country. I would sponsor them, too; I would sponsor everyone. Some of my brothers in Turkey support the CHP (Republican People's Party) (...) Some are for the AKP (...) My brother's a lawyer; his business partner is from the AK Party. His partner's brother is a mayor at the X municipality (...) Now, how can I make a distinction between them? On the one hand, my brother, who has ambivalent feelings, supports the HDP (Peoples' Democratic Party), and whose interest is in supporting who (...) Since

I'm a man of trade, I don't want to be seen much. (Interviewee 45, 31 years old, male).

Kurdish movers are seemingly more active than others in terms of monetary donations, mostly for political purposes. For some Kurdish movers, making donation is a sign of commitment to the Kurdish cause.[9]

I do it on a regular basis, without hesitation. I'd say the same thing if they take me to the police. (Interviewee 7, 63 years old, male).

Always... When I was single, I used to divide my income into three... I would use one portion for myself, one for the organization, and the last one I would send to my father. Now, I'm giving less. (Interviewee 6, 47 years old, male).

Of course we are. We do it voluntarily. Nobody can take it from anyone by force. (Interviewee 41, 50 years old, male).

Attention to political developments in the media and on the internet
Interest in and attention to political news is also an indication of political participation. We have explored what movers pay attention to and which country's news they follow most through the media and the Internet. First generations are more likely to be interested in home country politics, be it Cyprus issue or Kurdish issue. This fades away among later generations. Interviewee 53 explained this as follows:
There are usually two groups. You can see that. They shouldn't be misunderstood; more elderly people are watching Turkey and Cyprus politics, and younger people are paying attention to the politics here. For instance, there is one Turkish Cypriot here with me today. He's helped me. For example, he also follows UK politics, like me; he does not even look at politics abroad. But older people, older than me, come here [the association] and always talk about Turkey and Cyprus. (Interviewee 53, 53 years old, male).

In Turkish Cypriots associations, usually politics in Cyprus is discussed, campaigns are run for the recognition of the Turkish Republic

---

[9] During fieldwork and interviews, there was an intense activity concerning Kurds. Kurds gathered primarily through the Kurdish Community Centre and *Halkevi*, as well as other non-governmental organizations, and organized many support activities for migrants from Turkey living in London. Charity funds collected during these events were sent to conflict regions such as Rojava, Kobane, and Şengal.

of Northern Cyprus as a sovereign independent state and awareness is raised among the wider public:

> *I follow it very closely. I follow the Turkish Cypriots more. In my house, the Turkish Cypriot channels are always on. I think Turkish Cypriots go through critical periods. I'm one of the founders of the Federation of Turkish Cypriot students in the UK. We had joint meetings with left-wing organizations. But that stayed in the past. After 1974, when I saw the lobbying activities of Greek Cypriots, I returned to the association to protect the rights of Turkish Cypriots because I looked around and I saw that there weren't many people interested. I also pay attention to Turkey as much as I can, since they are related.* (Interviewee 3, 61 years old, male)

There is also a degree of frustration with the Cyprus politics and some tend to stay away from it:

> *Whether I follow Cyprus or not is an open question. I follow it, but I wouldn't say anything. It's Cyprus' situation; this is Cyprus (...) They have no reasons, neither the youth nor the others (...) The youth are doing what the leaders are doing. The youth are already getting their passports and leaving.* (Interviewee 60, 44 years old, female).

> *We watch it (Cyprus) sometimes on satellite television. In Cyprus, there's deadlock after deadlock. Our [side] is also contributing to the deadlock. Nobody wants to solve it. One of the simplest problems to solve is the Cyprus issue.* (Interviewee 33, 61 years old, male).

For second generations, the whole issue was pretty out of concern: Interviewee 46, who was born and raised in the UK, felt very British, rather than Turkish or Cypriot, and did not pay attention to Turkish politics, for example:

> *There's no Turkish channel in our house. There used to be. Now they've changed the satellite. We're not able to watch them. (...) I'm more British than Turkish (...) I don't follow it. We're not religious, either. I grew up here. If I were born and raised in Cyprus, it would have been a different story.* (Interviewee 46, 33, female).

Another one stated more interest in world affairs than Cyprus or Turkey:

> *I don't pay much attention to Cyprus and Turkey. I've followed things in English in particular, so it's a mix. But it's mostly English that's spoken; the English-speaking countries are the USA, UK, Europe*

(...) I don't use Twitter. I use Facebook a bit. There are certain forums on the Internet, so I follow them. I use Reddit a lot. There are certain Internet blogs; I follow them, both from the right and from the left wing, so I try to figure out people's opinions. (...) I'm banned quite a bit; I was kicked out of those places. [Laughs]. (Interviewee 35, 22 years old, male).

Political developments in Turkey, as opposed to what is happening in the UK, receive more attention from Turkish and Kurdish movers as they follow Turkish news closely as expressed by many respondents:

I pay attention to Turkey a lot, but not to this place [the UK]. The AKP, Recep Tayyip Erdoğan's activities, and his efforts have brought Turkey to a good place. I wouldn't have come here if it had been like this [then]. There was the devaluation in the 2000s. We came here because of that. It seems to me that Turkey is doing better than this place [the UK]. (Interviewee 4, 38 years old, male).

I feel I have to follow it because we're very upset lately. Besides, if there was not this party in power that I hate, I wouldn't follow things this much. Up until two years ago, I was planning to go back to Turkey. In fact, we were planning to own a place there. We searched for a place, and all. But we gave up these plans because of the point that politics has gotten to. I would probably have returned there if there were a different ruling government. (Interviewee 29, 37 years old, female).

Turkey's politics interest me more. My heart beats for Turkey. If Turkey is happy, I'm happy; if Turkey's on edge, I am too. (Interviewee 36, 53 years old, female).

I follow Turkey more than people living in Turkey. You can ask me any question on politics. (Interviewee 6, 47 years old, male).

Some interviewees even feel distressed about the news from Turkey. They feel helpless as they cannot do anything to undo or mend what is broken in Turkey:

Now, I've started not to follow the events in Turkey. I believe it's useless and meaningless. It started to give me a headache, so I'm more concerned with things here; I follow the UK more. In fact, both of them are equal for me, but Turkey began to make me so tired. Even though I'm not living there, it's such a disturbing situation to have the feeling that it's making me tired. (Interviewee 32, 19 years old, female).

As we mentioned earlier, one of the reasons that migrants are more interested in Turkey's politics is that they do not have full command of English. The lack of language proficiency, experienced by a significant portion of first-generation immigrants, prevents them from following - and thus participating, in the UK politics. Another reason relates to the integration of first-generation immigrants. Çağlar and Onay (2015) in their work on the issue of integration, draw on Berry's 'acculturation behaviours' to explain the process by using four different concepts: integration, assimilation, separation, and marginalisation (Berry, 1997; Berry et al., 2006). In this categorisation, the vast majority of first-generation migrants from Turkey would fall under 'separation'. Hence, first-generation migrants from Turkey were likely to socialise only within their own group and also experience language proficiency problems, are inevitably more interested in Turkey's politics. There is also the issue of political inefficacy as they feel that nothing will change in the UK politics.

I follow both. I don't have a Turkish television channel but most of the time, I follow political developments in Turkey. What has changed in the UK in the last twenty years? We don't worry about this place as much as we do about Turkey. Whether the Labour Party or the other [party] comes to power it is pretty much the same. The policies are very different here. There's no policy in Turkey. In Turkey, we still say people are Turkish, Kurdish, or supporters of Fetullah [Gülen][10]. There's nothing like that here. People look at how much tax they will pay and they make their decisions accordingly. It's very easy to decide here. (Interviewee 18, 49 years old, male).

I don't follow it [the politics of the UK]. Because we don't know how to read and write in English, and also there's not much that interests us here. An election can happen or not, if you do not know. I just go and vote for the Labour Party like a sheep. It's like the Alevis who vote for the CHP in Turkey like sheep. (Interviewee 6, 47 years old, male).

---

[10] Leader of the Gulenist "hizmet" movement which has been in clash with the Turkish government since 2013 and Turkey's President R.T. Erdogan launched a crackdown on the movement and his followers, particularly after the failed military coup attempt on July 15, 2016.

Photo: A pro-PKK demonstration in London, 2015.

At the time of the interviews, the referendum on the independence of Scotland was a major political debate and our interviewees paid almost no attention to it. Similarly, the UK national elections on May 7, 2015 were of little interest, if at all, to most of the interviewees; they were more interested in the elections in Turkey:

Well, I don't follow it, obviously. We pay attention to Turkey more (...) OK, we know something about it, but for instance, when there were presidential elections in Turkey, sometimes we didn't sleep that night. We don't get any news about the elections in the UK or who becomes prime minister. Indeed, it seems as if we live in Turkey. (Interviewee 1, 44 years old, male).

The first generation movers from Turkey believed that second and later generations and younger first generation movers were less interested in the Turkish political agenda, which was also due to parental guidance:

I think that the second generation is much better (...) They have no problems with English language. This is a more educated generation. So I find them very successful. Politically, we shouldn't expect much from them. Why? Because their first-generation parents try to make their children stay away from politics. 'Oh, they shouldn't go to the associations; oh, no, they shouldn't participate in any sort of politics.' I don't blame the kids. What would the children of families with this mentality do, in a political sense? The first generation did this. So this is the reason I go to Turkey. My family was Kurdish and Alevi; even they didn't want me to go to the associations. I was kind of in the mood to fight with them and run away to Turkey... Now, think about the other families. Most of them use the associations to obtain residency. They've already received their residency permits. The UK ones are in their pocket. 'Oh, don't get involved in politics; don't get into anything.' This is the idea given to the kids. So I find it quite normal for them to stay away from politics. (Interviewee 28, 43 years old, female).

Participation in political activities

In this section, we will look at to what extent migrants participate in political activities such as rallies, demonstrations, marches, petition campaigns, and boycotts, as well as to their participation in activities related to the UK's and Turkey's political agendas. By participating in this type of activities, individuals make an effort to influence government decisions and to call attention to the issues they see important and create public awareness.

Turkish Cypriots' interest in Cypriot politics was declining as the respondents see no solution in the foreseeable future as the number of activities they can join was declining.

No. In the past, I used to participate. There was a march for Cyprus. It was August 30 or something like that, a peace thing maybe; there was also the march for the recognition of Cyprus. I participated in it a couple of times. (Interviewee 31, 46 years old, male).

We used to join during my youth. It was mostly about Cyprus. (Interviewee 51, 67 years old, male).

A lot (...) But now we don't think we can march, so we left that business to young people. This is what we do against all forms of injustice... (Interviewee 54, 81 years old, male).

Our [people] don't organise these kinds of things so much. I'm always complaining. I complain away, poking their brains about it. We're a bit weak on this issue. (Interviewee 20, 58 years old, male).

Almond and Verba (1963) suggested that "if people are satisfied with their lives, they do not need political participation." As "the crisis of legitimacy of liberal democracy" stems from liberalism's attitude of confining its citizens to the private sphere and its approach of restricting participation mechanisms, rather than leading citizens to participate in politics. The downward trend in electoral participation, distrust in the political institutions, and a wide indifference towards public and political events appear today to be the indicators of a crisis of legitimacy for Western democracy" (Barber, 1995: 22; Bauman, 2000: 116). Turkish Cypriots' indifference to politics is not far from this: *Because they're relaxed. They're satisfied.* (Interviewee 39, 18 years old, female). *Because people found their comforts.* (Interviewee 33, 61 years old, male).

Most of the activities are about Turkey, Turkish movers in the UK or some other global issue, and they take place in North London. Therefore, those living nearby were more likely to participate in such activities compared to those living elsewhere. Even the south of London was seen as far away by some respondents: *No. Such things don't happen on our side [of the city].* (Interviewee 57, 76 years old, female).

The political sensitivities of Turkish migrants, living socially intertwined in North London, can be different. For example, Sunni conservatives described their political activities as activities organized often related to issues that concern the Muslim world.

I participated, but I have participated in things about the case of Egypt. We already participated in [activities] related to the events in Palestine and Egypt. I have a little activist spirit. (Interviewee 37, 37 years old, female).

Sometimes (...) The last time I participated in was the Mavi Marmara march. [His friend asks, "At the time of Rabia, so you were not here?"] No, I was not there in Rabia (...) The petition campaign against private education, I joined that. (Interviewee 26, 43 years old, male).

Because of the dominance of small family run businesses and prevalence of long working hours, many respondents felt that there was no time to participate in political activities.

The most active participation was observed among the Kurds. This was partly because of the fact that many of them arrived in the UK as asylum seekers often claiming involvement with the Kurdish movement in Turkey (See also Bilecen & Araz, 2015b: 198). Also there were many events organised around the Kurdish issue which made more Kurds to participate:

Yup. I joined a hundred of them in three months. I worked all day and stood in front of the parliament at night, and I went to work in the morning. (Interviewee 30, 38 years old, female).

I'm very much affected by the war in Kobane. I felt a sense of responsibility as a human being. When there's a good march, I participate. I join petition campaigns (...) Also for UK politics (...) especially if there are acquaintances, we act together. It can be in our neighbourhood or in our relationships at school. (Interviewee 14, 45 years old, female).

I participate. Here, for example, in the Haringey area, I'm the only one today collecting signatures for the leader [başkan in Turkish] Öcalan's freedom. I collected two thousand five hundred signatures. Everybody asked me, "What are you doing?" So we don't ask for anything bad. (Interviewee 7, 63 years old, male).

All of them (...) I try to attend all the events concerning us. Especially in the most recent period, our struggle, the party, the hunger strike organized by the Kurdish Community Centre, marches and campaigns— I'm trying to participate in all of them as much as I can. Rojava, Sengal, Kobane, all of them (...) I participate in all the marches related to support for workers and oppressed people, too, in the UK. I do my best not to miss any of them. (Interviewee 42, 38 years old, male).

Kobane protests, the capture of Serok [Abdullah Öcalan] (...) Newroz (...) I join all these protests (...) (Interviewee 41, 50 years old, male).

Apparently as time passes and movers settle in their new country, their interest in asylum policy and procedures declines which were two key important topics for Kurdish movers in early years as many of them were waiting for decisions on asylum applications. These organisations were organising events and offering services informing and guiding applicants in the asylum processes:

Sometimes we participate. In the first years, we were participating quite a lot. You move away from these activities, as you get more relaxed. (Interviewee 1, 44 years old, male).

One should not forget certain events had a powerful impact on political participation rates among Turkish and Kurdish movers. For example, the Gezi events[11] in Turkey in 2013 encouraged and attracted many who were not participating in any political activities in the community. The community from Turkey, meanwhile, has organized a series of activities. Forums, similar to those held in Turkey during the Gezi events, were held at various public parks and sites in London. During our field research, it was felt that Gezi mobilised more women compared to men in the community:

---

[11] For further information on Gezi protests in Turkey the relevan literature can be consulted: e.g. Gürcan & Peker, 2014; Gül et al., 2014; Arat, 2013.

I followed a lot, especially at the time of the Gezi events. (Interviewee 35, 22 years old, male).

Yes... I attended during Gezi Park protests. I participated in the one at Trafalgar Square (...) I went to the embassy (...) Also for the Berkin Elvan [little boy who lost his life during Gezi events] protest (...) I participated in the activities related to student fees, too. (Interviewee 39, 18 years old, female).

For example, very recently, I took part in the protests and marches during the Gezi protests. I attended the forums. (Interviewee 8, 36-year-old, female).

I joined the ones for the Gezi events. Other than that, I did not participate. (Interviewee 21, 31 years old, female).

Unfortunately, (...) I participated in the marches only because of the Gezi events. (Interviewee 12, 35 years old, female).

Direct or indirect contact with politicians

Another dimension of political participation is establishing direct or indirect contact with politicians. Establishing contact with politicians is an indicator of people getting the benefits of citizenship rights at the local level and taking responsibility for issues related to their social environment. In the narrow district electoral system in the UK, towns are divided into districts. Each region has a parliamentarian, and parliamentarians meet with the public from their district on certain days of the week. It is very easy to reach out to the district MPs in London. Another dimension of local participation is the town councils. In the local elections of 2014, the community from Turkey carried out an active political campaign. As a consequence, the community won seats on the town councils, initially in Enfield, but also on the Islington, Hackney and Haringey councils. For example, at the Enfield Council, among 41 town councillors, 13 originate from Cyprus and Turkey. This shows that the majority of town councillors (apart from the Turkish Cypriots) entered the council as a result of the *Cemevi*'s effective work in the region. The current mayor, Ali Bakır, was also elected in this way (Enfield Council, 2015). [12]

---

[12] There are also town councillors from Turkey in other municipalities of regions inhabited by the community from Turkey. There are two town councillors from Turkey in Islington, three in Haringey, and four in Hackney (Haringey.gov.uk, 2015; Hackney.gov.uk, 2015; Islington.gov.uk, 2015).

Based on the interviews, we see that Cypriot migrants have more contact with local politicians. Almost all of the Cypriot interviewees have direct or indirect contacts with politicians. All the interviewees implied that it was very easy to reach politicians in the UK. Established relations with politicians, rather than party loyalty, are essential to taking steps towards the solution of the existing problems and lobbying activities in the political sense. Cypriot migrants have more relations with local politicians compared to the community from Turkey. Their language fluency and knowledge of how local politics works play a significant role in this regard.

There are MPs I know, of course. We are closely acquainted with the Liberal MP, Simon Hughes, from this region (...) [The Minister of Justice from the Liberal Party at the time of the Liberal-Conservative coalition.] He also invites us to their meetings. He recently invited us to a party held in parliament. Other than that, there is Lord McKenzie (...) In the past, there was also Meral Ece. Our MP, Andy Love (...) We also have relations with the candidates. (Interviewer 3, 61 years old, male.)

Of course we had contacts. Our most recent contact was with David Lammy from the Conservative Party (...) About the Cyprus issue (...) Before that, we had relationships with our town councillors. (Interviewee 20, 58 years old, male).

Simon Hughes (...) the MP of the Liberal Democrats, is currently the Minister of Justice (...) He has been the MP who is closest to the Turkish Cypriot community. Once he was pro-Cypriot Greek, because his sister was married to a Greek. His general secretary is Selçuk Akıncı; thanks to him, he mingled with Turks. He got along well with us so far. (Interviewee 57, 76 years old, female).

If they feel a necessity, migrants contact town councillors in the region they live and MPs from that region.[13] Most of the interviewees we talked to know the names of most MPs from their respective regions, and they

---

[13] In the answers given to the question of direct or indirect contact with politicians, we found that the majority of the migrants from Turkey living in North London have contact with MPs from the region. There are especially close relationships between the regional MPs from the Labour Party and the community from Turkey. For instance, at the time when this chapter was first drafted, Jeremy Corbyn, a regional MP from Islington, who became the candidate for the Labour Party presidency, visited the Day-Mer, the Britain Alevi Federation, and the London Cemevi in order to win the support of the community from Turkey. (acikgazete.com, 2015, olaygazetesi.co.uk, 2015).

expressed that they could contact them in case of necessity. Some interviewees compared this situation with the one in Turkey.

Yes. We invited one MP and said look, we've done this kind of work. Here, with ten people, we had a meal together and asked questions. He came from the Labour Party and he didn't object to our invitation. If you call an MP and they don't come, that's a minus point for them. They talk with two or three people every day at the door. Very easy. If they'll do it, they say yes; if they can't do it, they just say no. There's no bribery or anything. It's not something that would happen with such humble people like us. They say, "talk to this person or that person," leading us. Otherwise, they just say that they also don't know and can't help. (Interviewee 18, 49 years old, male).

Of course, you can go now and tell your problems to the MPs. Wait your turn, talk, and come back (...) I haven't done it as of yet, but I have friends who go and talk. In Turkey, it's impossible. Here, they have to listen to the community. (Interviewee 13, 38 years old, male).

Very easy. Sometimes the MP from my region knocks on the door and comes in. That MP doesn't come with fifty security guards following, but just alone, by bike. (Interviewee 42, 38 years old, male).

Working in the food sector, especially, enables Turkish migrants to establish close relationships with the MPs from their region and with town councillors. Interviewee 25, manager of a cafe, suggests that he has hosted many politicians from the UK and Turkey in his workplace.

It happens directly. For instance, our Labour Party members gather here once a month. We can tell them our problems. Council members from the Hackney Municipality gather here. Simon Hughes, for example, comes here at least once every two months and has a meal here with his own team. We can tell them our problems. We're already in direct contact with the politicians from Turkey. Muharrem İnce, Uğur Dündar, and Ali Pekşen, all the brain team of the CHP came here. They always come through our connections. Two weeks ago, the president of the Iraqi Turkmen Front came here. (Interviewee 25, 52 years old, male).

The Green Lanes area, within the boundaries of Haringey Council in London, is home to an especially high number of ethnic restaurants and businesses. Their managers are usually Kurds, and restaurants with Turkish names serve other communities as much as the Turkish community. Another interviewee, who owns a restaurant in Green Lanes, said that he was almost proud of having many politicians at his restaurant.

I met with Ed Miliband. I met with two MPs (...) Town councillors (...) I recently met with the mayor. That woman likes me. An emotional bond was formed between us. [He shows a photo.] (Interviewee 45, 31 years old, male).

Kurdish immigrants sometimes get in contact with politicians, especially in order to make the Kurdish issue heard in the international platform at the British parliament, and they organize joint events at the parliament with those who are closer to them. In this regard, it is possible to say that Alevis are as active as Kurds. The Britain Alevi Federation is very active in the UK. The Federation works to increase the recognition of Alevis and to draw attention to the problems of Alevis in Turkey and the Middle East. As a result of the effective lobbying of the Britain Alevi Federation, the Charity Commission of England and Wales recognized Alevism as a religious belief in October 2015 (Cumhuriyet, 2015). The *Cemevi* in Dalston, besides being a religious centre, also hosts a variety of events and politicians.

In our region, there was a lady called Makbule and she's now become a member of the town council (...) We met her (...) They formed a group called Labour for Kurds. I'm thinking of joining, but I couldn't find the chance yet. So, I mean, I want to join their group. (Interviewee 28, 43 years old, female).

We sometimes go and present our files to the parliament in the name of the Kurdish Community Centre. They sometimes come to our events. Sometimes our people come, too. For example, I listen to the MPs from the CHP. But I don't go to the ones from the AK Party and I don't want to. (Interviewee 30, 38 years old, female).

Over the course of a few decades of migration, migrants from Turkey seem to have a fairly good understanding of the dynamics of the UK political system. However, as we have previously noted, issues of integration arising from closed-off socialisation, language issues, the tendency to approach political life in the UK through the lens of Turkey, etc. all keep first-generation immigrants away from UK politics. A Cypriot interviewee offers a critique concerning this issue in the following way:

We don't know politics. We don't know how to establish relations. Our active politicians are gradually rising. We saw it in the municipal elections. In the last elections, new names won in the municipal elections, but how far can they go? We stand here as separate communities— Cypriots, Kurds, Turks, Alevis, Sunnis, or whatever, nobody would take us seriously. But if we gather under the umbrella of a Turkish-speaking community, or rather as I call it, the British Turks (...) Sometimes Kurdish friends don't like it. You have to give it a title. This is something that you can perceive in English. That's the only way to be a power. (Interviewee 58, 44 years old, female).

Trust in politics

In the literature, there is a direct and positive relationship between citizens' political participation and their trust in politics. In this relationship, trust in politics also creates a ground of legitimacy for political participation (Fennema and Tillie, 2010). Given this, interviewees were asked how much they trust political institutions and the legal structures of the system in the United Kingdom, Turkey, and/or Cyprus. The responses to this question provide us a satisfying amount of data concerning which political system migrants would prefer as they make comparisons between the countries of settlement and of origin.

A majority of Cypriot interviewees said that they never trust the political institutions in Cyprus, while they have more trust in political structures and legal mechanisms in the UK. Lack of trust in the political structure of the TRNC is related to key issues such as disbelief in the resolution of the Island's political problems, political instability, corruption, and bribery.

If we consider the TRNC, I believe that people's rights aren't given over there, due to the issue of connections. They go to the door of politicians. People are in need of politicians to make their works done. So they go to the door of politicians. (Interviewee 47, 24 years old, female).

They say that there's democracy in Cyprus, but there's not actually. There's a lot of corruption there. Connections and everything (...) There's really too much injustice in Cyprus (...) It's about the people, not about political parties; the people (...) Because of all that corruption and injustice, I don't trust it at all. But at least here there are human rights, so even if corruption exists here—we don't know at the high level—there's a balance. There's an equilibrium. So it gives us some more trust. (Interviewee 52, 36 years old, female).

It's better not to consider Cyprus. There's no such thing as Cyprus, rather the island of the mafia. Corruption, everything. The UK is an island too, but there's a system here. (Interviewee 60, 44 years old, female).

The non-recognition of the TRNC in the international world and its dependency on Turkey when it comes to internal matters are both issues that adversely affect some interviewees' trust in the political institutions of this country. On the other hand, Turkish Cypriots cannot vote in the TRNC elections from the UK. This emerges as another reason for this existing distrust.

So you know, Cyprus is a non-recognized country. Due to this non-recognition, anyone can do anything they want there. At voting time, they manipulate votes. Some votes are stolen. And Cyprus can't decide on its own. Since it's dependent on Turkey, whatever comes from them [Turkey], they [Cyprus] must do it. That's why I'm sure that we can't do some things we want to do. (Interviewee 55, 42 years old, female).

Almost all the Cypriot interviewees expressed that they have more trust in UK politics. They justified this position by citing factors such as equality before law in the UK; equal opportunities; the absence of discrimination; and the absence of people intervening in the functioning of institutions for their own interests.

Of course, this country gives you more trust. Because there are no connections. In Turkey, Hasan is Huseyin's son, and he's a police or military officer. It gives him an advantage. But in the UK whoever you are, it doesn't make much difference (...). This place is certainly much better in terms of the law. (Interviewer's 23, 39 years old, male).

Of course, the UK is a place that gives you more confidence. In fact, Cyprus should reproduce all the things in the UK system. But they can't do it. It's supposed to be like that, but it can't be done. So now people do things based on whatever their interests are. It's similar in religion. That's my opinion. They can even turn milk black, that's my opinion (Interviewee 33, 61 years old, male).

This place is (...) the UK (...) a place where the legal system is not 100%, but it's at least more democratic than Turkey and Cyprus and more settled. So it's not easy to change the existing law. It's not the case that one person or two people would decide to change such-and-such an article in the constitution. (Interviewee 34, 54 years old, female).

When it comes to trust in politics, even those who think of the UK as the lesser evil share a sense of trust in the UK's legal system. Most Cypriot interviewees share the idea that everyone is equal before the law in the UK.

Unfortunately, here (...) I did work in this country for many years. I haven't had even one day of trouble at my work. The letter arrives on one day or the next, but it arrives every time. There's always someone to answer the phone. So the bureaucracy is super. There was no problem, I'm telling you. 40 years have gone by. (Interviewee 51, 67 years old, male).

When we look at the answers of migrants from Turkey on the question of trust, conservative Sunnis and the Turkish side have an extreme trust for Turkey's politics. For this reason, among Sunni conservatives, the desire to return to Turkey is more dominant (Bilecen & Araz, 2015a).

Of course, the one in Turkey (...) Here things are corrupted, lying, criminal, capitalist (...) I'm saying everything openly; this is who I am (...) (Interviewee 36, 53 years old, female).

If we compared my life in Turkey, in terms of politics, political and religious habits, my life was better in Turkey. It gives me more confidence, obviously. If I had the opportunity now, I would go back. I would have done something. But unfortunately, we have to follow our choices and live accordingly. (Interviewee 22, 32 years old, male).

The notion of equality before the law in the UK leads migrants from Turkey to have more trust in UK politics compared to Turkey. One female interviewee mistaken the question of trust as a question of personal security and indicated that she felt more confident in the UK.

The UK definitely gives you confidence. I don't trust anything in any way in Turkey. The law gets violated, rights get violated. It's pretty difficult for us to trust in Turkey's politics. You have to be pretty blind. It's also debatable how democratic the UK is, but still, they don't violate the law. If the laws are violated, it's penalized. In Turkey, so many women are killed, but those men are walking free on the streets like nothing happened. If something like that happens here, the man gets punishment, but in Turkey you're putting the man who murdered his two wives on a woman's TV show. What are you going to trust in? (Interviewee 32, 19 years old, female).

Kurds in general answered the question of trust in politics by saying that they did not trust the political and legal system in Turkey at all and that they felt trust for the political system in the UK. Among Kurdish interviewees, an emphasis on human rights stands out in their trust for UK politics.

Of course, the UK (...) The system... it's not fully socialist, but human rights are more at the forefront (...) also social rights... As a woman, I don't think I can find these conditions in Turkey. Maybe I can be more comfortable economically, but as a woman, I don't feel free in Turkey (...) (Interviewee 14, 45 years old, female).

As a socialist, I know the system in the UK very well. Despite its inadequacies and its wrongs, I believe it's more democratic and it's a system prioritizing human rights at a level incomparable to Turkey. (Interviewee 17, 52 years old, female).

Certainly, the UK (...) So we can see the results (...) The system in Turkey is absolutely unreliable. I don't trust it. It didn't give me a sense of trust. If a man throws a stone and is sentenced to 15 years in prison, how can you trust that? (Interviewer 43, 40 years old, male).

The UK (...) It gives me trust because there's something called human rights, women's rights. I think none of those is ever developed in Turkey. (Interviewee 50, 25 years old, female).

Even though feeling more trust in UK political institutions is a common tendency among Turkish and Kurdish interviewees, some immigrants have doubts about political institutions in the UK that include discriminatory and pragmatic elements.

Is there a legal structure left in Turkey? (Laughs) No, we don't trust either of them, but on the other hand, I don't think there's anything left of the legal system in Turkey. (...) There was a little bit of trust in the law. The man erased that. So, he pretty much erased it. Me and my husband, for example, always discuss the UK. I think of it as more democratic, and I feel more secure. He always says, do something that doesn't suit their interests; then you'll see what happens. The same thing happened three to five months ago. Women chained themselves in front of the Parliament and they took them away by beating them. See, we're in the most democratic country. This is such a hypocritical democracy. (Interviewee 28, 43 years old, female).

Among these migrant groups, trust felt for political institutions in the UK does not translate into a motivation for political participation. This is especially a result of the factors listed in relation to the situation of first-generation immigrants.

General patterns of political participation

Turkish Cypriots have shown the lowest political party loyalty among the respondents. They seem to choose the party to vote for by examining party programs and rhetoric. Turkish Cypriots had the lowest participation in elections too. Party membership is extremely low among Turks and Kurds from mainland Turkey. Most Turkish movers we have spoken had a tendency to vote for the Labour Party because of its policies towards migrants. Non-working female movers had a lower level of political participation compared to men. It seems mainly due to their limited language skills and their absence from public life. Long working hours is another reason for low level of political participation.

Community organizations referred to as 'institutions' make an important contribution to the socialization of movers. These organisations tend to link with certain socialist political factions in Turkey. Participation in such civil society activities were lowest among Turkish Cypriots and highest among the Kurds. Religious associations, such as *Cemevis* and mosques, offer religious services while also enabling movers to develop religious identities.

Political donations were more frequent among the Kurds and very rare among Turkish Cypriots. These donations were often directed towards religious purposes and associations and to the socialist and Kurdish movements. For some Kurdish movers, making donations indicate a strong commitment to the Kurdish cause. Generally, movers trust in political institutions and legal mechanisms in the UK but not in the places of origin.

Older generations are more likely to follow politics in media, whereas later generations are seemingly more interested in world politics. Language proficiency is one reason barring some participants from following the UK politics. The Kurds and Alevis were politically more active and interested in both Turkish and the UK politics. As a result of this interest and increasing participation, in recent elections, they gained a considerable number of council seats in London.

Chapter 4. Ankara Agreement and the new wave of movers

International human mobility and the ways in which people move are often shaped by the drivers uprooting people in home countries as well as admission rules and regulations in destination countries (Massey, 2015). People manoeuvre to overcome legal and practical barriers and exploit every possibility to achieve the desired move. When there are wars, like in the cases of Syria and Iraq, refugee flows become dominant, when there are no legal entry routes left, irregular moves follow. In this chapter, we focus on a new and relatively small stream of population movement from Turkey to Britain: movers of the Ankara Agreement, one of the European Community Association Agreements. This agreement's resident permit clause allows Turkish citizens to migrate to the UK without going through the normal work visa process. Although the agreement was signed in 12 September 1963 between Turkey and the European Economic Community (EEC) of the time and the UK became bound by it in 1973 when it joined the EEC; Turkish citizens first attempted to benefit from this agreement in 2002, when getting work permits and refugee status through usual channels became rather difficult. This is a route more suitable for the entrepreneurial and professional visa applications, as these movers often differ from other migrants in terms of having higher education and skill levels including language fluency. Nevertheless, as we will discuss below, they do not differ much in terms of the fact that their moves were also a response to various conflicts and perception of human insecurity in Turkey as well as not differing in terms of facing various difficulties and tensions in the UK as suggested by the "conflict model of migration" (see Sirkeci, 2009).

This chapter draws upon a field study based on semi-structured interviews conducted with 20 respondents who were recruited through snowball sampling in London in 2015. The interviews were conducted in different places and lasted between 30 to 80 minutes from 15th February to 15th May 2015. The respondents included eight women and 12 men with an average age of 35. Typically, they moved in their late 20s and were living in Britain for about five years at the time of the research. Except for three, all interviewees were single. 12 interviewees were university graduates, four had master degrees, three completed high school and one completed primary school. 10 interviewees identified themselves as Turkish while four were Kurdish, one Turkmen, one Zaza, one Hamsheni and two were self identified as mixed.

To ensure confidentiality, names of the respondents were replaced with numbers which are cited in this chapter. For recruitment and to immerse in the research environment, Turkish migrants' associations, community centres, culture centres, restaurants, cafes, pubs, and university canteens were visited. Work places of immigrants were also visited. To obtain information about the legal and financial aspects of the Ankara Agreement based visas, interviews were conducted with two attorneys and an accountant with knowledge and experience in the field.

Four broad topics were covered in the interviews: Demographic backgrounds of respondents; reasons for migration and problems faced in the visa application process; adaptation and relations with the Turkish community and other communities; feelings, perceptions and future expectations. The total numbers and statistics on people who moved within Ankara Agreement scheme were obtained from the Home Office.

What is Ankara Agreement?

Ankara Agreement (officially the "Agreement Creating An Association Between The Republic of Turkey and the European Economic Community") was signed between Turkey and the EC in 1963 in Ankara and aimed to sustain economic and then political integration of both sides. This integration process is composed of three consecutive stages which are preparation, transition and completion. When the UK joined the EC in 1973, it became party to this agreement. Provisions about the workers' free movement of the "Treaty on the Functioning of the European Union" were put under the "Free Movement of Services and Capital" in Articles 45, 46, 47 and 48. Later on, clauses about free movement had been interpreted again with several revisions (e.g. Additional Protocol, Association Council Decision etc.) (Sevimli & Recber, 2014). This agreement entitles Turkish citizens to apply for a residence permit in all EU member countries.

This agreement came handy for Turkish citizens who want to move to the UK after the court decided in favour of Veli Tum and Mehmet Dari in 2007 confirming that the Ankara Agreement allows Turkish citizens to move to the UK freely for business purposes. Veli Tum, from Germany, came to the UK from France by boat in 2001 and Mehmet Dari, from France, came to the UK from France by boat in October 1998. When their applications for asylum were refused with a deportation order, they applied to the European Court of Human Rights and eventually won the case and granted permission to stay (Sevimli & Recber, 2014: 430).

To start a business or to be employed in Britain, Turkish citizens can benefit from the Ankara Agreement. The applicants in this scheme are required to prove that their earnings in Britain will be sufficient to maintain themselves. Initially a one-year leave to remain (residence permit) is given to applicants through this Ankara Agreement scheme. After this one-year period, the applicant must apply to renew the residence permit and convince the Home Office about the viability of their businesses and earnings (Home Office, 2015c). In the past, Home Office had issued three-year extensions of residence permits after the first year but recently it was also the case that some applicants were issued only one-year extensions at a time. After completion of four years, the person can obtain the permanent resident status. Until 2009, applications were only possible after arrival in the UK. Following a European Court of Justice decision, since 7 September 2009, applications made from Turkey were also allowed.

Social factors in migration decision

Half of the respondents came to the UK for language courses while the remaining cited education or tourism for their reason to move. Four interviewees had applied for entry clearance through Ankara Agreement while they were in Turkey. These were a musician, a graphic designer who was avoiding military service and looking for better living standards, an entrepreneur, and an academic who were under political and social pressure. Similar motivations were observed among other respondents who filed their applications after arriving in the UK.

Existence of a 'migration culture' is believed to be a driver for further migrations (Cohen and Sirkeci, 2011). Improved communication and transportation systems along with established migration experience facilitate two way population flows (including circular migration) between countries as is the case with Germany and Turkey (see Zeyneloglu & Sirkeci, 2015: 218). King and Skeldon (2010) draw attention to the importance of social connections when examining internal as well as international migration. As shown in Figure 4.1, Turkish and Kurdish migrants follow a step-wise migration; in other words, they have internal migration experience prior to their international move and they continue to move internally at the country of destination too. These moves can also be linked to the fact that there are certain places where migrants with similar backgrounds concentrate in destination countries.

Figure 4.1. displays migration trajectories of the respondents where the first column shows their places of birth in Turkey and the other columns indicate their migrations in Turkey and in the UK. It is clear that all respondents had migration experience prior to their move to the UK and they moved from their birthplaces to metropolitan areas, mostly to Istanbul. In this small group of respondents, the fact that many were from provinces of Maras, Tunceli (Dersim), Kayseri and Sivas also indicates that migrant networks play a role in their moves and destination choices since these provinces are common among the places of origin of Turkish and Kurdish immigrants in London.

Figure 4.1. Respondents' stepwise moves

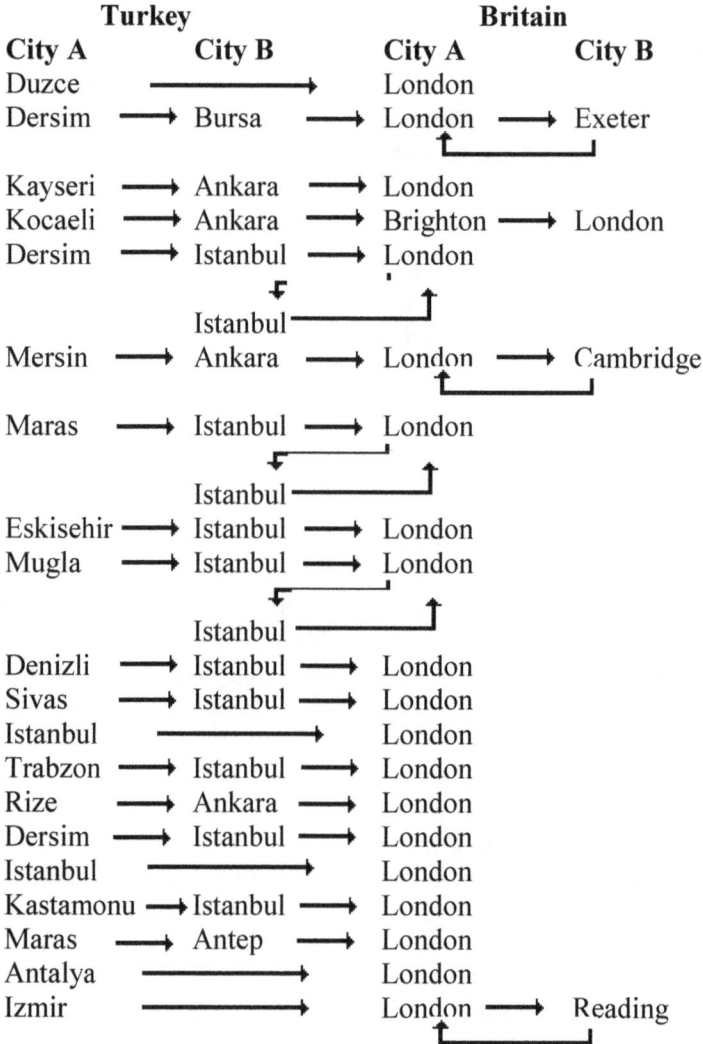

	Turkey		**Britain**	
City A	**City B**		**City A**	**City B**
Duzce	⟶		London	
Dersim	⟶ Bursa	⟶	London ⟶	Exeter

Kayseri	⟶ Ankara	⟶	London	
Kocaeli	⟶ Ankara	⟶	Brighton ⟶	London
Dersim	⟶ Istanbul	⟶	London	
	Istanbul			
Mersin	⟶ Ankara	⟶	London ⟶	Cambridge
Maras	⟶ Istanbul	⟶	London	
	Istanbul			
Eskisehir	⟶ Istanbul	⟶	London	
Mugla	⟶ Istanbul	⟶	London	
	Istanbul			
Denizli	⟶ Istanbul	⟶	London	
Sivas	⟶ Istanbul	⟶	London	
Istanbul	⟶		London	
Trabzon	⟶ Istanbul	⟶	London	
Rize	⟶ Ankara	⟶	London	
Dersim	⟶ Istanbul	⟶	London	
Istanbul	⟶		London	
Kastamonu	⟶ Istanbul	⟶	London	
Maras	⟶ Antep	⟶	London	
Antalya	⟶		London	
Izmir	⟶		London ⟶	Reading

Few of the respondents returned to Istanbul and then remigrated to London. Similarly, perhaps, those who moved to other cities in the UK also returned to London, where upto 70 % of Turkey-linked populations reside and maintain a strong ethnic enclave. Typically, people moved to join their families, friends and relatives:

My brother was living here [in London]. He arrived here in 1966. He is still here with his family. His children, my sister and my aunts are also here [in London] like all others who came from Maras. My brother helped me to move here. (Interviewee 7, Male, 29 years old)

Similar to the case of Turks and Kurds in Germany (see Sirkeci, 2006), such social networks and family ties are assumed to reduce the risks associated with migration. Hence this also indicates a need for "human security" in relative insecurity of the destination. Having relatives and prior experience of London as a student or a tourist have helped movers to choose London as a destination. Only four of our interviewees had no prior experience or social networks in the UK. Nine have been helped by people who have lived in London. In this regard, movers by Ankara Agreement scheme are no different than other movers. For example, one respondent who is an opera singer was influenced by her sister who lives in London:

My sister has been here. She is a British citizen. I wanted to join her. I do not mean staying with her in the same house as she is living with her family but at least being in the same city comforts me psychologically. (Interviewee 16, Male, 38 years old)

Respondent 20 came to the UK on a tourist visa and his brother was already living in Reading:

I came here to visit my brother. After one week, he told me to stay and insisted. Then I decided to stay and lived in Reading for three months and moved to London. (Interviewee 20, Female, 31 years old)

Interviewee 1, a 27-year-old-woman, also came to visit her sibling and her relatives in London. Despite her intention was to stay for one month, her relatives "so to speak, detained her and would not let her go back". Apparently she has a large network of relatives in the UK. They comforted her a great deal and she ended up staying longer. After four months, she, under the influence of relatives, has decided to stay permanently. Her sister had come to the UK five years earlier to settle.

Family and social pressure and political factors

It was important to understand what made this particular group of people move abroad, or flee Turkey. Our sample was largely composed of professionals who left their careers to move abroad and university graduates who were potential white-collar workers in Turkey. Why do such people move, despite all the costs, risks and difficulties? Why does one move knowing that he or she would have relatively better living conditions back in Turkey compared to London?

Conflicts experienced by an individual with his/her family and/or social environment could sometimes trigger the desire to migrate. For example, the Interviewee 19 said that following the central university entrance and placement exam in Turkey, she had to attend a university that she did not want, simply because of the pressures of her family and relatives. Turkey was a restrictive place for her. These pressures had a significant impact on her desire to leave Turkey. Hence, she secretly attended a language school without telling her family; and then travelled to the UK relying on bank loans.

Turkey became restrictive to me, it really did. I came here after many adverse incidents in my life. I couldn't find what I wanted for my education. It wasn't a place that I wanted and loved (...) I applied to come here by myself. I came here by taking out a bank loan. My parents didn't even know about that. (Interviewee 19, female, 32 years old)

Speaking about family pressure, Interviewee 11 also said, "I ran away in order to live." His conflicts with his family significantly affected his decision to migrate:

There's always family pressure. 'Look, he did this; your aunt's son did that.' He lived an unhappy life, he married at an early age, he had economic problems, and then I have to do this or that. You know what they say: everyone is born, but only some people live. But in our country, my own family was among those who were born, but weren't able to live. I escaped in order to live, so I could live. When I came here, the first week, I felt like I was living. (...) You live there at home with your family, and [it's always] someone did this or that. They pull you into the dark. And unfortunately, they're successful at it. Unfortunately, those ignorant people get you down in a deep hole some way or the other. You're questioning what happened to you, or they take you to their own circles [networks]. I came here to get away from this a little. (Interviewee 11, male, 31 years old)

According to Bakewell (2010: 1705), the conventional migration literature is unable to adequately explain 'forced' and 'voluntary' migration. In order to consider a situation of 'forced migration,' the individual compelled to migrate need not be living under conditions of war or civil war, or be the victim of physical violence. Rather than looking at the forced or voluntary characteristics of international migration, the conflict model instead assesses migration as a quest for human security or as a desire to escape from insecure conditions (Sirkeci, 2012: 356). Some of the interviewees stated that factors in their decision to migrate included societal pressures and the extreme political atmosphere of Turkey. For instance, Interviewee 10 resigned from his job as a university professor because of political circumstances. It was not an easy decision, but he then moved to London from Turkey with his wife through the Ankara Agreement:

First of all, the main reason I've come here is the political situation that's gained momentum in the last ten years. (...) We were just thinking of leaving. It was just an idea that was entirely about going somewhere, because Istanbul really stifled us. We got really bored. (...) The condition of universities in Turkey, the political situation, the socio-political situation on the streets, everywhere I went, it all started to make me feel a bit constrained. My wife was the same way. In the last three or four years, we've started to talk quite seriously about where we can go. (Interviewee 10, male, 35 years old)

Interviewees told us that they were looking for a relatively secure place where they can live and they were comparing social and political conditions between the two potential destinations:

I don't know, after a certain point, you start to like the multiculturalism, the colourful atmosphere here. You realize that there are actually very good opportunities here (...) The problematic things in Turkey are settled here, and they aren't spoken of. These things shaped my mind here, a bit. I decided to stay in this country based on these things. (Interviewee 2, male, 35 years old)

Even though Interviewee 3 experienced many difficulties in the first year after he arrived in the UK, he did not want to return to Turkey; he noted that the ethnic and religious discrimination that he experienced in Turkey, particularly at work, had a significant impact on his decision. Looking at the political conditions in Turkey, he believed that he had made the right decision in living in London:

Now, obviously Turkey wasn't very promising in terms of working conditions. The job I was doing in Turkey would go well sometimes, and it would go poorly the rest of the time. Or, I don't know, if you have a different political position and ethnic origin, they might not give you a job based on that ethnic origin and political background. (...) Here whatever your culture, religion, ideology, belief is, they don't care. They even encourage you; they say, 'come and do this job,' but the opposite is at play in Turkey. They're trying to stop you. (...) And when you see recent political developments in Turkey, you say, 'it's a good thing that I came here.' (Interviewee 3, male, 42 years old)

Interviewee 14, who left his secure office job in Turkey and moved to London by benefiting from the Ankara Agreement, said that he did not want to return to Turkey. It was not, he said, because he would be seen as a failure but rather because of possible public pressure and exclusion in Turkey. He thought he would not be able to sustain a life he wanted to have and would not be able to find a better job there:

I gave up a job as a civil servant that wasn't that bad. (...) The shared environment, the way people behave towards one another. (...) The neighborhood pressure (...) You can't be yourself. (...) Being judged by people (...) I don't know what else. You can't freely express your religious beliefs in the workplace, or among friends. The job doesn't come before these things. I just said this before. (Interviewee 14, male, 33 years old)

Another source of conflict, we have come across in the field research was about gender security. Women and homosexuals who do not feel secure in their country of origin move to places where they can express their sexual identities freely. After finishing his graduate studies in the UK, Interviewee 4 decided to stay in the UK. He implied that his sexual orientation affected his decision to stay:

I didn't suffer from sexual harassment much in Turkey, because I didn't seem [gay]. But I still think that London being the 'gay capital' could have had a bit of an effect. I wanted to know a bit more about London's gay life (...) Oh, I know, if somebody acts in a homophobic manner toward me, I go to the police and that person gets screwed. There's this guarantee. This is a good thing. (...) You're living in London with the perspective of being a gay person from Turkey. It has an effect; do you get that? You're in a gay capital [of the world]. When I lived in Turkey, it was my dream. I preferred Brighton, a little, because of this. That's why sexuality is important in one's life. It does have an effect. I really liked that idea: right now I'm in one of the gay capitals of the world and I won't die without having experienced it. I've seen that, too: what people really live. Because in Istanbul and Ankara we live our lives deprived of many things. (Interviewee 4, male, 30 years old)

A female interviewee explained her reason for moving to London as no longer being able to 'define' herself and feel safe in Turkey:

It was because I couldn't define myself in Turkey anymore. I didn't know what the next step would be and what would happen. I didn't feel safe. Maybe it was actually in order to have a break and look at things that I came here for a language school. (Interviewee 6, female, 44 years old)

One interviewee, a therapist, said that, as a woman, she was disturbed by the way women are seen and treated in Turkey, and this strongly affected her desire to live in London:

When I think about my life, the way people view women always gets on my nerves. Even when I'm watching it on TV, it's annoying. I also get pissed off watching ads, so that I'm in a constant state of nervous breakdown, even when I'm on holiday. I feel so uncomfortable that I don't want to go back. (Interviewee 12, female, 29 years old)

Migration does not always resolve the conflict. It may even lead to more conflicts and these may lead to further migration. These can be expressed and unfolded at different levels; in relations between individuals (the micro level), within the family and society (the meso level), or between states (the macro level) or systems or across these levels (Sirkeci, 2012: 356; Sirkeci and Cohen 2016: 385). For example, compulsory military service in Turkey had driven two male interviewees to move and settle in the UK:

Honestly, military service and unemployment pushed me here. If you work in a country other than Turkey legally for three years, you don't have to do military service and you then have the right to pay not to do military service. So I decided to settle here in 2012. (Interviewee 7, male, 29)

Economic reasons and opportunities for a better career
It is estimated that every year 2.3 million people in the world migrate from underdeveloped countries to developed ones (Hugo, 2014: 245). The reasons—limited job opportunities and socio-economic factors, such as poverty and low wages in the countries of origin—can be seen as sources of conflict that do not involve violence. Therefore, migration for economic reasons is defined based on an individual's desire to be economically secure for him/herself and his/her family (Sirkeci and Cohen, 2016:382).

These conflicts trigger the move and the destination choice is often influenced by social networks and others' recommendations. Interviewee 2 said that he decided to move to the UK because of the influence of one of his friends after his movie business declined in the 2009 economic crisis. His social connections influenced this decision:

My friend came here before me. I was working in the film business in 2009. When the business stopped for economic reasons, I decided to come over here, influenced by that friend. (Interviewee 2, male, 35 years old)

Some others did a thorough search and made comparions between potential destinations. Interviewee 17, for example, a lawyer who applied from Turkey, chosen the UK over Germany, the United States and other countries. For him, London was the most appropriate place to move as the city was known as a legal hub and on the central time zone relative to the rest of the world:

In fact, I developed my own business here. (...) I chose this place because of my job. The reason why I chose the Ankara Agreement is that I'd have done this work anyway. I had to decide in which country I would do it. When I was considering this place, people said that there was something called the Ankara Agreement, and that I could use it. After I'd chosen this place [London], I learned of the Ankara Agreement. (Interviewee 17, male, 45)

People working professionally in the art industry preferably used the Ankara Agreement because of the lack of opportunities to practice their profession, financial problems, and their general discomfort with the politics of art in Turkey -or with the involvement of politics in the arts. Interviewee 15, who received a bachelor's degree in Art Management and supported herself economically by painting and working in the design sector, indicated that the politics in Turkey made it impossible for people like her to continue in their professions in economic terms:

What you can do in Turkey is limited if you're especially interested in art. So I came here to specialize in my own profession, and also to widen my horizons a bit and to see how I'd reflect this multicultural structure in my work. That was my first reason. The second reason was the terrible drop in the incomes of people in the arts business because of the government in Turkey. (...) 10 years ago, the salary we got was at least around four to five thousand [Turkish lira per month]. Ten years later, it fell to 1500 (...) (Interviewee 15, female, 38 years old)

Multiple factors affect individuals' desire to leave a location or not. Interviewee 5 does not have language proficiency in English, so in order to support himself economically, he is dependent on the community from Turkey. He makes his living by playing the *bağlama* (a string instrument) and singing folk songs at weddings. His desire to move was mostly driven by economic and political reasons:

I'm an artist (...) I'm supposed to make a name for myself. In Turkey, there should be some tolerance for artists. [Turkey] has to make agreements with other countries. Just like businessmen can come and go with ease, artists should be free in this, too. (...) There are obviously economic reasons. Maybe you can earn more here. That's right. There were political reasons in the 2000s. They sent us to the DGM [State Security Court] and we went on trial. The lawyers were even going there instead of us. Our album was banned. We couldn't place newspaper ads. We can't sing everywhere in our native language, in Kurdish. (Interviewee

5, male, 50 years old)

Another interviewee, an opera singer, saw favouritism and the lack of institutionalisation as the main obstacles for him to practice his profession:
Obviously, one factor that made me come here is the lack of a system in Turkey. I was aware that I couldn't progress there in my profession. Crony relationships are in play, just like in other sectors. (...) So it's wherever I feel comfortable professionally. I go wherever I can actualize my ideals. Currently, the best place for me is London. The day after tomorrow or so, another place will present itself, and then I'll go there. (Interviewee 16, male, 38 years old)

Interviewee 9, an actress, thought that she would overcome the depression she experienced after breaking up with her partner by traveling. She then decided to settle in London after arriving as a tourist and then realizing that the city was a promising place for her career. At the beginning of her stay in London, she spent time seeing plays at various London theatres and noticed the problems and weaknesses in the Turkish diaspora community. Despite having just a few months remaining until she received her permanent residency, she accepted an offer to play in a movie and decided to return to Turkey. So this was an open ended process for her and she did not like the conflict which resulted in disappointment in the place of destination and made her to return to Turkey.

Moving for education
It is shown in the literature that many international students stay after completing their studies abroad. For example, students stay in the US after completing their studies and often get job offers; half of students from Turkey intend to remain as such and 31% received job offers (Rizvi, 2005:179). This is a pattern for Turkish students in the UK as well. Given the pace of developments in communications, transportation and rights, the mainstream neoliberal thinking on migration is inadequate in understanding contemporary human mobility (See Cohen and Sirkeci, 2016). The opportunities such as Ankara Agreement enable many movers to delay their decisions to settle or move. For example, some Turkish students use the Ankara Agreement to avoid visa issues while remaining undecided about their final destinations (Olay Gazetesi, 2013). We have also come across such similar cases: Interviewee 12 moved to London because she was unable to find better professional career opportunities back in Turkey. She was informed through student networks and friends who returned. Those who returned, she heard were unhappy. She also wanted to avoid the hierarchical relations at work in Turkey. Hence she

Sirkeci, Bilecen, Çoştu, Dedeoğlu, Kesici, Şeker, Tilbe, Unutulmaz

decided to stay in the UK:

All my returning friends are extremely unhappy due to the working conditions there. There were lots of people who I was in MA studies with during the same period. All of them returned to Turkey and they are all very unhappy; some still couldn't find a job. The ones who did find a job are so unhappy and they're trying to get back here. They say, 'don't come here.' I get tired mentally when I go there, as if the environment is one of too much ambition. There's a hierarchical thing in [my] workplace. It's something that bothers me. When it comes to private therapy areas [the respondent is a therapist], there's a boss at those centers. And the boss dominates. There's a certain hierarchy. You have to work for long hours. You get quite a small amount of money. Blah blah blah (Interviewee 12, female, 29 years old)

Desire to be mobile and meaning of a British passport

Our respondents in general did not intend to return to Turkey. However, this does not necessarily mean that they would continue living in London. One of the interesting narratives emerged from the interviews is that after receiving the British passports, most immigrants intend to move on to other countries. The passport is seen as a ticket to freedom to wander and not to settle in Britain necessarily. Despite challenges, ability to move elsewhere excites those movers:

This place is still 'challenging' for me, I still feel like I can experience something new here. If I go to Turkey, I would feel like as if I'm living in my own neighborhood again, with people from Turkey. I'll retreat into myself again. The idea of being foreign here opens up a space for me. (Interviewee 4, male, 30 years old)

Interviewee 18, who left her work as a bank employee in Turkey, moved to the UK with the purpose (or perhaps the pretext) of pursuing a language education. She described this experience as an 'escape.' She was disappointed in London, and felt a constant uncertainty about whether to return or not but eventually returned. Nevertheless, she decided to move back to London once more as she was disappointed in options in Turkey too. Many decided to "endure a difficult life" in London in the hope of getting a British passport to avoid the conflicts, risks, dangers and unhappiness in Turkey. The following excerpts from interviews show common feelings and desires to be free to travel at wish:

I will stay here until I get permanent residency. Because when I was in Turkey, I thought that (...) Europeans' being able to travel so easily was about the visa and completely about their decision to travel. There's no need for anything else. I just said that if you want to travel the world, you need to have a good passport in your pocket. [After receiving the passport] like I want, I can either stay in Turkey or I can travel the world. When I return here, it won't be any trouble, because I'll have the visa. Imagine that you go back to Turkey, you regret it, and then you can't move to London; I don't know. (...) For example, if you're searching for yourself, you can do it more comfortably with your visa. (Interviewee 18, female, 32 years old)

So, the prize is so big. You know that you're getting citizenship at the end of the fifth year [Note: permanent residency, not citizenship is possible after five years]. *For a Turk, getting a British passport could be one of their dreams, probably. Now you can go anywhere without a visa. I don't know (...). (Interviewee 13, male, 28 years old)*

In this political environment, no, I don't think I would return, but I can say it could be another country. All my life, I wanted to travel and see different places and live in their cultures. This is partly the reason I'm waiting for citizenship. This is the reason I'm trying to get citizenship. I find that I have this ability to go somewhere else. I don't know how I can make it, in the economic sense. I think it might be a European country, I don't know. I need to look around. I always had Greece in mind, but it might be a different place. Maybe Africa, Latin America could be it. (Interviewee 6, female, 44 years old)

There are people who, after becoming a citizen of this country, go to Germany, Spain, Norway, or the US. There are people going to Canada. I'm thinking about something like this. (...) I could go to different countries other than Turkey. I don't know, for example, it might be Canada. Or European countries. (...) Friends sometimes say, 'let's go to other countries, other countries are much better.' I can go when I get the passport. To have a look. (...) If there are opportunities there, I can stay. (Interviewee 3, male, 42 years old)

My goal is Europe. The world would open its doors to me. (...) I just want a British passport. (...) Now this is all I want. Let the borders come down. (Interviewee 7, male, 29 years old)

I swear, mister. I'm 45 years old (...) I'll live comfortably for 20 more years. Wherever I find the comfort (...) I mean, I'm at peace here (...) I grew my business here (...) I'm trying to grow it even more. I want to travel in the world. If I open my business to the world, I'll be a man working with the world. I've already done what I'm going to do in Turkey. (Interviewee 17, male, 45 years old)

The Ankara Agreement: the best available channel to move

The conflict model suggests that at 'macro level' there can be friction between sending, transit and receiving countries. Visa policies of the countries may not match and this may lead to tensions. Overall policies can be at contrast, such as some countries having a liberal approach whereas others being more restrictive. Prohibitionist approach in many European countries aim to "stop" or "control" immigration from within and outside the European Union (Hugo, 2014: 254; Salomoni, 2015; Kulu-Glasgow, Leerkes, 2013).

UK immigration policies have been geared towards more restrictions since the 1960s when the 1962 Immigration Act was introduced. After a short spell of relatively liberal immigration policies in the late 1990s and 2000s, the UK also turned towards even tighter immigration regime recently. Nevertheless, as argued elsewhere, legislation often follows the practice and movers find ways to overcome immigration barriers as they are rather motivated by the conflicts, discomfort and tensions in places from where they originate (Sirkeci and Cohen, 2016). Turkey has been such a country of insecurity with abundance of conflicts constantly pushing this or that group of people towards moving abroad (Sirkeci, 2017). In the British case, movers try to find appropriate mechanisms and means of migration or getting access to the UK territory. Hence securing permanent residency in the UK via the Ankara Agreement emerged as an option to migrate as other channels were closing down. Interviewee 1 travelled to London and decided to live there because some family members and close relatives were also there:

I didn't have much of a chance to stay here [in London]. I could have received a student visa but for people coming here with a visitor's visa, we're not allowed to get a student visa here. Here, I can apply either for the Ankara Agreement or for a marriage visa. I wasn't much inclined towards the marriage visa. Actually, at that time the laws were more favorable. They would give residency after two years. They didn't make you go through hardships. The laws have changed since then. Marriage didn't make sense for me. I then applied through the Ankara Agreement scheme. (Interviewee 1, female, 27 years old)

The Ankara Agreement movers seem to have a higher level of educational attainment and/or a professional career. However, this route as a last resort also appeals to those who failed in their asylum applications or marriage plans:

76

Those [who apply] through the Ankara Agreement are at roughly similar levels. I'm not saying this because of university graduates. Some left their good professions, some didn't. Some tried to marry, but it didn't work; some tried to start a shop, or to get asylum, but it didn't work, and the Ankara Agreement was their last hope (...) But those I met recently, who came after me, would have pursued their careers or did pursue their careers there, but came here to try their chances. (Interviewee 9, female, 33 years old)

There were examples of others who failed in securing a visa but eventually managed to move to the UK via the Ankara Agreement:

Between 2007 and 2013, they [the British Consulate in Turkey] gave me approximately five rejections. After 2001, if they would've treated me fairly during my entry and exit to and from this country, I wouldn't have needed to use the Ankara Agreement scheme. In the literature, there is such a thing. When we applied in 2012, I received a rejection again. We appealed. We used our right to appeal against [their decision]. The court case was happening here. I was writing back and forth via my lawyer. I won the case while I was writing letters. The six-month visa. (...) It took a year of litigation. One day, they called me from the consulate; they said, 'you should come and receive your passport; you won the case.' Three days later, I got my visa. As soon as I arrived, I applied through the Ankara Agreement. I stayed a year without any problems. As soon as the year ended, I applied for three years, and they gave it to me without hesitation. (Interviewee 5, male, 50 years old)

This is also a case illustrating how movers overcome immigration barriers. When rules for the acceptance of immigrants become more restrictive, individuals and groups vary their migration strategies, methods of migration, and their migration routes in response (Sirkeci, 2012: 359). In an interview titled, 'Asylum replaced by the Ankara Agreement,' published in the magazine called *Aksiyon* on June 8, 2015, manager of a law firm in the UK said that today, the Ankara Agreement has taken the place of asylum as a mode of migration, and that because of the political climate in Turkey, the firm's clientele has grown 100% in the last a couple of years (Aksiyon, 2015).

The UK Conservative-Liberal coalition government from 2010 introduced more regulations making immigration more difficult. It was argued applications slightly fallen after 2011 (Londra Gazetesi, September 4, 2014). However, these numbers are likely to rise again in the aftermath of the failed military coup and purges in Turkey since 15 July 2016.

The Home Office (2015a) data shows that (Table 4.1), the number of entry applications with reference to Ankara Agreement have sharply increased after 2007 which was mainly due to fact that the status was recognized by the UK Home Office in 2007. The numbers remained modest and gradually declined in the last five years. 290 of 4,820 applications were refused or rejected and since prescreening introduced in 2012, some applications were not allowed to proceed with their applications. The total number of applications pending decision exceeded 150 from 2004 to 2014 while there were 125 applications in the first quarter of 2015. Further details provided by the Home Office shows that the vast majority of applicants were 21 to 40 years of age and they were predominantly males (see Figure 4.2).

Table 4.1. Applications under Ankara Agreement, 2002-2015

	Accepted	Refused	Rejected	Other	Pending	Total
2002		*				*
2003		*				*
2004	5	10		5		20
2005	25	5		5		35
2006	55	20		10		85
2007	100	20		5		130
2008	265	20		10		300
2009	575	35		15		625
2010	815	35		25		875
2011	750	25		15		790
2012	625	20	10	25		680
2013	540	25	45	20		630
2014	480	10	5	5	25	530
2015					125**	125
Total	4,240	230	60	135	160	4,820

*Source: (Home Office, 2015a) * Numbers under 5 are not disclosed for confidentiality purposes. ** First Quarter only.*

Aiming to limit the number of applications and make the selection process more difficult, the British government has chosen to introduce some more restrictions. For example, citizens from Turkey living in the UK were required to apply two years in advance (ahead of the expiry of their current visas) in order to obtain indefinite leave to remain for their families (olaygazetesi.co.uk, 2015). Similarly, the right to appeal for those rejected under the Ankara Agreement was abolished and replaced instead by the right to an administrative review with the new law in 2014, which was implemented in 2015 (Home Office, 2015b). This was followed by more restrictive interpretation of the provisions of the agreement.

Figure 4.2. Age and sex distribution of Ankara Agreement movers

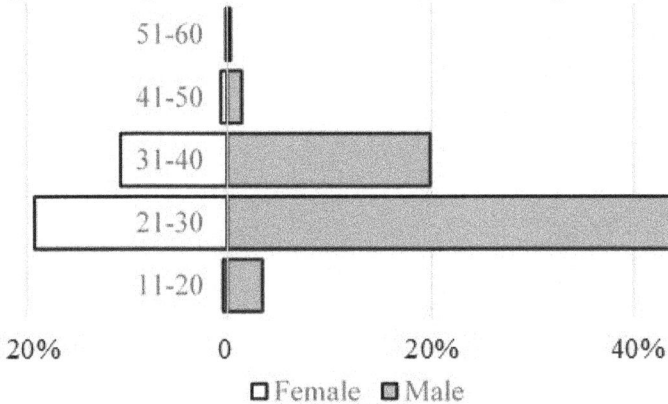

Source: Home Office

Settling in and socio-cultural conflicts

The concept of 'adaptation' refers to the commitments and support networks of a community, which also involve the sense of belonging, the desires to participate and to help others, and has social, cultural, economic, and political dimensions (Laurence, 2011; Jacobs & Phalet, 2007: 146). Language skills; ethnic, religious, or sectarian backgrounds; relations with the host society; position in the labor market; ethnic make up of the settled community; socio-political situation; national policies; cultural similarities and differences; and lived experience of discrimination all have an impact on the integration processes (Seker, 2015: 23; Hugo, 2014: 257). In recent years, especially in countries where the extreme right is on the rise and xenophobic political discourses are spreading, immigrants are often singled out as the scapegoats of the economic crisis (Sonmez Efe, 2015: 63).

The Ankara Agreement movers we interviewed were typically living in areas with large Turkish diaspora populations such as Hackney, Haringey, Islington and Enfield. Like other movers, this enables them to socialise as well as, offering solidarity in housing, finding jobs and easing off the burden of moving into a new place. With exceptions, these movers usually connected with other movers from Turkey and elsewhere. Hence they are integrating into an immigrant Britain where most friends are also immigrants.

Figure 4.3 Number of respondents by London boroughs

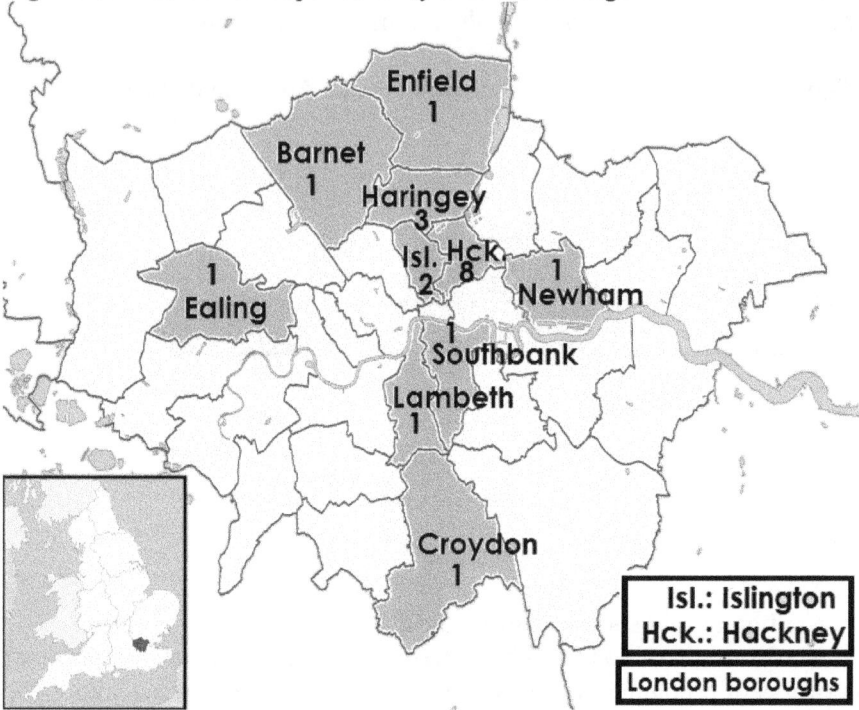

Our respondents contacted others from Turkey and joined their social activities at initial stages and then slowly reached out to make friends in other immigrant and non-immigrant groups. These networks were particularly helpful in overcoming the bureaucratic and economic problems associated with the Ankara Agreement. Joining community organisations formally or informally some respondents felt that life in London in these circles were restricting too:

London is Dogville. I've said this before. (...) This place is a tiny village. People claim a right over you after a while (...) For a while, I tried to understand why they do this. Then I came to the conclusion that this place is a pool, and there are people in the pool with no stairs to climb. If some people climb out using a rope, they pull you back in because they want you to stay here. (Interviewee 9, female, 33 years old)

There were also occasions when newcomers felt those movers who arrived long ago were less open-minded than their cousins left behind in Turkey:

For example, I got this sort of a response that was so strange for me. I said that I rented a room with a French girl. My father said, 'oh, my girl, you did well.' When I told the same thing to my cousin who lives in London—so, my cousin, meaning my father's niece—she said, 'don't tell my husband you're going to share a room with a stranger.' I was shocked. We're people of a certain culture. We come from the same place. I can't say Alevis are also obviously bigoted. When I look at my own community, they're a bit more open. I was extremely shocked. She's lived here for twenty years. Still foreigners are like that (...); 'when my son is getting married, it should be an Alevi.' Imagine, there are still people who want this. (Interviewee 18, female, 32 years old)

Living with someone outside of one's own ethnic group was perceived differently by those in Turkey and those in London in the above case. This has also led to newcomers forming networks of their own. Perhaps differences in such cohorts of movers are similar to generation gaps:

Yep. Let me tell you how to get foreign friends. Our environment comes from Turkey, but it's not an environment of the Turks who settled here, because they are so different. We can't adapt to them. However, we can do things only with people who came recently, like we did. (Interviewee 19, female, 32 years old)

There were also tensions between those who arrived as refugees and those others including the Ankara Agreement movers. Sometimes, the former treated the latter with less respect because they are not viewed as suffering as much as those political refugees:

There is an oppressor-oppressed relationship. Guys are like—I witnessed them saying such things to me, all of them using the same logic. 'Now, you had a university education in Turkey, you worked at a bank in Turkey, what are you doing here,' or, 'look at that person, I came from a village, I'm a primary school graduate, and you work as my waitress. (...) I own a car, I own a house,' and I don't know (...) 'So you wasted your time with education.' He thinks he has opportunity [to insult and humiliate me]. He says 'I'm oppressed.' What I'm saying is that when he came in the eighties or in the nineties — again, our people [regular migrants who arrived earlier] have oppressed him. They don't have a visa or anything because they arrived illegally. They aren't like us. They lived in poor camp conditions, like refugee camps. They struggled with problems that we cannot even imagine. If we're going to talk in percentages, maybe 80% of them are like this. The guy practically says 'I was oppressed then; and you're going to be oppressed now.' In the beginning, I couldn't believe it. How come?! (Interviewee 18, female, 32 years old)

This tension has also a class and qualification dimension appearing time and time. It is sometimes education, sometimes refugee status, or political standing marking the line:

They [referring to those who arrived as asylum seekers] were acting as psychologically superior. This is because they're uneducated. Our generation is educated; some even speak English. They [asylum seekers of the time] experience frustration because of this. They're trying to satisfy themselves by being oppressive. They practically look down on us [educated and/or skilled migrants] and think 'that person graduated from university, but they need the money I give them.' (Interviewee 6, female, 44 years old)

My other observation is related to the attitudes towards the ones [who came] with the Ankara Agreement (...) There's an attitude like, 'so you studied at a university, so what. Look again, there is this attitude: 'you're working with me, you're serving me.' (Interviewee 19, female, 32 years old)

I heard this expression from those who came earlier, 'why do you work.' I love you. You work very well, but you steal the jobs of the migrants here, of the children of the families who had taken asylum, and so on. (...) Coming here for political reasons seems more valid for those people. I feel like I've come here unnecessarily and I'm taking up space. (Interviewee 12, female, 29 years old)

Another dimension of conflict within the Turkish diasporic community and relating to the Ankara Agreement movers is employment and businesses. Turks and Kurds in London are well represented in such businesses as kebab shops, convenience shops, off-licenses (the UK name for shops selling cigarettes and liquor), restaurants, and cafés. In these businesses, access to cheap labour from the community is important. The newly arrived migrants and students in London provide cheap labour for the ethnic economy (Dedeoğlu, 2014: 53). The Ankara Agreement movers were also complaining about disadvantages faced in these sectors:

They hire you with a very low salary. For a normal employee, for instance, they give half the salary that they have to give. This is a big inconvenience for the working person. What's more, if their papers are complete, it's never okay to give these people this amount of money. That's the odd part. For example, you're doing a job, and that job deserves to be paid 400. Turks will never pay people. Everybody knows that. Turks never pay! (Interviewee 1, female, 27 years old)

As we will discuss in the next two chapters, in the ethnic economy working conditions are characterised by low wages (often below minimum wage) for long working hours. Hence this is not exclusive to the Ankara Agreement movers. Even some movers who acquired British citizenship or permanent residency were accepting these unfavourable conditions due to various related issues. For example, occasional informal income coming through these networks would prevent social welfare benefits from stopping. Some accept these jobs because they lack other skills. With an uncertain future and lack of citizenship protections, the Ankara Agreement movers were occasionally disadvantaged in the ethnic economy:

Honestly, they don't care much what the Ankara Agreement is at first. You're just a person working for three to five pounds an hour for [the employer in the ethnic economy] (...) [The settled immigrant] might work, but with a few social assistances from the state and housing benefits, that person doesn't have any rental costs. He/she is getting housing benefits, child benefits, and disability benefits from the state. On top of that, he/she works for five pounds an hour to make additional income. So, that person can work, but it's different for me. I'll pay rent with that money and so forth. (Interviewee 14, male, 33 years old)

After applying under the Ankara Agreement scheme, it takes about five to six years on average for an applicant to obtain the British citizenship. During this period, immigrants go through a difficult time, economically, socially, and psychologically. The obligation to work; regularly reporting to the Home Office; fear of rejection in the visa process; inability to travel while their visa applications are being processed; further restrictions on the duration of travel abroad per year; ineligibility for social welfare benefits and support; and tensions with settled movers are among the factors that adversely affect movers' psychology. Language proficiency (or the lack thereof) also plays an important role in the adaptation of movers in the host country (Alexander et al., 2007: 784, Seker, 2015: 20). Six interviewees in our study reported to have very good English, while six were at intermediate and two at poor levels of language proficiency. Understandably, those educated in the UK or attended language courses in the UK reported to have good English, but for the rest, language was a significant barrier leading to psychological issues such as losing confidence:

I said, 'how can I travel the world?' I said, 'I should start by learning English.' I came here, and I got distracted from my goal, of course. I left the school. I didn't make any effort to learn English, blah blah. When I lost my purpose, I also lost my faith in myself. (Interviewee 18, female, 32 years old)

When we go somewhere, when we sit down somewhere or go shopping, or when going to government agencies, they treat us so differently from how they treat a British person. Especially when your English is not very good (...) Or, you know, if you're having adaptation problems, you definitely experience lots of problems. (Interviewee 1, female, 27 years old)

There are studies suggesting that involvement in social organisations where movers can use their native languages can make learning the language of destination country difficult (Ersanilli & Koopmans, 2011: 211). There were narratives emerged in our interviews that some Ankara Agreement movers felt that but it was more of paradox as these movers also benefited from the solidarity in these communities which may help in adaptation:

As soon as I came, I fell into this community. Somehow, I couldn't get out of this community so easily. (...) (Interviewee 3, male, 42 years old)

I almost never have any foreign friends, because we've had language problems. Our friends are from Turkey and Kurdistan. (...) (Interviewee 5, male, 50 years old)

Another aspect of the challenge in immigrant integration is about that feeling of life in limbo. Many movers constantly question their decisions to move when they face difficulties: 'Did I do the right thing by migrating?' These kind of feelings may prevent movers to make an effort to integrate and settle as their minds are occupied with the question of return. Interviewee 2, who has been living in the UK for six years at the time of the interview said that he could not get his life together as he felt challenged and confused:

(...) I came here in 2009. If you look back and say what you really did in this six-year period, for example, there's obviously nothing, really. But there is serious work and stress. There are little things that offer you something positive. You say, 'I should learn the language,'; but it isn't easy to learn a language. Because after the second and third years, you can understand everything more easily, but you still have problems with speaking. Because you can't mingle with foreign friends. Because it takes time. In order to socialize, you need money. (Interviewee 2, male, 35 years old)

Interviewee 7, a university graduate in Radio, Television, and Cinema working as a photographer for a local newspaper published by the community from Turkey in London was in the same boat contemplating about returning to Turkey and he even bought return tickets several times but never returned:

Up until a few months ago, I would give up every week. I would buy a ticket. I would give up. I would say, 'only a few months left; a little more patience, a little more patience.' My goal is not to receive the permanent residency then relax. Not to apply for social assistance. (Interviewee 7, male, 29 years old)

Return was not considered as an easy option either. The movers considered integration problems in Turkey if they return while also feared of being perceived as a failure by others in Turkey:

There were many who gave up. I have many friends around me who left. I have many friends who left and then came back again (...) You're surrounded by abundance in Turkey. Food, environment, friends, social affairs, these things are absolutely paradise—in contrast with this place. But there's such a political environment in Turkey; there's such neighborhood pressure. People come here, live for one or two years, and when they return to Turkey again, they can't adapt. (Interviewee 7, male, 29 years old)

We would say that at the worst, we can return at the end of a year; an adventure for a year. (...) The thing that bothered me most at that time was the possibility of return. If I returned at the end of that year or so, I didn't want to say, 'I went to the UK and stayed there for just a year'. (...) Though I loved London; not to stay here would have upset me. (Interviewee 13, male, 28 years old)

Avoiding being seen as a failure but also avoiding wasting valuable time and money invested in this process of settling in the UK appeared to be a dilemma troubling some people. The end was expected to be good and all compromises were worthy:

We get so tired in all these, we want to return so much. It is an effort, the lawyer's fee, the accountant's fee, taxes, working in poor conditions: all of it will end after four years, so it isn't so easy to give it up. This is a very important factor. So it shouldn't be wasted. (Interviewee 12, female, 29 years old)

However, the outcomes and expectations do not always match. There were mixed feelings among respondents. Some felt that the whole process of visas and settlement occupy one's mind to an extent that you are mentaly unable to process anything else; cannot read a book or newspaper as you would otherwise. Some also felt that intellectually and socially, living in London was less satisfactory than living in Turkey. The price also comes with the busy working life in London leaving practically no space for anything else:

Over the years, you ask yourself this. When we're being a bit idealistic, we say we could do work related to education. But you couldn't find time to do that because your mind is constantly occupied with something. If you stay at home doing nothing (...) you can't even read two or three pages of a book. You just read the newspaper, but what efficiency can you get? (Interviewee 2, male, 35 years old)

I lagged behind. If I lived in Turkey, I would have benefited more. The intellectual atmosphere was different there. You can discuss things more, because you speak the same language you read in. The political environment here is more backward. It never satisfied me. It's the same socially. (...) The relationships I made with people from Turkey never developed. This kept me back. This is something so depressing. In economic terms, it was already unsatisfying. (Interviewee 6, female, 44 years old)

Nevertheless, some interviewees were happy with what they have achieved believing that they built a better life in London in comparison to their life in Turkey. They found public life in London to be more comfortable and; professionally more satisfying. For some, life in London was calmer.

What does Ankara Agreement mean?

The Ankara Agreement movers are not so different than other movers. This appears just as another mechanism to enable movement. Until 2015, about five thousand applications were filed and many more might have been lodged since then. Changes in British politics after the Brexit referendum are likely to affect this particular category of movers as the Ankara Agreement is part of the European Union integration process.

These movers we have interviewed faced various difficulties were and burdened with a heavy psychological cost as it takes 5-6 years to settle as a permanent resident or a British citizen. The integration process begins within the ethnic community in the UK. It is a resource the movers benefit from greatly but could also be a source of tension. The Ankara Agreement movers are relatively better educated than others and less involved in active politics. These sometimes appear as cause for friction between these groups.

Similar to other migration cases, these movers also do exhibit patterns and effects of an established culture of migration. They move into areas where earlier movers from the same groups reside. They are encouraged by the presence of these early immigrants. It is also important to underline that many movers were more interested in obtaining British passports than settling in Britain. For many, this was perceived as a ticket to the world of free movement.

An area of concern is the ethnic economy and patterns of employment and interwoven relationships at the axes of politics, society and economics. In the next two chapters, we will elaborate the employment relations in the ethnic economy in London of Turks, Kurds and Turkish Cypriots.

Annex. Full Text of The Ankara Agreement

Agreement Establishing an Association Between the European Economic Community and Turkey (Signed at Ankara, 1 September 1963)

PREAMBLE
HIS MAJESTY THE KING OF THE BELGIANS,
THE PRESIDENT OF THE FEDERAL REPUBLIC OF GERMANY,
THE PRESIDENT OF THE FRENCH REPUBLIC,
THE PRESIDENT OF THE ITALIAN REPUBLIC,
HER ROYAL HIGHNESS THE GRAND DUCHESS OF LUXEMBOURG
and
THE COUNCIL OF THE EUROPEAN ECONOMIC COMMUNITY
of the one part, and
THE PRESIDENT OF THE REPUBLIC OF TURKEY,
of the other part,
DETERMINED to establish ever closer bonds between the Turkish people and the peoples brought together in the European Economic Community;
RESOLVED to ensure a continuous improvement in living conditions in Turkey and in the European Economic Community through accelerated economic progress and the harmonious expansion of trade, and to reduce the disparity between the Turkish economy and the economies of the Member States of the Community;
MINDFUL both of the special problems presented by the development of the Turkish economy and of the need to grant economic aid to Turkey during a given period;
RECOGNIZING that the support given by the European Economic Community to the efforts of the Turkish people to improve their standard of living will facilitate the accession of Turkey to the Community at a later date;
RESOLVED to preserve and strengthen peace and liberty by joint pursuit of

the ideals underlying the Treaty establishing the European Economic Community;

HAVE DECIDED to conclude an Agreement establishing an Association between the European Economic Community and Turkey in accordance with Article 238 of the Treaty establishing the European Economic Community, and to this end have designated as their Plenipotentiaries:

HIS MAJESTY THE KING OF THE BELGIANS:

Mr. Paul-Henri SPAAK,

Deputy Prime Minister and Minister for Foreign Affairs;

THE PRESIDENT OF THE FEDERAL REPUBLIC OF GERMANY:

Dr. Gerhard SCHRODER,

Minister for Foreign Affairs;

THE PRESIDENT OF THE FRENCH REPUBLIC:

Mr. Maurice COUVE DE MURVILLE,

Minister for Foreign Affairs;

THE PRESIDENT OF THE ITALIAN REPUBLIC:

Mr. Emilio COLOMBO,

Ministry for the Treasury;

HER ROYAL HIGHNESS THE GRAND DUCHESS OF LUXEMBOURG:

Mr. Eugene SCHAUS,

Vice-President of the Government and Minister for Foreign Affairs;

HER MAJESTY THE QUEEN OF THE NETHERLANDS:

Mr. Joseph M. A. H. LUNS,

Minister for Foreign Affairs;

THE COUNCIL OF THE EUROPEAN ECONOMIC COMMUNITY:

Mr. Joseph M. A. H. LUNS,

President in Office of the Council of the European Economic Community and Minister for Foreign Affairs in the Netherlands;

THE PRESIDENT OF THE REPUBLIC OF TURKEY:

Mr. Feridun Cemal ERKIN,

Minister for Foreign Affairs;

WHO, having exchanged their Full Powers, found in good and due form,

HAVE AGREED AS FOLLOWS:

TITLE I. PRINCIPLES

Article 1

By this Agreement an Association is established between the European Economic Community and Turkey.

Article 2

1. The aim of this Agreement is to promote the continuous and balanced strengthening of trade and economic relations between the Parties, while taking full account of the need to ensure an accelerated development of the Turkish economy and to improve the level of employment and living conditions of the Turkish people.

2. In order to attain the objectives set out in paragraph 1, a customs union shall be progressively established in accordance with Article 3, 4 and 5

3. Association shall comprise:
(a) a preparatory stage;
(b) a transitional stage;
(c) a final stage.

Article 3

1. During the preparatory stage Turkey shall, with aid from the Community, strengthen its economy so as to enable it to fulfil the obligations which will devolve upon it during the transitional and final stages.

The detailed rules for this preparatory stage in particular those for aid from the Community, are set out in the Provisional Protocol and in the Financial Protocol to this Agreement.

2. The preparatory stage shall last five years, unless it should be extended in accordance with the conditions laid down in the Provisional Protocol.

The change-over to the transitional stage shall be effected in accordance with Article 1 of the Provisional Protocol.

Article 4

1. During the transitional stage the Contracting Parties shall, on the basis of mutual and balanced obligations:
- establish progressively a customs union between Turkey and the Community;
- align the economic policies of Turkey and the Community more closely in order to ensure the proper functioning of the Association and the progress of the joint measures which this requires.

2. This stage shall last not more than twelve years, subject to such exceptions as many be made by mutual agreement. The exceptions must not impede the final establishment of the customs union within a reasonable period.

Article 5

The final stage shall be based on the customs union and shall entail closer coordination of the economic policies of the Contracting Parties.

Article 6

To ensure the implementation and the progressive development of the Association, the Contracting Parties shall meet in a Council of Association which shall act within the powers conferred upon it by this Agreement.

Article 7

The Contracting Parties shall take all appropriate measures, whether general or particular, to ensure the fulfilment of the obligations arising from this Agreement.

They shall refrain from any measures liable to jeopardize the attainment of the objectives of this Agreement.

TITLE II. IMPLEMENTATION OF THE TRANSITIONAL STAGE

Article 8

In order to attain the objectives set our in Article 4, the Council of Association shall, before the beginning of the transitional stage and in accordance with the procedure laid down in Article 1 of the Provisional Protocol, determine the conditions, rules and timetables for the implementation of the provisions relating to the fields covered by the Treaty establishing the Community which must be considered; this shall apply in particular to such of those fields as are mentioned under this Title and to any protective clause which may prove appropriate.

Article 9

The Contracting Parties recognize that within the scope of this Agreement and without prejudice to any special provisions which may be laid down pursuant to article 8, any discrimination on grounds of nationality shall be prohibited in accordance with the principle laid down in Article 7 of the Treaty establishing the Community.

Chapter 1. The customs union

Article 10

1. The customs union provided for in Article 2 (2) of this Agreement shall cover all trade in goods.

2. The customs union shall involve:

- the prohibition between member States of the Community and Turkey, of customs duties on imports and exports and of all charges having equivalent effect, quantitative restrictions and all other measures having equivalent effect which are designed to protect national production in a manner contrary to the objectives of this Agreement;

- the adoption by Turkey of the Common Customs Tariff of the Community in its trade with third countries, and an approximation to the other Community rules on external trade.

Chapter 2. Agriculture

Article 11

1. The Association shall likewise extend to agriculture and trade in agricultural products, in accordance with special rules which shall take into account the common agricultural policy of the Community.

2. "Agricultural produces" means the products listed in Annex II to the Treaty establishing the Community, as at present supplemented in accordance with Article 38 (3) of that Treaty.

Chapter 3. Other economic provisions

Article 12

The Contracting Parties agree to be guided by Articles 48, 49 and 50 the Treaty establishing the Community for the purpose of progressively securing freedom of movement for workers between them.

Article 13

The Contracting Parties agree to be guided by Articles 52 to 56 and Article 58 of the Treaty establishing the Community for the purpose of abolishing restrictions on freedom of establishment between them.

Article 14
The Contracting Parties agree to be guided by Articles 55,56 and 58 to 65 of the Treaty establishing the Community for the purpose of abolishing restrictions on freedom to provide services between them.

Article 15
The rules and conditions for extension to Turkey of the transport provisions contained in the Treaty establishing the Community, and measures adopted in implementation of those provisions shall be laid down with due regard to the geographical situation of Turkey.

Article 16
The Contracting Parties recognize that the principles laid down in the provisions on competition, taxation and the approximation of laws contained in Title I of Part III of the Treaty establishing the Community must be made applicable in their relations within the Association.

Article 17
Each State party to this Agreement shall pursue the economic policy needed to ensure the equilibrium of its overall balance of payments and to maintain confidence in its currency, while taking care to ensure a continuous, balanced growth of its economy in conjunction with stable prices.

Each State party to this Agreement shall pursue a policy with regard to rates of exchange which ensures that the objectives of the Association can be attained.

Article 19
The Member States of the Community and Turkey undertake to authorize, in the curency of the country in which the creditor or the beneficiary resides, any payments or transfers connected with the movement of goods, services or capital, and any transfers of capital or earnings, to the extent that the movement of goods, services, capital and persons between them has been liberalized pursuant to this Agreement.

Article 20
The Contracting Parties shall consult each other with a view to facilitating movements of capital between Member States of the Community and Turkey which will further the objectives of this Agreement.

They shall actively seek all means of promoting the investment in Turkey of capital from countries of the Community which can contribute to Turkish economic development.

With respect to arrangements for foreign capital residents of all Member States shall be entitled to all the advantages, in particular as regards currency and taxation, which Turkey accords to any other Member State or to a third country.

Article 21
The Contracting Parties hereby agree to work out a consultation procedure in order to ensure coordination of their commercial policies towards third countries and mutual respect for their interests in this field, inter alia in the event of subsequent accession to or association with the Community by third countries.

TITLE III. GENERAL AND FINAL PROVISIONS

Article 22

1. In order to attain the objectives o this Agreement the Council of Association shall have the power to take decisions in the cases provided for therein. Each of the Parties shall take the measures necessary to implement the decisions taken. The Council of implement the decisions taken. The Council of Association may also make appropriate recommendations.

2. The Council of Association shall periodically review the functioning of the Association in the light of the objectives of this Agreement. During the preparatory stage, however, such reviews shall be limited to an exchange of views.

3. Once the transitional stage has been embarked on the Council of Association shall adopt appropriate decisions where, in the course of implementation of the of the Association arrangements, attainment of an objective of this Agreement calls for joint action by the Contracting Parries but the requisite powers are not granted in this Agreement.

Article 23

The Council of Association shall consist of members of the Governments of the Member States and members of the Council and of the Commission of the Community on the hand and of members of the Turkish Government on the other.

The members of the Council of Association may arrange to be represented in accordance with its rules of procedure.

The Council of Association shall act unanimously.

Article 24

The office of President of the Council of Association shall be held for a term of six months by a representative of the Community and a representative of Turkey alternately. The term of office of the first President may be shortened by a decision of the Council of Association.

The Council of Association shall adopt its rules of procedure.

The Council of Association may decide to set up committees to assist in the performance of its tasks, and in particular a committee to ensure the continuing cooperation necessary for the proper functioning of this Agreement.

The Council of Association shall lay down the terms of reference of these committees.

Article 25

1. The Contracting Parties may submit to the Council of Association any dispute relating to the application or interpretation of this Agreement which concerns the Community, a Member State of the Community, or Turkey.

2. The Council of Association may settle the dispute by decision; it may also decide to submit the disputc to the Court of Justice of the European Communities or to any existing court or tribunal.

3. Each Party shall be reguired to take the measures necessary to comply with such decisions.

4. Where the dispute cannot be settled in accordance with paragraphs 2 of this Article, the Council of Association shall determine, in accordance with Article 8

of this Agreement, the detailed rules for arbitration or for any other judicial procedure to which the Contracting Parties may resort during the transitional and final stages of this Agreement.

Article 26
This Agreement shall not apply to products within the province of the European Coal and Steel Community.

Article 27
The Council of Association shall take all appropriate steps to promote the necessary cooperation and contacts between the European Parliament, the Economic and Social Committee and other organs of the Community on the one hand and the Turkish Parliament and the corresponding organs in Turkey on the other.

During the preparatory state, however, such contacts shall be limited to relations between the European Parliament and the Turkish Parliament.

Article 28
As soon as the operation of this Agreement has advanced far enough to justify envisaging full acceptance by Turkey of the obligations arising out of the Treaty establishing the Community, the Contracting Parties shall examine the possibility of the accession of Turkey to the Community.

Article 29
1. This Agreement shall apply to the European territories of the Kingdom of Belgium, of the Federal Republic of Germany, of the French Republic, of the Italian Republic, of the Grand Duchy of Luxembourg and of the Kingdom of the Netherlands on the one hand and to the territory of the Turkish Republic on the other.

2. The Agreement shall also apply to the French overseas departments so far as concerns those of the fields covered by it which are listed in the first subparagraph of Article 227 (2) of the Treaty establishing the Community.

The conditions for applying to those territories the provisions of this Agreement relating to other fields shall be decided at a later date by agreement between the Contracting Parties.

Article 30
The Protocols annexed to this Agreement by common accord of the Contracting Parties shall from an integral part thereof.

Article 31
This Agreement shall be ratified by the Signatory States in accordance with their respective constitutional requirements, and shall become binding on the Community by a decision of the Council taken in accordance with the Treaty establishing the Community and notified to the Parties to this Agreement.

The instruments of ratification and the notifications of conclusion shall be exchanged at Brussels.

Article 32
This Agreement shall enter into force on the first day of the second month following the date of exchange of the instruments of ratification and the notification referred to in Article 31.

Article 33
This Agreement is drawn up in two copies in the Dutch, French, German, Italian and Turkish languages, each of these texts being equally authentic.

PROTOCOL No 1. Provisional Protocol
THE CONTRACTING PARTIES,

RECOGNIZING the importance to the Turkish economy, particularly in the preparatory stage, of exports of tobacco, dried grapes, dried figs and hazelnuts;

DESIRING to adopt the Provisional Protocol provided for in Article 3 of the Agreement of Association,

HAVE AGREED AS FOLLOWS:

Article 1
1. Four years after the entry into of this agreement, the Council of Association shall consider whether, taking into account the economic situation of Turkey, it is able to lay down, in the form of an additional Protocol, the provisions relating to the conditions, detailed rules and timetables for implementing the transitional stage referred to in Article 4 of the Agreement.

The additional Protocol shall be signed by the Contracting Parties and shall enter into force after completion of the respective constitutional procedures.

2. If the additional Protocol has not been adopted by the end of the fifth year, the procedure laid down in paragraph 1 shall be set in motion again after a period which shall be fixed by the Council of Association and which shall not exceed three years

3. The provisions of this Protocol shall continue to apply until the additional Protocol enters into force or until the end the tenth year, whichever is the earlier.

If, however, the additional Protocol has been adopted but has not entered into force by the end to the tenth year, this Provisional Protocol shall be extenuated for more than one year.

Should the additional Protocol not have been adopted by the end of the minth year, the Council of Association shall decide on the arrangements to be applied in respect of the preparatory stage from the end of the tenth year.

Article 2
From the date of the entry into force of this Protocol, the Member States of the Community shall open the following annual tariff quotas for imports originating in and coming from Turkey:

(a) 24.01 - Unmanufactured tobacco: tobacco refuse

Belgo-Luxembourg Economic

union 1 250 metric tons

Federal Republic to Germany 6 600 metric tons

France 2 550 metric tons

Italy 1 500 metric tons

Netherlands 600 metric tons

Each Member State shall apply to products imported under these tariff quotas the customs duty which it applies to imports of like products within the framework of the Agreement of Association signed by the Community of 9 July 1961.

(b) ex 08.04 - Dried grapes (in containers of a net content not exceeding 15 kg)

Belgo-Luxembourg Economic

Union 3 250 metric tons

Federal Republic of Germany 9 750 metric tons

France 2 800 metric tons

Italy 7 700 metric tons

Netherlands 6 500 metric tons

Each Member State shall apply to products imported under these tariff quotas the customs duty which it applies to imports of like products within the framework of the Agreement of Association signed by the Community on 9 July 1961.

(c) ex 08.03 - Dried figs (in containers of a net content not exceeding 15 kg)

Belgo-Luxembourg Economic

Union 840 metric tons

Federal Republic of Germany 5 000 metric tons

France 7 000 metric tons

Netherlands 160 metric tons

In the case of dried figs imported under these tariff quotas each Member State shall, pending the final alignment of the national rates of duty of Member States are finally aligned on the Common Customs Tariff, the Community shall adopt, for dried figs, the tariff measures necessary to ensure that Turkey retains commercial advantages equivalent to hose which it has under the preceding paragraph, taking into account the provisions of Article 3.

(d) ex 08.05 - Nuts, fresh, or dried, shelled or not: Hazelnuts

Belgo-Luxembourg Economic

Union 540 metric tons

Federal Republic of Germany 14 500 metric tons

France 1 250 metric tons

Netherlands 710 metric tons

Each Member State of the Community shall apply an ad valorem customs duty of 2-5% to products imported under this tariff quota.

Furthermore, on the entry into force of this Agreement, the Member States of the Community shall abolish all intra-Community customs duties on this product and shall apply the Common Customs Tariff in its entirety.

Article 3

From the date the final alignment of the national duties applied by Member States of the Community to products mentioned in Article 2 with those of the Common Customs Tariff, the Community shall each year open tariff quotas in favour of Turkey equal to the total of the national quotas open at the date of that final alignment. This procedure shall be implemented without prejudice to any decisions which may have been taken by the Council of Association pursuant to Article 4 in respect of the following calender year.

As regards hazelnuts, however, this procedure shall not be implemented until the national duties of Member States of the Community for all the three other products have been brought into line with those of the Common Customs Tariff.

Article 4

From the second year following the entry into force of this Agreement, the Council of Association may decide to increase the tariff quotas referred to in Article 2 and 3. unless the Council of Association should decide otherwise, these increases shall remain in force. Any increase shall take effect only from the beginning of the next calendar year.

Article 5

If this Agreement does not enter into force at the beginning of a calendar year, member States of the Community shall, for the period from the date of entry into force of this Agreement until the beginning of the next calendar year, open tariff quotas of one twelfth of the tonnages mentioned in Article 2 for each month between the date of entry into force of this Agreement and the beginning of the next calendar year.

From the date entry into force of this Agreement, however, the Council of Association may decide to increase the tariff quotas opened pursuant to the preceding paragraph so as to take into account the seasonal nature of exports of the products in question.

Article 6

At the end of the third year after the entry into force of this Agreement, the Council of Association may take appropriate measures to promote the disposal on the Community market of products other than those mentioned in Article 2.

Article 7

Once a common agricultural policy has been introduced for tobacco hazelnuts or dried figs, the Community shall take any measures necessary to ensure that Turkey retains export openings equivalent to those which it has under this Protocol, taking into account the arrangements laid down for that common agricultural policy.

Article 8

If the Community should open tariff quotas for products mentioned in Article 2 of this Protocol, Turkey shall not, as regards the rates of customs duty chargeable within the framework of those tariff quotas, be treated less favourably than a country which is not this Agreement.

Article 9

Turkey shall endeavour to extend to all Member States of the Community the most favourable treatment which it grants to one or more of them.

Article 10

From the beginning of the preparatory stage each Contracting Party may bring before the Council of Association any difficulties regarding the right of establishment, the provision of services, transport or competition. Where necessary, the Council of Parties any appropriate recommendations for the solution of such difficulties.

Article 11
This Protocol shall be annexed to the Agreement.

PROTOCOL No 2. Financial Protocol
THE CONTRACTING PARTIES,

DESIRING to promote the accelerated development of the Turkish economy in furtherance of the objectives of the Agreement of Association,

HAVE AGREED AS FOLLOWS:

Article 1
Request for the financing of investment projects which will serve to increase the productivity of the Turkish economy and further the objectives of the Agreement of Association, and which are part of the Turkish development plan, may be submitted by the Turkish State and by Turkish undertakings to the European Investment Bank, which shall inform them of the action taken thereon.

Article 2
Projects for which requests approved shall be financed by loans. Theses loans may be contracted up to a total of 175 million units of account, which may be committed in the five years following the entry into force of this Agreement.

Article 3
Requests for financing submitted by Turkish undertakings shall not be approved without the agreement of the Turkish Government.

Article 4
1. Loans shall be granted on the basis of the economic features of the projects which they are to finance.

2. Loans, especially those for investment projects the return on which is indirect or long term, may be made on special terms such as reduced rates of interest, extended repayment periods, interest-free periods and, where appropriate, any other special repayment terms which may facilitate the servicing of such loans by Turkey.

3. Any loan granted to an undertaking or to an authority other than the Turkish State shall be subject to a quarantee from the Turkish State.

Article 5
1. The Bank may make the granting of these loans subject to public invitation to tender or other tendering procedures. Participation in such public invitations to tender or other tendering procedures shall be open on egual terms to all natural and legal persons who are nationals of Turkey or of Member States of the Community.

2. Loans may be used to cover expenditure on imports or domestic expenditure, where such expenditure is necessary for carrying out approved investment projects.

3. The Bank shall ensure that the funds are used in the most judicious manner

and in accordance with the objectives of this Agreement.

Article 6
Turkey undertakes to allow recipients of these loans to obtain the currency necessary for the repayment of the loans and of interest thereon.

Article 7
Assistance provided under this Protocol for carrying out certain projects may take the form of participation in financing operations in which, in particular, third countries, international finance organizations or credit and development authorities and institutions of Turkey or of Member States of the Community may be concerned.

Article 8
Aid to Turkish economic and social development under the conditions set out in this Agreement and in this Protocol shall be Supplementary to the endeavours the Turkish State.

Article 9
This Protocol shall be annexed to this Agreement.

In witness whereof, the undersigned Plenipotentiaries have signed this Agreement.

done at Ankara this twelfth day of September in the year one thousand nine hundred and sixty-three.

For His Majesty the King of the Belgians,

For the President of the Federal Republic of Germany,

For the President of the French Republic,

For the President of the Italian Republic,

For Her Royal Highness the Grand Duchess of Luxembourg,

For Her Majesty the Queen of the Netherlands.

FINAL ACT
The Plenipotentiaries of

His Majesty the King of the Belgians,

The President of the Federal Republic of Germany,

The President of the French Republic,

The President of the Italian Republic,

Her royal Highness the Grand Duchess of Luxembourg,

Her majesty the Queen of the Netherlands, and

The Council of the European Economic Community,

of the one part, and

The President of the Republic of Turkey,

of the other part,

meeting at Ankara, on the twelfth day of September in the year on thousand nine hundred and sixty-three,

for the signature of the Agreement establishing an Association between the European Economic Community and Turkey,

have adopted the following texts:

Agreement establishing an Association between the European Economic

Community and Turkey and the Protocol listed below:

Protocol No 1: Provisional Protocol

Protocol No 2: Financial Protocol

The Plenipotentiaries have furthermore:

- adopted the declarations which are listed below and annexed to this Act (Annex I):

1. Declaration of Intent on dried grapes, in connection with Article 2 of the Provisional Protocol,

2. Interpretative Declaration on the value of the unit of account referred to in Article e2 of the Financial Protocol,

3. Interpretative Declaration on the definition of "Contracting Parties" used in the Agreement of Association,

- and taken note of the Declarations of the Government of the Federal Republic of Germany which are listed and annexed to this Act (Annex II):

1. Declaration on the definition of the expression "German national",

2. Declaration on the application of the Agreement to Berlin.

The Plenipotentiaries have agreed that the Declarations annexed to this Act shall be subjected, in the same manner as for the Agreement establishing an Association between the European Economic Community and Turkey, to any procedures that may be necessary to ensure their validity.

In witness whereof, the undersigned Plenipotentiaries have signed this Final Act.

done at Ankara, on the twelfth day of September in the year one thousand nine hundred and sixty-three.

For His Majesty the King of the Belgians,

For the President of the Federal Republic of Germany,

For the President of the French Republic,

For the President of the Italian Republic,

For Her Royal Highness the Grand Duchess of Luxembourg

For Her majesty the Queen of the Netherlands.

Declaration of Intention concerning dried grapes with reference to Article 2 of the Provisional Protocol

The Community declares that it does not envisage the establishment of a common organization of the market in dried grapes.

****

Interpretative declaration on the value of the unit of account in the context of Article 2 of the Financial Protocol

The Contracting Parties declare that:

1. The value of the unit of account used to express the amount mentioned in Article 2 of the Financial Protocol shall be 0-88867088 grammes of fine gold.

2. The parity of the currency of a Member State of the Community in relation to the unit of account defined in paragraph 1 shall be the relation between the weight of fine gold contained in the unit of account and the weigh of fine gold corresponding to the par value of that currency communicated to the International Monetary Fund. If no par value has been communicated, or if exchange rates

differing from the par value by a margin exceeding that authorized by the International Monetary Fund are applied to current shall be calculated on the basis of the exchange rate for a currency Member State to current payments, on the day of the calculation, and on the basis of the par value communicated to the International Monetary Fund for that convertible currency.

3. The unit of account defined in paragraph 1 shall remain unchanged throughout the period in which the Financial Protocol is in force. If, however, before the end of that period a uniform proportionate change in the par values of all currencies in relation to gold should be decided by the International Monetary Fund under Article 4, Section 7, of its Articles of Agreement, the weight of fine gold contained in the unit of account shall alter in inverse ratio to that change.

If one or more Member States do not apply the decision taken by the International Monetary Fund as referred to in the preceding subparagraph, the weight of fine gold contained in the unit of account shall alter in inverse ratio to the change decided by the International Monetary Fund. The Council of the European Communities shall, however, examine the situation thus created and shall take the necessary measures, acting by a qualified majority, after receiving a proposal from the Commission and the opinion of the Monetary Committee.

Interpretative Declaration on the definition of the expression "Contracting Parties" used in the Agreement of Association

The Contracting parties agree that for the purposes of the Agreement of Association "Contracting Parties" means the Community and the Member States or alternatively the Member States alone or the Community alone on the one hand, and the Turkish Republic on the other. The meaning to be given to this expression in each particular case is to be deduced from the context of the Agreement and from the corresponding provisions of the Treaty establishing the Community. In certain circumstances "Contracting Parties" may; during the transitional period of the Treaty establishing the Community, mean the Member States, and after the expiry of that period mean the Community.

****

Declarations by the Government of the Federal Republic of Germany

1. Declaration on the definition of the expression "German national"

All Germans as defined in the Basic Law for the Federal Republic of Germany shall be considered nationals of the Federal Republic of Germany,

2. Declaration on the application of the Agreement to Berlin

The Agreement of Association shall apply equally to Land Berlin unless the Government of the Federal Republic of Germany makes a declaration to the contrary to the other Contracting Parties within the three months following the entry into force of the Agreement.

Chapter 5. Work and social relations in London

Working practices of migrants in host countries are largely governed by the social relations and practices in which a particular migrant community is embedded. Many migrants do business or work within ethnic niches and these ethnic economies and migrants' work practices reflect social relations and practices that are common in a specific community. In this chapter we examine working conditions, working hours and days of Turkish, Kurdish and Turkish Cypriot migrants working in the Turkish ethnic economy in London in relation to their daily lives, social relationships, and social integration.

Immigrant communities referred to "as movers from Turkey" in this book are a heterogeneous mix in terms of ethnic, religious, political characteristics. The main groups are the Kurds, Turks, and Turkish Cypriots each of which is also divided along the sectarian lines of Sunnis and Alevis as well as political stances. In this chapter, we draw upon the findings of a 12-month field research carried out between September 2014 and September 2015 in London. Community associations, coffee houses, workplaces and houses were visited and informal interviews were conducted to understand this community of movers from Turkey. We particularly focused on those resident in boroughs of London, where larger concentrations are identified as presented in the first chapter: Enfield, Haringey, Hackney and Islington.

We have conducted 60 interviews including 20 with Kurdish, 20 with Turkish, and 20 with Turkish Cypriot movers, representing the three largest groups. Respondents included workers, employers, self-employed, unemployed, and retired people. Semistructured interviewers with people we reached through a snowball technique by mobilising contacts within the community, associations and businesses. We have probed interviewees with questions about their work experiences, social and business relationships and migration histories while also collecting basic information about their personal characteristics.

Working hours in Britain

Working hours[1] are important for understanding the link between labour markets and family and social networks of workers. Thus, understanding working times regulations in Britain in general is useful to examine migrant workers' experiences in the labour market.

The working hours in Britain are regulated pursuant to domestic law and European Union (EU) directives. It is prohibited to work longer than

---

[1] See GOV.UK (2015).

48 hours a week on average, unless the worker waives from this right under a written contract. Workers aged 16-17 cannot work for more than 8 hours a day and 40 hours a week. Full-time working means working for 36-40 hours a week and part-time working means working for 35 hours or less a week.

Normal working hours are determined under the employment contract and overtime means working hours above the determined normal working hours. Employers are not liable to make any extra payment for overtime other than normal working hours, provided that average wage of worker is not less than the minimum wage. Employment contracts mainly contain details on how to work and how much shall be paid for overtime and, if specified in the contract, employee is liable to work overtime. It should be also noted at this point that there is a type of flexible employment contract called as "zero-hours contract". In the framework of this contract, employers may require workers to work whenever there is a need without guarantee. These workers are paid on an hourly-rate basis. There is generally no sick pay in these type of contracts, but there should be holiday pays pursuant to regulations on working hours.[2]

Night work is normally between 11:00 pm and 6:00 am; but workers and employers are required to arrange it between midnight and 5:00 am by mutual agreement.

If an adult worker works for more than 6 hours a day, he/she has the right to take a break of minimum 20 minutes during working hours. Workers have the right to rest for minimum 11 hours between workdays. Workers also have the right to rest for a minimum uninterrupted period of 24 hours a week.

If a worker younger than 18 works for more than 4.5 hours a day, he/she has the right to take a break of minimum 30 minutes during working hours. Such workers have the right to rest for minimum 12 hours between workdays and the right to rest for a minimum uninterrupted period of 48 hours a week.

These regulations simply follow the minimum standards imposed by International Labor Organization, but very often the ethnic economy does not even meet these minimums.

Ethnic economy of movers from Turkey

The term ethnic economy refers to businesses run by co-ethnics from a single immigrant group or it can include members of different ethnic groups as is the case in some parts of London. These ethnic economies are also considered as part of economic integration process (Dedeoğlu, 2014).

---

[2] See Department for Business Innovation & Skills (2013).

In an ethnic economy (or ethnic enclave), there typically are businesses such as wholesalers, retailers, restaurants, cafes, and other small or medium size businesses which usually serve to co-ethnics and recruit labourers from the co-ethnic populations and involve a good deal of family businesses (Ojo et al., 2013: 592). Chrysostome and Lin (2010: 78) argue that, besides economic benefits, immigrant entrepreneurship facilitates development of dynamism within ethnic communities, social integration and recognition of immigrants as well as supporting entrepreneurial spirit and providing role models for immigrants.

There is evidence that movers from Turkey in western Europe mainly work in respective Turkish ethnic economies. Early movers from Turkey to Germany and few other European countries were recruited to work as industrial workers in manufacturing. After the 1973 energy crisis, unemployment among immigrant workers gradually increased and some of these workers started their own businesses within ethnic enclaves. In this process, ethnic food such as *yoghurt* and *döner kebab* found their way into these destination countries and over time, reached beyond immigrant consumers (e.g. Sirkeci, 2016; Panayiotopoulos, 2010). Approximately 70% of movers from Turkey who are self-employed in European Union (EU) work in Germany (Constant et al., 2007). These self-employed businesses in the ethnic economy like restaurants, coffee houses, liquor stores, markets and particularly döner-kebab shops, became popular in other European countries and as well as in Britain over time (Dedeoğlu, 2014; Sirkeci, 2016).

The history of ethnic economy of the movers from Turkey in Britain is similar to that of those in Germany. In the 1980s and 1990s, most movers worked in factories, especially in textile/ready-made clothing sector. After the closure of those factories, movers started setting up small businesses which created an ethnic economy:

I worked in a factory for 13 years and worked as a manager in another factory for 7 years. I was responsible for 35 machine operators (...) At one point, factories started closing down and textile was moved to Romania. After the factory I was working was closed, we opened here (a café/restaurant). And now, I am here for 12 years (Interview 15, 48 years old, female).

This may be considered as an outcome of the neoliberal restructuring which caused unemployment to grow among industrial workers and it is also a reaction to lack of employment opportunities for ethnic minorities (Dedeoğlu, 2014: 43).

As one of the largest metropolitan cities of Europe, London entertains a majority overseas population (Sirkeci & Açık, 2015: 143-144). As described in chapter one, London is also home to majority of movers from Turkey resident in Britain. Turkish ethnic economy in London has been established to an extent with savings accumulated by migrant workers in the textile factories. It also emerged in our interviews that small businesses like coffee houses, restaurants, döner/kebab shops, markets, liquor stores, taxi driving, import-export companies are mostly family-run businesses where the owners actively work.

Since market-entry is relatively easy in ethnic economies, there is a price competition rather than quality competition, which is one of the factors facilitating exploitation of labour within these communities (Rath & Kloosterman, 2000). For example, Aldrich (1977) claims that there is an intense internal exploitation based on long working hours, low wages etc. experienced by the self-employed business owner and his family. This is often the only option for these businesses to survive in a competitive environment. Dedeoğlu (2014: 62) observed the same in Turkish ethnic economy in London. We have seen similar evidence too:

It is 9 am - 5:30 pm for workers, excluding me [he laughs]. For me, it is from 7:30 am to 7 pm for 6 or 7 days. Oh, work is very busy during the day, it never stops. It is pretty intense. Workers are OK, they are alright. They have a lunch break of 1 hour, everybody goes out for lunch between 1 and 2pm (Interview 53, 53 years old, male).

I used to work for 15-16 hours a day. Of course, the shop was ours and we would work if there was an unfinished work. We used to work for 7 days a week. We would not work on Sunday; we would go for cleaning sometimes (Interview 54, 81 years old, male).

(...) You run your business under hard conditions. Well, maybe you are an employer, but employers have problems. Whether you go or not, there is a problem. Actually, there is no difference between employer and worker in England, one of them earns more than others, that's it. I can also say some are completely exploited. (Interview 49, 48 years old, male).

There were also evidence illustrating within family exploitation which is common in these businesses with a few employees, where usually the employer's wife, sibling(s), relatives or co-ethnics are employed:

I stated here with an employer from my own village. He gave 500 liras to everyone, but 150 liras to me. It was because we did not speak English or know the right way (Interview 4, 38 years old, male).

It is also worth noting that London's movers from Turkey, who are employed in the ethnic economy, often can only find employment in the service jobs in restaurant and café and off-license shops with long working hours, etc.

Working hours and days of movers from Turkey

According to Eurostat, working week has gradually shortened into the 2000s in Europe in general. Similarly, in Britain, average weekly working hours for full-time workers went down from 48.3 hours in 1956 (Lee et al., 2007: 26) to 43.7 hours in 2003 and to 42.9 hours in 2014. Nevertheless, we have observed that working hours were very long and working conditions were hard generally in the ethnic economy:

Working from 9 am to 7-8 pm is generally normal, it is sometimes longer. I sometimes work on weekends, at least for one day. There may be meetings or I need to finish a work that I could not finish in weekdays (Interview 58, 44 years old, female).

We used to work for at least 60 hours in the market (Interview 51, 67 years old, male).

Working hours are at least 10 hours a day for us. Nobody works for less than 10 hours. I work for 11 hours a day. I normally work for 6 days a week, but it is 7 days for now (Interview 43, 40 years old, male).

I have never seen a person who worked with Turkish people and worked for 8 hours a day. There is no one working for less than 12 hours here. Because they generally work in workplaces of Turkish people and it is always 12 hours. They generally work for 6 days (Interview 1, 40 years old, male).

(...) when I gave consultancy services, most of my customers were Turkish (...) they always earned less than minimum wage and work for 40-50 hours. They suffered a lot and I believe it is the same in many Turkish companies (Interview 58, 44 years old female).

It is known that when working hours are long, average hourly wages are low (Lee et al., 2007: 37, 120-123). For example, in Philippines, more than 90% of workers working for more than 48 hours to earn more (Mehran, 2005: 4). Similar evidence was found in studies on labour markets in Turkey too (Messenger, 2011: 303; Toksöz, 2008: 36). However, working hours differ from sector to sector. For example, the longest working hours are in agriculture, construction, hotel and restaurant sectors in the EU (Parent-Thirion et al., 2007: 19). Often number of immigrant workers are relatively high in these sectors. It is common in London too: Movers from Turkey mainly work in service sectors and some interviewees were aware of the wage implications:

You work for 10 hours if you need, work for 5 hours if you don't (Interview 33, 61 years old, male).

Of course it is very difficult for people from Turkey. They work for very long hours and earn very little. So, when I work at a Turkish place, I go out immediately if it is closing time, because I know about these jobs. I worked in such places; it is very hard (Interview 24, 41 years old, female).

Long working hours in the service sector are also related to limited work opportunities in other sectors and/or out of ethnic economy due to skill mismatch between the skills required for jobs and qualifications of the workers (Johnston *et al.*, 2010). It is also linked to high unemployment rates. In London, unemployment rate is higher among immigrants compared to the mainstream white population (ONS, 2015). Sirkeci and Açık (2015: 124) show that economic activity levels among movers are lower than the white British. Among Muslim minority women it is even lower. This is probably the case for movers from Turkey. However, in the interviews it became also clear that many respondents work in the informal sector despite appearing economically inactive. Some people also work informally but continue receiving some welfare benefits while some work part time in two jobs but declare only one to avoid losing welfare benefits. At the same time, most of these people were on very low wages even if they work in multiple places.

Most of our workers work informally; [at the moment] there are two or three undocumented workers for instance. We look after the man, pay him cash. He cannot object, can he? There are also two or three workers who prefer to declare themselves as part-time workers and receive benefits from the government. Now, does this man have a chance to refuse [the low pay]? (Interview 18, 49 years old, male).

We seem working part-time. Because if we don't, we cannot live here. Rents are high, expenses are high and we have to do this (Interview 1, 40 years old, male).

Additionally, some interviewers state that this is a common behaviour in the community:

As you know, many people do not declare that they work. They seem unemployed to the government and they receive benefits. But rather, they go and work. What happens when they work? The government does not know after all. And it serves to the purpose of the man (Interview 1, 40 years old, male).

There is an apparent pattern here regarding undeclared work, long hours, and low wages within the ethnic labour market in London. We believe there are multiple factors shaping this triangular relationship: Regulations, high tax levels, high salary expectations in the mainstream labour market perhaps push these small business owners towards informal labour. Another factor is the availability of such low paid labour within the ethnic community. As shown in other studies, on the other hand, skills mismatches and the dynamics of international worker mobility along with the fact that some ethnic workers have either incompatible skills or limited language skills or are unfamiliar with the labour market make them accept these low paid jobs irrespective of other existing disadvantages and discrimination (Khattab et al., 2011; Sirkeci et al., 2014). The trust and loyalty dynamics within immigrant ethnic communities also play a role in generating these patterns of low paid and often undeclared work.

Working hours, conditions of work and social relationships

Intra-community socioeconomic relationships and social integration to British society are not to be considered separate from the working conditions described above. Earlier migrants usually have better command of English and they seem to have integrated well compared to late-comers. In our case, Turkish Cypriots are better integrated than Turkish and Kurdish movers who arrived later in Britain, which was mentioned by some interviewees:

As we have a Cyprus passport, that passport is a European Union passport and unconditionally and 100% accepted by the EU. Because it is a passport accepted in all circumstances, we have the right to live and work here. However, people from Turkey do not have the same opportunities of working and living (Interview 20, 58 years old, male).

I think Cypriots are welcomed more. It is because they are more acquainted and it is generally easier for Cypriots to adapt to English society (Interview 35, 22 years old, male).

Unlike Turkish Cypriot movers, most of Kurdish and Turkish movers were in contact with community organisations such as *Halkevi, Kurdish Community Centre, Cemevi, Day-Mer* and this was often because they did not know about the procedures of acquiring British citizenship or other legal procedures, and they have limited language skills. These organisations offer such advisory services. Even daily contacts requiring English language proficiency such as speaking to a landlord on the phone can be a challenge for some movers who seek the help of these organisations and people working with these organisations. This is, of course, preventing or slowing down the integration process in a sense as direct connections with the mainstream population is further limited. When it coincides with the long working hours and heavy workloads, what is social and what is work is mixed up and there is hardly any time and energy left to build such relationships beyond the ethnic enclave:

I have never attended [social activities]. Actually, I do not have the chance and time to attend. I never have the spare time to go to such places (...) I mean people develop a political apathy here. You have no social life due to long working hours. I mean, everybody is just focus on economy (Interview 7, 63 years old, male).

I think working hours are too long in restaurants and shops like liquor stores of people from Turkey, as some of which open very early or some are even open for 24 hours. My father, who is a chef, sometimes works for 52-54 hours a week. And this is not normal, as we are not machines/tools. I believe that people from Turkey work too much in restaurants of people from Turkey which are open all day, 24 hours (Interview 46, 33 years old, female).

Society here is not open to foreigners, English people. They shop from each other, work with each other, and do everything with each other. Then what happens? You cannot learn the language (Interview 1, 40 years old, male).

In other lines of businesses though these small shops enable contact with a wide range of other people. For example, owner of a liquor store who works 7 days a week and 10-12 hours a day used to chat with a great number of customers as they check out. These small talks encourage interaction and integration. Legal affairs, relations with wholesalers and banks involved in these businesses also offer opportunities for exchange with the wider society:

I always talk to foreigners, my customers, as much as possible about everything. I talk about politics, trade, family (...) (Interview 7, 63 year old, male).

My wholesalers are Turkish and Pakistani, but mostly Pakistani. 90% of wholesalers with which Turkish society works are Pakistani (Interview 49, 48 years old, male).

On the other hand, it was expressed that these long working hours and heavy workloads usually have an adverse effect on social relationships:

Working hours for people from Turkey are too long (...) especially for men. They do not have any social activity with their families. I think these working hours are caused by them to an extent. I see that they love and make much of money, looking at things, houses, cars that others things to buy. At the end, children either drift away from their families or develop a very different personality. They cannot raise their children as they want. They cannot keep their family together. As an example, I am from a broken family (Interview 14, 45 years old, female).

It gets harder when compared to the past. It was subcontracting in textile, but it was kind of better than the current workmanship. It is because you had spare time in weekends, you could go to a picnic or other events with your community, neighbours or others. But now, there is no chance, it has all broken away, you cannot even imagine, people have completely drifted away from each other (Interview 49, 48 years old, male).

I cannot attend due to my intense work, but I want to. I have a busy pace in my work life and I do not have the time (Interview 48, 30 years old, male).

Another aspect of the ethnic economy is the lack of jobs for women, in other words, the exclusion of women from work outside of home. Patriarchal tones pinning children's poor school results or other social ills such as violence, using drugs and bullying put pressure on women in the movers' community. Thus, women are pushed away from paid work towards housework, child care, and other unpaid family work. This has limited their integration prospects:

Housework and child care are very tiring; I generally prefer taking care of my children. Yes, I do the housework after they sleep. I mean we have a busy day (Interview 50, 25 years old, female).

Housewives from Turkey generally want to work, because domestic life tires them out. Wake up in the morning, have children prepared, take them to work, come back home, cook, welcome guests (...) You feel suffocated after a certain point, because it is always the same works. You get bored and then want to work (Interview 10, 31 years old, female).

Some women do work as well as taking care of domestic chores and children; but then they have no time to social activities and are excluded from public in this sense:

I work and I do not have time for such things. I am here for 7 days a week. I leave here and run to home, because I need to cook before Hakan and Rahime come [husband and daughter]. There is housework, laundry, dishwashing, ironing (...) I mean I do not have the time to do such things [social activities]. I would maybe attend if I had time (Interview 15, 48 years old, female).

Poor working conditions, long working hours, low wages and widespread exploitation in family businesses are common characteristics we have observed in the Turkish ethnic economy in London. Although there are some differences between ethnic, religious and political groups, general patterns are illustrative of various disadvantages and discrimination in wider labour markets. These work patterns have adverse effects on integration processes as either there is no time to invest in establishing social relationships beyond and even within the ethnic community or no time to gain basic skills such as language to have any meaningful exchange with others. Compared to men, women are in a relatively worse position as they are often pushed towards domestic roles. In the next chapter we focus on their experiences.

Chapter 6. Women's labour in the Turkish ethnic economy in London

While strolling through Green Lanes in Haringey, one comes across many restaurants with Turkish names, such as *Antepliler, Diyarbakır Kitchen, Gökyüzü, Hala, Yayla* and many others. A quick look is enough to see that there are not many women workers in these restaurants. The most visible ones are those working as waitresses. During the day, one can see women pastry-makers through the shop windows where they appear to be sitting and making pastry. This is the most visible type of female labour in the Turkish ethnic economy, but it is only the tip of the iceberg. There are many other categories of women involved in the ethnic business. This chapter examines the role of women's labour in the advancement of Turkish ethnic economy in London and the possible role of this work on women's social position.

The previous studies have investigated the relationship between women's work and the ethnic economy in different locations. Floya Anthias, in her pioneering work, (Anthias, 1992), shows that the use of female kinship labour has even been considered a necessary 'building block' for the development of ethnic minority enterprises in Britain. Although the role and use of female labour has been seen as necessary for the development of ethnic minority enterprises in Britain, gender sensitive research shows that ethnic economies do not necessarily support the professional advancement of women as much as they do for men and can keep them in a subordinate position, thus preventing their integration into the host society. It is proposed that female immigrant workers are 'generally captive by other relationships than that of a wage' (Panayiotopoulos, 1996: 455). The predominantly male-controlled, labour-intensive nature of many ethnic economies is marked by 'social structures which give easy access to female labour subordinated to patriarchal control mechanisms' (Phizacklea, 1988: 22).

This chapter argues that women's work in the Turkish ethnic economy has been central to its development and success, but their work has been invisible both to their households and to their community as well as to the outside world. The material presented here explores how women have been silent contributors to the expanding family-based establishment of the Turkish ethnic economy in Britain. It further shows how women's work in the ethnic economy and their role in social ties and networks on which this economy depends preclude their social integration within the wider society. The agency of women in maintaining community networks and representing ethnic/national identity has been essential in the establishment and success of the Turkish community, which places more emphasis on women's traditional gender roles as mothers and wives. In this framework, women are seen to be under the control of patriarchal and ethnic ties of their community.

Turkish women baking in North London (*Photo by Arif Bektas*)

Forming an ethnic economy in London

Movements of Turkish-Cypriots, mainland Turks and Kurds of Turkey were driven by deep socio-economic inequalities, conflicts and violence imposed upon certain ethnic and religious groups. These populations from Turkey found refuge in London and set to begin a new life.

Most migrants in London define themselves either by their religious sect, such as *Sunni* or *Alevi*, or call themselves Turkish, which refers to their status as Turkish citizens rather than their ethnic origin. The most common signifier of identity was their place of origin in Turkey, such as being from Maraş, Adana or Kayseri. By using the place of birth people also explicitly refer to their ethnic and religious identities without openly stating them. A further important characteristic of Turkish migration to London is that most first generation migrants are refugees who sought asylum in the UK. The chain migration from Turkey has been facilitated by migrant networks. The earlier arrivals facilitated the arrival of new migrants from their own families and communities left behind in Turkey. As social networks are extended and strengthened by each additional migrant, potential migrants were able to benefit from the presence of social networks and ethnic communities. As a result, there are many people from the same place of birth living in London, and close networks of families from same places of origin maintain traditional social and cultural practices.

These close networks and family connections constitute the basis of Turkish ethnic economy in London. Turkish ethnic economy is a Europe wide phenomenon and understood to have contributed to national economies due to their capacity to create employment. The growth of the ethnic economy was an outcome of neo-liberal industrial restructuring that left many industrial workers including Turkish guest-workers in Germany unemployed. Initially, the ethnic economy served the Turkish movers but products such as *döner-kebab* helped it to reach beyond the coethnic markets. Thus, Turkish migrants emerged as self-employed entrepreneurs in almost all Western European countries. Germany has also emerged as a key country to supply wholesale Turkish ethnic food for the rest of Europe. *Döner-kebab* businesses including manufacturers and suppliers of machinery have helped to standardize the ways in which kebabs were served and the skill levels required to run a kebab shop were reduced with the help of new tools (e.g. slicers, vertical warmers, etc.) introduced. From wholesalers and *döner* factories to kebab shops and *imbisses*, these businesses were run by and employed Turkish movers generating a considerable amount of employment for Turkish communities in Europe.

In the UK, the Turkish ethnic economy of London has been rapidly expanding since the early 2000s, and it became the main economic activity of Turkish migrants after the closure of garment workshops in London. Despite the limited data available it is estimated that the *döner-kebab* business has an annual contribution of over £2.2 billion to the British economy (Sirkeci, 2016). This is no small business serving to a sizeable clientele. Turkish movers are the main entrepreneurs in the *döner-kebab* businesses but their ethnic entrepreneurship is not only limited to *döner-kebab* and has been diversified in recent years to include corner off-licence shops, coffee shops, and restaurants.

Based on small-scale shops, family labour and resources, the Turkish case in London is a typical ethnic economy. Families used their own savings accumulated in hey days of garment production to open their shops and utilised mainly family labour to run these shops. Many people opted to form a partnership with another family member or a relative to start their businesses which required heavy work load and long hours as we discussed in the previous chapter. Running a shop for almost 20 hours a day would not be possible without such family labour exploited freely.

Fathers work with their sons or brothers work together are the most common forms of business partnerships established in the community. The second generation's contribution (i.e. their input of English language skills and knowledge of the British system) played a significant role in the expansion of the Turkish ethnic economy. Ethnic solidarity and trust are the building blocks of this ethnic economy; thus when there is a need for labour, it is mostly recruited from within the ethnic community. The economic cooperation among movers living at the margins of British mainstream success is only possible with the extreme exploitation of labour and communal sacrifice for very small returns and marginal incomes.

Women movers from Turkey and work in London

Presence of women from Turkey is more significant and visible in migration to Britain compared to the patterns of Turkish migration to Germany which was rather characterized by family reunification. Migration from Turkey to Britain has been somehow gender balanced possibly due to the regulations facilitating family unification and the nature of economic activities Turkish migrants involved in London. Since the early 1980s, movers had worked in the garment industry in London, which positively affected female migration, as women were considered to be better at garment making, which helped to push up the number of women moving to London. Census results in the UK also show that the number of movers from Turkey are equally distributed between men and women.

We focused on two generations of women who moved to the UK in different time periods whose access to and patterns in economic activities differ. Those who arrived earlier in the 1980s worked in the textile industry, which brought power and status for women in their families and in the community. Recent arrivals had no such opportunity to work in factories and most of them became unpaid family workers or low-wage workers within the Turkish ethnic economy. For some women, the expansion of catering based family shops resulted in a retreat of women from paid work. This has facilitated women's return to traditional roles as mothers and wives and ends their income generating activities.

The employment opportunities for the movers from Turkey in London had been limited to a small number of sectors for decades. Garment industry was a leading sector and since the early 1980s, and it remained as the main employment sector for movers from Turkey until the early 2000s when this industry declined and gradually moved overseas. Women were the dominant work force in this industry. Migrant women's work in the textile industry in Western countries is well documented and is linked to women's migration statuses in host countries (Chin, 2005; Bastina, 2007). In her analysis of Bolivian women in Argentina, Bastina shows that undocumented women who have fewer work opportunities when they migrate have to take up jobs in the garment industry. Working in a garment workshop meant staying in dimly-lighted workshops for long hours with no health and safety measures in place. Their workday might have lasted 12 to 17 hours, often for six days a week (Bastina, 2007). Turkish women's experiences in London were no different from that of the Bolivian workers in Argentina. However, there is a difference as Turkish women mostly moved to London with their families and not as solo independent workers.

A woman attending kids at a community event (*Photo by Arif Bektas*).

The textile industry not only provided for the community and for migrant families, but it also increased women's status in the community as workers and earners. For most women, working in the textile industry was their first industrial job, as they often had a rural background and had never worked outside home, or only worked in their family-owned farmland. This did not mean that women were freed from their traditional roles and family obligations; they remained responsible for domestic chores and childcare. Women's domestic roles and identities had an impact on their working patterns, and some women preferred working from home while caring for their children.

Although women had the option to arrange their workload around their domestic responsibilities, textile work still involved long hours and tedious work. Thus, these textile worker women were working either with their co-ethnics in a workshop or in isolation in their own homes with minimal contact with others. However, women's work during this period was visible to their families and the community as it generated good financial returns and economic rewards. However, it did little to overhaul the traditional gender relations because the work itself took place within the ethnic circle and women remained confined in their traditional roles with little prospect of changing them. In fact, this type of work joined the psychology of being a migrant and the desire to save up as much as they could so that they had enough savings to secure a better life after their return to Turkey.

Women's work in the Turkish ethnic economy in London

Women's work in ethnic economies is usually conceptualized within the framework of their contribution to family-based ethnic businesses as an unpaid family worker or low paid worker. It is also accepted that few economic opportunities exist for immigrant women outside the ethnic enclave (Hillmann, 1999). This is also true for the first generation Turkish migrant women in London. Turkish women's work in the ethnic economy helped the success of the ever-expanding ethnic businesses which became part of a Europe-wide Turkish ethnic economy too. Women contribute to this ethnic economy in many diverse ways, but paid-employment opportunities for women have generally decreased in the ethnic economy period and most of women have been pushed back to the position of unpaid family workers with roles of wife, mother, daughter-in-law etc. as a reflection of traditional, patriarchal and social gender relationships.

With the rise of Turkish ethnic economy in London, Turkish female movers gradually were less involved in economic activity in contrast to their leading and visible roles in the textile work. Women were not completely retreated from the labour market but, rather, their contribution has become less visible and more under-recognized. This was due to the nature of these ethnic businesses and gender roles within the diaspora community. Turkish ethnic economy has increasingly become a male-dominated environment often involving serving strange and unrelated men, mostly in the catering sector. Working for the catering industry means working at shops which remain open until late serving customers from various backgrounds, mostly men. With Islamic tones, in traditional Turkish culture, women's contact with unrelated men is not welcome. Therefore, male business owners do not allow their wives or mothers to work at the counter in their shops in late hours, even though their businesses rely on extensive use of family labour and kinship-networks.

Due to the widespread nature of family-run shops in the forms of döner-kebab shops, off-licences and coffee shops, women's labour is mostly used and referred to as 'help'. This 'help', however, is not actually helping the main work, but is really a part of the main work because it takes the form of cleaning the shop, cutting the vegetables, doing the dishes and making pastry to sell. Although women work hard for family businesses and contribute in diverse ways, the owners of these shops are almost always men, either the father or husband of the unpaid female family worker. Running an ethnic business is a public sphere activity requiring a constant interaction with the outside world and it is believed that men are more suitable for this job, as women are perceived to have more home-bound duties and their contribution is considered as 'help'.

Families running a shop usually expressed the fact that it was very difficult to run a shop without a large family. Different family members offer different contributions to the family business. They provide a reliable and low-cost workforce of which families not only utilize physical labour but also their English language skills and other administrative knowledge that is necessary to conduct a business. In this regard, grown up children are the best option for families aspiring to own their business and aiming to pool their resources as their English language skills are a must for the success of these businesses. In some cases, it is reported that children are prevented from pursuing higher education so that they can help with the family business.

In London's Turkish ethnic economy, female family members seemingly are expected to show their loyalty to their families and to the community by offering their labour. Offering their unpaid labour is a way of confirming their domestic roles as mothers and wives. In this regard, what Sharma (1986) calls 'household service work', in which domestic tasks extend beyond meeting the physical needs of household members to providing and maintaining ties with kin, neighbours and friends, who are a source of information and aid, is a useful framework for explaining women's work and contributions to the ethnic economy. By combining their household work with ethnic business activities, unpaid family workers play a vital role in connecting the areas of production and reproduction. Yet these women consider themselves to be just housewives.

Women's roles in ethnic businesses differed depending on their domestic roles and positions in families. For example, mothers were less involved in businesses than wives. The mothers were from the older generation whose contributions came from the financial means they accumulated in the textile days. For this generation of the family, the ethnic businesses were usually supported to secure the future of their grown-up children and were left to their management. In Dalston, London, for example, there was a coffee shop owned by a family and run by two brothers with the help of their father and mother. The mother of the brothers was in her early 50s, and, in principle, she said that she did not intervene with the business of her sons. Even though she said that she did not get in their sons' way, she visited the coffee shop every day, and stayed there for a few hours. She helped with the dishes, and sometimes she made Turkish pastries to be sold.

These family enterprises were often organized through a labour hierarchy. Positions within the family translate into working identities for men and women, and family members usually participated in the family business by offering services that directly or indirectly contribute to the success of the business. In return, some were unpaid workers, while others received payments for their contributions. For the Turkish immigrant women in small-businesses, their work was an extension of their domestic responsibilities, and they often did the cooking and cleaning. As such, many of the Turkish immigrant small-businesses were built on the back of Turkish female movers' unpaid labour. It seems true to say that this form of work results in women's extreme isolation and family dependency. Thus, women's contributions within their domestic roles and identities usually remain unpaid, invisible and unrecognized by the family and community.

Nevertheless, not all women workers in the ethnic economy were family members or relatives. Although most family members were involved in family-based work, in some cases it became necessary to hire extra help. The help usually came from close family circuits. This was also true for women's labour where ethnic establishments obtained their required female labour from their own social networks. This also shows a hierarchical relationship between families who have the resources to own their shops and those who do not have access to similar levels of financial resources so have to be employed by those who have. This divide was most apparent for those who migrated in the mid-1990s or later, who could not accumulate enough financial means to open their own shops. Thus they became a source of cheap labour for other families who had enough capital to run their own shops.

For women, working in a family-owned ethnic establishment perpetuated the existing gender and social relations based on kinship. The intimate connections with kin and friends working at the same place were maintained outside the home. In the interviews, many informants emphatically expressed the fact that a family or friend connection had helped them to get their current jobs, suggesting that women's entry into the labour market was constrained to the places where they had acquaintances. Moreover, women always felt obligated to those who had given them job opportunities, and kept those relational ties going. The sense of obligation and respect compelling them to work hard and show dedication to their employers created a work ethic and commitment to the workplace, as if it were their own home. As a result, women sometimes found it difficult to change jobs, even when they had better opportunities elsewhere. White (1994:47) calls these social relations based on reciprocity and trustworthiness the 'power of debt', which leads people to feel obligated to one another in return for a favour, such as offering a job or lending money.

These women in the Turkish ethnic economy either worked as a pastry-maker or cleaner, or cook for other staff members. Women's wage work in the ethnic economy was structured around their obligations in their family circles and they often had access to these jobs through their relatives and family members; hence they reinforced their identity as mothers and wives as well as assuring their group membership. Another important aspect was that this work carried out by women was not seen as a means for making a living but for earning pocket money or additional income to help the family budget. Thus, work was perceived and portrayed as extra, additional, not essential and temporary for women, and it never challenged their traditional patriarchal roles within their families and the community dictated by patriarchal social structure.

Hence, in this chapter we have demonstrated that Turkish immigrant women have been silent contributors to the expanding family businesses in the Turkish ethnic economy in the UK. There were many categories of women involved in the ethnic businesses. Women contributed to the ethnic economy as mothers who were the main financiers, or as wives who offered their unpaid work and time as "casual" workers. Some of these women worked as unpaid family workers in family-owned businesses but some became low paid wage-workers to provide additional income for their families and children. Moreover, some men who were married to the second generation of immigrant women utilized their wives' knowledge of the British system and language ability to run and improve their businesses. However, women's contributions remained largely invisible, and they were confined to domestic chores as well as giving birth and rearing children in many cases. Another way that women made a contribution was in the role they played in social reproduction in which women expanded their role in the private sphere to generate more time for men to work longer hours in the ethnic economy, or in their role in fostering the social ties and relations that were the very foundation of the Turkish ethnic economy.

In this chapter, we have also evaluated the major shift in women's economic activities in London. Women's invisible work in the ethnic economy caused them to retreat from the public spehere as was the case with the textile work they used to do in the 1980s and 1990s, to the domestic sphere and sidelined but their important "help" with ethnic businesses owned and run by men.

Chapter 7. Remittances to Turkey

Movers are carriers of ideas, opinions, views, politics, skills, knowledge and wealth. These all fall under social or financial remittances. In this chapter, we rather focus on the latter. Remittances, thus, can be defined as money (or valuable items) transfers by migrants to their families, relatives, friends and/or communities left behind in the country/area of origin or in a third country. These are often person-to-person transfers in relatively small amounts. It is also known that governments may intervene time to time and change the definitions and scope of remittance transfers. Although most transfers are from migrants to others, migrants appear as recipients in a rare number of transfers (Yiadom, 2008:98). These small transfers can be domestic or international. Remittances are key component of their GDPs for many small countries (e.g. Tajikistan and Nepal) while certain countries receive the largest sums (e.g. India and China), but they are often vital for families left behind in developing countries.

Movers' remittances from abroad were once very important for Turkey's cash balances, but still a sizeable amount of money is sent to Turkey every year as remittance receipts were reported to be about 0.1% of Turkey's GDP recently (IFAD, 2015:37). Arrival of over 3 million Syrian refugees (Sirkeci, 2017; Yazgan et al., 2015) along with growing number of other movers is likely to increase the amount of money sent to Turkey as well as remittances from Turkey. In this chapter, we focus on these money transfers with a focus on money transfers from the UK and mechanisms used by Turkish and Kurdish diasporas.

Given the small size of the Turkish and Kurdish movers population in the UK (see chapter 1), the (financial) remittance flows to Turkey is expected to be small. Turkey's total remittance receipts grew from about 100 million US$ per annum in the mid-1960s to over 1 billion US$ per annum in the early 1970s (the peak of guest-worker flows). The largest annual receipt was historically recorded in 1998: 5.8 billion US$ (Tansel & Yaşar, 2012: 340). The remittance flows to Turkey was shy of 2 billion US$ per annum throughout the 1980s and grow over 3 billion in the 1990s and placing Turkey in the sixth place among the top 20 developing country recipients of workers' remittances (Ratha, 2003:162). Fluctuations in official remittance flows to Turkey are moderated by various factors including the duration stay abroad (i.e. maturity of diasporas), economic and political crises, cost of sending money, and availability of informal channels (Tansel & Yaşar, 2012). Growing traffic between Turkey and the UK (i.e. number of tourists soaring, number of Brits settled in Turkey and Turkish residents in the UK growing) may have also facilitated in person money transfers which are largely undocumented. It is difficult to accurately estimate these informal remittance flows but some studies suggested that the size of these would range from 10 to 50 percent (Puri and Ritzema 1999; El-Qorchi et al., 2003). One should not forget the good share of irregular migrants who often do not have access to formal channels of sending money.

Money transfer shop in London (Photo by yell.com)

Total volume of remittances was about 531 billion (US$) in 2012 and gradual growth is expected to continue in the second half of the 2010s. In 2014, migrants in European countries led by Russian Federation were sending 109.45 billion (US$) to other countries. Developing countries are estimated to have received about three quarters of all remittances. Due to large share of its diaspora population's concentration, 84% (947 million US$) of remittances received in Turkey were from European countries in 2014 (IFAD, 2015:24). In 2014, 48% (544 US$ million) of remittances received in Turkey were from Germany.

In 2014, the total volume of remittances sent was about 17.2 billion (US$) from the UK where a relatively small but sizeable Turkish and Kurdish immigrant population is present. The volume of remittances sent from the UK to Turkey also remains low. Top five largest remittance recipients from the UK are Nigeria, India, Pakistan, Poland and China. These are also countries of origin for the UK's largest immigrant groups.

Table 7.1. Top 6 Remittance sending countries to Turkey, 2010-2014 (million US$)

	2010	2011	2012	2013	2014
Germany	640	701	607	547	544
France	69	76	66	95	94
Netherlands	46	51	44	74	74
Austria	38	41	36	58	58
USA	26	28	24	40	40
Belgium	22	24	21	35	35
Switzerland	16	17	15	31	31
United Kingdom	17	18	16	30	29

Source: World Bank Migration and Remittances Factbook 2015.

Table 7.2. Remittances from the UK and to Turkey, 2010-2014 (million US$)

	2010	2011	2012	2013	2014
Total Remittances from the UK	21,057	23,159	23,601	23,917	25,115
Total Remittances to Turkey	993	1,087	940	1,135	1,128
Remittances from the UK to Turkey	17	18	16	30	29
% of total Remittances from the UK	0.08	0.08	0.07	0.12	0.12
% of total Remittances to Turkey	1.71	1.66	1.67	2.61	2.61

Source: Bilateral Remittance Matrix 2014, 2013, 2012, 2011, 2010 http://www.worldbank.org/en/topic/migrationremittancesdiasporaissues/brief/mig ration-remittances-data (Retrieved: 03.03.2016)

According to the World Bank estimations based on Ratha and Shaw's methodology (2007), total remittances from the UK were expected to rise from about 21 billion US$ in 2010 to over 25 billion US$ in 2014 (about 20% rise for the period) (Table 7.2). In the same period, remittances from the UK to Turkey are expected to rise from 17 million US$ to 29 million US$. Although the total volume nearly doubles in five years, we should note the modest size of all remittances from the UK to Turkey constituting less than a tenth of a percent of total outgoings from the UK and about

2.5% of all receipts in Turkey. We can also speculate that the average annual amounts of remittances per immigrant sent to Turkey are about the same when Germany and the UK compared when we take official number of Turkish born populations in each country respectively.

One should not overlook the fact that these figures provided in estimates and government statistics reflect the remittances sent through formal channels. However, our own study and many others show that migrants often resort to informal channels to send money abroad. Total flows through these informal channels are estimated to constitute between 20 to 75% of all remittances depending on the countries involved and money transfer corridors (see Sirkeci et al., 2012; Ratha and Sirkeci, 2010).

Money transfers remittances mechanisms

Movers use both formal and informal transfer mechanisms interchangeably for various reasons. Strictness of ID checks, documents need and transaction costs play a role in this choice of channel. However, personal networks and preferences along with past experiences and cultural characteristics are also important. Hence it is not solely based on economic concerns.

In some cases, legal requirements are more stringent, and services are inconvenient and expensive. It is known that undocumented population without access to bank accounts tends to use informal channels more extensively (Endo et al., 2011:1). However, we believe majority of migrant remittances are sent through formal channels. A study by the Bank of Uganda (2010:11) showed that the most frequently used channels to remit are international money transfer operators led by Western Union and Money Gram (32.6 percent), followed by commercial banks (23.5 percent) and friends and relatives in Uganda (21.8 percent). There was also a decrease in the percentage of households using informal remittance channels from 41.6 percent in 2008 to 37.4 percent in 2009 (Ansala, 2012: 41).

The total volume of remittances was estimated to be larger than foreign aid and on par with foreign direct investments and remittances are the most resilient cash flow to developing countries (Sirkeci, Cohen & Ratha, 2012). The informality or irregularity in remittances is also linked to reporting issues. Small businesses which are not money transfer agents or banks are hardly reported in these global statistics (Martinez, 2005: 28). Even money transfer companies and post offices are not fully reported (Martinez, 2005: 6). Moreover, one should not ignore the fact that the line between informal and formal is always blurry. Thus estimations vary greatly too (Gupta et al., 2007; Sander, 2004; EC, 2004; Freund & Spatafora, 2005). For example, about a third of remittances sent from the UK was estimated to be through informal channels (Blackwell & Seddon, 2004). Thus there is no reason to expect remittances from the UK to Turkey would be different. In fact, our survey carried out in 2015 in London shows several mechanisms of informal money transfers are used by Turkish immigrants. Here we would like to expand upon these informal channels.

IRS (Informal Remittance Systems) are remittance systems that exist and operate outside of (or parallel to) conventional regulated banking and financial channels (Buencamino & Gorbunov, 2002:1). Nevertheless, it is noted that what is legal or regular in one country may not mean the same in another. Different names have been used to refer to the informal remittance systems. For instance, these systems have been called "underground banking systems", "informal funds transfer systems", "alternative remittance systems", "ethnic banking", and "informal value transfer system" (El-Qorchi et al., 2003:6). The World Bank and IMF have been explicit in using the term "Informal Funds Transfer Systems (IFTS)" for very specific reasons (El-Qorchi et al., 2003).

Yet, there is no clarity about the definitions and terms referring to informal money transfers. According to Passas (2005:15) two types of informal value transfer systems (IVTS) can be distinguished: Informal funds transfer systems (IFTS) and informal value transfer methods (IVTM). Passas argues that IVTM involves networks and organizations, employing methods of transferring both money and value informally and, partly, illegally (2005:16). These various channels are summarised in Table 7.3. In this chapter, we particularly focus on individual movers' remittances and it covers fund and value transfers including financial and in kind transfers. Informal remittances are defined as any such transfers occuring outside the formal, regulated channels (e.g. banks, money transfer organisations (MTO), etc.).

Informal remittance systems ("informal value transfer systems" in jargon) have been in place for thousands of years and used in almost every part of the world often along with formal remittance channels. Turkish and Kurdish movers we have interviewed in London do also use both informal systems and regular channels. Some of these look very similar to "hawala type" while in some other occasions they appear closer to gift services as listed in Table 7.3. "Hawala" is used in some countries to refer to formal money transfers in commercial banking too. The most common reference to Hawala, however, is in reference to informal financial systems (Hariharan, 2012:277-278).

Table 7.3. Informal value transfer systems (IVTS) (Passas, 2005)

Informal Value Transfer Methods (IVTM) (Passas, 2005, s.16).	Informal Funds Transfer Systems (IFTS) (Passas, 2005, s.25).
• In-kind payments/transfers • Gifts services • Gift and money transfer services overseas via special vouchers and internet web sites (Africa and Asia) • Invoice manipulation • Trade diversion schemes • E-payments (internet based payments/transfers) • Stored value (e.g., hundi, chits, pre-paid telephone or credit cards, bearer instruments) • Credit/debit cards used by multiple individuals • Use of correspondent bank accounts • Use of brokerage accounts • Options/futures trading • Use of bank guarantees • Charities	• Hawala (it means "transfer" in Arabic and "reference" in Hindu) – India, United Arab Emirates (UAE), and the Middle East • Hundi (akin to a bill of exchange or promissory note; it comes from a Sanskrit root meaning "to collect") - Pakistan, Bangladesh • Fei ch'ien (flying money) - Chinese • Phoe kuan - Thailand • Hui k'uan (to remit sums of money) - Mandarin Chinese • Ch'iao hui (overseas remittance) - Mandarin Chinese • Nging sing kek (money letter shop) - Tae Chew and Cantonese speakinggroups • Chop shop - foreigners use this term for one of the Chinese methods • Chiti banking – (refers to the "chit" used as receipt or proof of claim in transactions introduced by the British in China; short for "chitty", a word borrowed from the Hindi "chitthi", signifying a mark). • Hui or hui kuan (association) - Vietnamese living in Australia • Courier services and physical transfer methods (self-carry and courier) • Door to door, padala – Philippines • Certain internet based payments/transfers • Debit and credit cards used by multiple individuals • Black market currency exchange – South America, Nigeria, Iran • Stash house (for casa de cambio) - South American systems

"Hawala-type transaction involves a sender, two trusted intermediaries and a recipient. If one wants to send money to a friend in Pakistan, he or she would contact a local IRS operator, who will keep a small commission or make a profit out of the exchange rate difference between the official

and the kerb price of US$ in Pakistan. He will contact by telephone, fax or email his counterpart, who will make the delivery. The accounts between the two IRS operators will be settled through compensatory payments (i.e. when someone from Pakistan sends money to the US)" (Passas, 2005:25).

In many of these methods used by movers to send money and goods, there are concerns about the transacation costs, speed of delivery, security and trust plays an important role in the process.

Hawala-type transfers are often money taken to home country by family, relatives and friends (Martinez, 2005:10) while some migrants also send money by special couriers (Maphosa, 2007), but this second type is something we haven't seen among the Turkish movers in London. In person transfers are known to be common around the world (Pendleton et al., 2006; Truen et al., 2005). It is important to understand why movers choose this or that method when it comes to formal and informal.

Among several reasons to resort to informal channels, failure of conventional financial infrastructure, their simplicity, efficiency, reliability and low cost (Buencamino & Gorbunov, 2002:13). There can be cultural preferences and language issues playing a role (Kosse & Vermeulen, 2014; Orozco, 2003; Sander, 2004), as well as the immigration status of the sender (Orozco, 2002; Endo et al., 2011).

What do Turkish and Kurdish movers in London do?

These movers in London were no different than other movers around the world in terms of remittances behaviour as far as we have observed in our field research. There is no reason to believe that irregular movers are more likely to use informal channels compared to regular ones. We did not see much evidence to argue that higher amounts are transferred by formal channels as several cases we have come across were involving very large transfers despite the risks known to senders.

Some used informal channels as they did not have access to formal ones due to immigration statuses but also there was confusion regarding what is required by formal channels and the risks involved:

"I can send money by Turkish Bank with my Turkish ID card. I can send money upto 10,000 Pounds without opening a bank account. When I need to send beyond this limit, I send it by relatives. There is also Moneygram but I prefer Turkish Bank. Since then it goes in Pounds; Pounds have very high value in Turkey. With Moneygram it is low as they send it in Euros." (Ahmet 2, 28 years old, male)

"We can send it through our shop too. They opened an account and gave us a device. We can send money through that. Upto 600 Pounds, we don't ask anything. Above 600 Pounds, you need an ID. To verify your identity, ID is needed. Then you enter ID details and send. If I had

an ID, I could send directly too. Agents don't worry about how much. State does not ask me why do I send that much money. They need ID to verify my name. Otherwise, you just print your name on the form and send. I can send for example 100 lira in your name, who will figure out. Receipient's name is also important. If you misspell you can't send."
(Can, 26 years old, male)

Turkish Bank in Central London (*Photo by turkishbank.co.uk*)

We have reviewed information provided by banks and money transfer companies and clearly our respondents were often misinformed about the identity verification requirements and payment amount limits imposed by banks or other regular channels. Despite common belief among immigrants, some transfer operators, at the time of our research, were accepting transactions up to 600-700 Pounds without ID requirement. Avoiding formal channels come with its own risks but there was anxiety in sending through formal channels too. Money being seized at airport controls was as bad as additional questioning by agents when sending money in somebody else's name. However, traditional ties and trust present among co-ethnics help to overcome these:

"Moneygram is better. When you send it in somebody else's name, you have to do a lot of explanation, beg for it. They don't accept, they don't send. They tell you lots of things. It does not work. Moneygram is comfortable." (Hasan, 30 years old, male)

"People are scared of carrying cash here. It is very likely they seize your cash, when caught as they will ask the source of money/income. People are scared of sending large amounts of money. Therefore, you go to other banks and send it in small installments. Or you give 1,000 Liras to the person taking money [to Turkey], so he should not face difficulty. If he is caught they will seize the money anyway. I can't proof that here. He may provide evidence for source of money but he takes

his own money too. So there is some fear [about this]." (Serkeftin, 30 years old, male)

Due to their immigration statuses, irregular migrants are limited in using formal channels to send money. Therefore, it was common that they send money with the help of regular immigrants. However, in countries where source of income is questioned such as the UK, this is not easy either. Many immigrants we have interviewed were on low incomes and many used to declare low income to be eligible for welfare benefits. Therefore, irregular immigrants who want to send money through somebody else need to find a businessman or a regular immigrant who do not declare low income and persuading to help is another hurdle:

"There was that guy here; he found out that I am a footballer. He asked me if I have a bank account. I said yes. He said: can we send that much money through your bank account? I said no. He even offered me some commission." (Ozan, 51 years old, male)

Although our respondents pointed out that they generally had difficulties in this respect, traditional solidarity networks still facilitated these transactions. However, it will make us get the wrong end of the stick to say that this method was used by irregular immigrants only. Regular migrants, who underreport their incomes to the taxman to be eligible for receiving social welfare or pay less taxes, also resort to informal channels frequently.

"I used to send through Moneygram in the period when I stayed there informally. For instance, it required passport when you go beyond a certain amount. Sometimes we didn't take such a risk. We used to tell somebody else, and they were sending it for us. For example, I used to divide it into two when the amount was very high." (Mehmet, 38 years old, male)

"Well, I never sent money on my behalf when I was a fugitive (...). For instance, I used to give someone else and he was sending for me. Someone who had residence... For example, my brother-in-law had residence here. I used to give him the money and he was sending it on his behalf." (Sevgi, 41 years old, female)

"Once, I sent 6,000 Pounds but I could not send it in person. I used to work illicitly in those days. My boss sent 4,000 liras of such on his behalf, and 2,000 liras was sent by his son on his behalf, because you

have to indicate your account sheet when the amount is high." (Çiko, 40 years old, male)

Persons helping money transfers in some organizations have several business transactions with Turkey and do transfer large sums frequently. Thus they are able to make transfers on behalf of those who are unable to transfer money due to their legal status through their own transfer instruments. There are also some larger firms taking a bigger commission and sending large sums without much questioning.

"Here, (...) is also making this. Say that there are some business owners here, monies enter into their accounts but they never see those sums. Let's say that you would like to send 10,000 [Turkish Lira], they tell you; "Give me 500, I will send it for you" and no questions about the source of the money. Employees do so... ("director is an employee anyway" he laughs). " (Mustafa, 40 years old, male)

"Germans had opened a firm here for higher amounts (...). the money is given to them. And they say they would charge 10% commission, and send your 100,000 TL from here to whomever you want in Turkey. They don't have any problem to show the source of the money; anyway he has a company here. And that money serves him as well." (Dino, 28 years old, male)

Although Hawala-type transfers are not used frequently by Turkish and Kurdish movers, its exists as an option though seemingly operate in a transnational fashion:

"Let me point out this; we have a border with Iraq, and it is open there now, a citizen from Turkey comes and sends money there, how? There is a system there; for example, a person visits you, take this TL 5,000, how much is the fee, let's say 50 TL, he takes it, well then you call your family and tell them that Ahmet will come, I gave him TL 5,000, I mean this is a transfer based on promise. I saw this and it is such a system that the English can't cope with it. Such vast amount of money is transferred that nobody is able to understand. For example, in this system there is an agent here and another one in Iraq. Suppose that you would like to send the money, you should give it to the agent here, and say that it should be immediately taken by the agent in Iraq. They make a deal in between, and counterparty is called orally, the one in the other side delivers the money at once, and they settle their accounts with each other afterwards based on the money you delivered. As the borders are open, nobody asks anything, there are several ways of doing this, there are always some acquaintances that will never end.

130

However, if you are caught and money could not be identified, such money will be assumed to be related with money for drugs and this will be deemed as a smuggling. Suppose that you go to a bank, you have some money in the bank, you withdraw it and the bank provides a receipt, you go to Turkey, but there is no control on the road, you just pass through and such receipt is not checked. You come again and can send money with the same receipt again and again (...). It is for sure that they charge less money than the banks. You have no right to send, you are exposed to an interrogation even if you send it through legal means. Therefore, you send your money upon promise without any interrogation (...). But, it is reliable anyway (...). Well, let me clarify this, it is generally based on the structure of the society. Because the society has tribal relations, nobody is alone there, I mean, there is someone behind even a small child wandering the streets, to do whatever is desired. That is to say; nobody is alone, everyone has a leader. It is not mafia, but how should I put it; I mean the structure of the study: should I call it a 'tribe' or 'family line' there is something like that." (Mustafa, 40 years old, male)

Indirect (non-)transfers similar to what *Transferwise* do also used. Money is transferred informally through official channels, however; limit is not exceeded and practically money does not cross borders. Therefore, this method is relatively inexpensive for sending remittances. Short-term visitors coming from Turkey for 6 months or 1 year create such opportunities for the movers settled in the UK. The visitor needs money in Pounds in the UK and the movers likes to send money to Turkey. So, the visitor gets the pounds in London and hands in or transfers the equivalent amount to the remittance recipient in Turkey.

"Well, in fact there are many big tricks here. You know, there is the act of money laundering. Now, the most reasonable thing is; certainly, its conversation took place in some occasions, suppose that, I need pounds here, you give me pound here, I give you TL there. I mean, for instance; I sent 11,000-12,000 Pounds in this way. I gave 10,000 Pounds here, and he gave my family TL equivalent to such pounds for instance." (Ahmet, 36 years old, male)

Sometimes, the transfer was through property purchase.

"I bought a house for myself [in Turkey], I gave the money to the owner here and I had the title to the land (property) registered in my name in Turkey." (Mustafa, 40 years old, male)

Apart from money transfers, many things in kind are also sent to Turkey too. Irregular movers send these goods through their friends or relatives, visiting Turkey. These include, for instance, mobile phones, chocolate, blood pressure monitors, tea, and shoes. Sometimes, apparently cash found its way into the gift wraps. Sending jewelry also falls in this category as they are relatively easy to exchange for cash. However, due to significant value loss in exchange, it was not that common among the respondents in London.

Physical transfer methods were another method used as we have surveyed. Some movers travel to Turkey by private cars and they hide cash to pass through controls. However, the controls are stricter now than in the past and in many cases cash was found by the officers and the method became less popular.

"Generally those who travel by car take away the money. For instance, my cousin had bought a house, they went by 2, 3, 4 times. They put 5,000 Pounds inside the car (...). We also know and hear about those, whose 40,000, 50,000 Pounds for instance, were caught while passing through the customs." (Bayram, 39 years old, male).

Carrying in person or the method of sending through somebody else is one of the methods that was used for a long time. Irrespective of migration status, regular or irregular, this is the informal money transfer method used by Turkish and Kurdish movers frequently.

"I sometimes send by those, who go on a holiday. Some of them of course do not accept. Because, they seize the money after a certain amount at the airport. This is why, they don not accept if there are people going with a lot of money with them. There are also the ones, who take big sums with them. I don't know in detail how they pass but there is an occasion as follows, that depends on the attitude of the security official at that time. Sometimes you go and have 250,000-300,000 liras passed but there is no control or search performed at all. But there are in some other months, I don't know exactly how that happens, there are stricter controls. Well, there are many people losing their money in those months. Then they bring to trial and there are some who can get back. They can take if they can make it suitable for formality, but there are also others who fail to do so and lose their money." (Doğan, 40 years old, male)

However, it was clear that our respondents felt that in the aftermath of the September 11, 2001, customs controls have become stricter. This had forced movers to find out new methods to transfer money. Hiding small amounts of cash inside the socks, in their bras, or in gifts such as tea packs along with sewing money inside the lining of suitcases appeared as new ways to send money, though risk of being caught was no less than other methods.

"I saw that money was put inside the tea packs, then there comes putting inside the clothes in the luggage or placing inside the gift chocolates (...). Then, they also put inside the socks. They put it inside the lining of the suitcase at the bottom, then it is not seen. 1,000 TL does not draw that much attention if you put them in £50 notes" (Ahmet 2, 28 years old, male).

"Ladies, in fact, know better how to hide. Now people have also learned about these ways but it doesn't mean that there aren't methods, they are sending money in such things that one can't imagine. For example, the tea we drink, I mean those smuggled teas with which we are familiar, they send a lot of money inside that. They stuck it among the tea, they fill it up with tea and embed the money inside. It is what we know as smuggled tea. Its name is smuggled tea in homeland, but it is called English Breakfast tea here. Some merchants sell them in some territories, there they are not factory packaged in packs. Of course, it has stickers, you remove it, and if you put the money inside it, there will be no problem such as dog etc, as long as it passes through X-Ray device, many people transfer the money in this way, I mean, I saw many instances of this." (Kadir, 36 years old, male)

"There are some people, they stuck it under the goods and send in that way. They go on a holiday, they have prepared large suitcases, of 4-5 persons in the family for instance. When it comes to per kilos, you have a right for 20-30 kilos for example. Suppose that it consists of 100 kilos of material, the police officers do not always open all of them. They place them under some special things, and hide them there, they sometimes doubt, let the dogs check in order to search and find. You know, there are dogs at the airports, this is generally applied. They send more or less, 10,000 liras for instance. They do not risk much of that, if he fails to document such money, he loses it. He retains some of it, he sends some amount of the money through the bank, he gives some amount to you and he sends some, he gives some amount of the money to somebody else and that person sends some of it, he takes away some amount with himself to carry, they deliver it a lot through these ways." (Kadir, 36 years old, male)

"One of my relatives has just took 50 thousand liras to Turkey recently with him. He put all the money inside a bag and took it away in that way. The fellow, put it inside the rug sack and took it away, I mean. He takes it secretly. Home office manager asks him, if there is money inside the rug sack. He replies 'No.' He asks; How much is there inside? 'I have 1,000 liras as my pocket money' he replies. 'Is that really that much?' he replies 'Yes.' He passes through the device, the machine sounds an alarm of course, as all of the money is in 50'. They don't let him because there is a chip in 50' banknotes. When the chip sounds, the fellow says that, 'Hey! there is a lot of money on you, how come?' 'No it shouldn't be, no, how come?' The fellow, pours down the bag, but there is no money. He had torn the bottom of the suitcase. He placed the money inside the letter of the suitcase and sewed it back. When the man tears it with knife, he sees that there are all £50 banknotes inside. They had taken the money, and sent him away. Anyway, he should thank god that he was not sent to prison (...). They seized such 50,000 liras, he lost the money. He can't prove it. And he won't be able to get rid of the problem if he chases after. Because, they will say that, you receive social welfare and you are the caretaker of your wife. They further say that; we are giving you money to the extend you can earn your life. How do you earn this much money then?"
(Hasan, 30 years old, male)

Another method we have heard from interviewees was "classified envelope method." This method seems being developed mainly to get through the questioning about the source of the money. Those movers, who had a relative visiting Turkey put the cash in separate envelopes addressed to different recipients in Turkey. The travelling person, if needed, provides the controlling officers the names and contact numbers of the recipients and hence the story can be confirmed directly with the recipients. This requires quite a bit of organisation and preparation and may not always go as planned according to our respondents.

"I told them that 500 pounds of this belongs to my friend, the name of my friend's father, his address, everything is written on the envelope. I had several times taken my friend's money in this way in advance too. I told them that 1,500 pounds of the money is mine, remaining 500 hundred is my friend's. Here is his address, if you want you can phone and ask him." (Aynur, 45 years old, female).

Declaring the source of the money

The real risk in pocket transfer method is that officers may seize the money at the airport until the source is proven. Sometimes, movers show photos, videos and other evidence of weddings where traditionally money and jewellery are pinned on wedding dresses. Still the carrier has to prove that there was a real wedding.

Another method our respodents said they resorted is to claim that they borrowed the money from friends.

"They had done this, I heard. They had asked one of the ladies at the airport, they asked her; 'You receive social welfare, what you do with this much?' One of the man, among the Turks I mean, appeared and had told them that, 'I know her, I have my own business, I lent the money to her.' That was how the lady had managed to pass." (Can, 26 years old, male)

Some movers claim the money was collected at a "day". Day is some kind of a social solidarity gathering among women operating on an informal membership principle to enable members to build savings. Members meet periodically and at each meeting, the host receives set amount of money or valuable (e.g. gold coins) from each participant. Thus, women had also claimed these gatherings as source of the cash they carry travelling to Turkey or they deposited the collected cash to a bank account.

"My mom was confined to bed in Turkey, we decided to buy a house rather than making her stay on rent. We bought a house. Moreover, the house was not only in my name. It was owned by me and my elder-sister. We bought it jointly (...). We organized days. You know ladies organize such days. We paid with that money with my elder-sister, for seven years; one month her turn, one month my turn". (Sevgi, 41 years old, female)

Another way to declare the source of money was that the mover deposits a certain amount of money to a bank account and withdraws it day before the travel and produces the receipt at the airport if caught. The amount has to be same as the amount he or she keeps at home in cash to take to Turkey. Upon return from Turkey, the same amount is deposited back to the bank account.

In this chapter we have explained the ways in which informal channels are used by movers to send money to Turkey. Apart from regular channel such as banks, money transfer agents, post office or other online services, Turkish and Kurdish movers have also resorted to informal channels and even invented new ways of carrying money and multiple ways of declaring the source as the regulations and controls have been tightened in recent decades. The reasons behind using informal channels as we heard from the interviewees were in line with the literature as the transaction costs, trust issues and practicalities were mentioned. However, a key feature was the employment and business patterns, against the costs and need to juggle to maintain a decent life while being able to save and invest, was forcing many movers towards informal work. Hence, it was not just irregular movers but also regular ones often resorting to informal channels to transfer money and clearly they have come up with innovative methods and narratives.

The patterns and cases discussed in this chapter seem compatible with the patterns explained in two previous chapters. Understanding both the employment and remittances in the context of movers in London is important for devising appropriate policies to deal with banking regulations, social security as well as integration.

In the next two chapters, we will turn our attention to identity and culture again and provide a snapshot of spiritual life and identity formation through sports among the Turkish movers in London.

Chapter 8. Turkish religious communities

Muslims in the UK have been a part of the British social and cultural landscape for almost a century and a half and they continue to constitute and increasingly significant share among minorities in today's Britain (Khattab et al., 2011). This population emerged as a result of migration inflows from Muslim countries many of those were former colonies of the empire. In this chapter, we highlight the organisational and practical aspects of the religious life of Turkish speaking communities in Great Britain. Thus, based on systematic observations, existing Islamic discourses, varying religious communities and organizations, and activities in mosques and prayer rooms are examined in this chapter.

For movers abroad, religion often plays an important role in identity formation and protection of heritage culture. While most Muslims in Great Britain share a common religious identity, the expression of their faith is likely to be shaped by their ethnic or national origins (Gilliat-Ray, 2010).

As we have explained in chapter two, Sunnis represent the largest group among the movers from Turkey in the UK, closely followed by Alevis but also a significantly large group with no religion (see tables 2.4 and 2.5).[1] This was in line with the selectivity of migration argument regarding ethnic or religious minorities such as Alevis who are often overrepresented among diaspora populations. According to the Department for Communities and Local Government (DCLG), 83% of the migrants born in Turkey, and 26% of the migrants born in Cyprus were Muslims and the majority were Sunnis, mainly adhering to the Hanafi School of thought. Sunni Kurds, who are originally from eastern Turkey, tended to follow the Shafi School of thought. There are also Alevis, Ismailis and Jafaris (DCLG, 2009).

The first attempt of Turks living in Britain, towards being organised as a religious community was in the early 1970s. However, in these years, religious life for the Turkish communities was confined to private homes. The first generation movers had a limited religious life practising and observing the basics. Small spaces were rented or bought to practise these duties (Atay 1994; Küçükcan, 1996; 1999). In conjunction with Turkish movers settling in Britain permanently, population growing significantly, and declining hopes of return to Turkey, some of these temporary and limited arrangements for practicing religion became insufficient. At the face of growing needs of the community, a need for institutionalised and systematic organizations arose.

---

[1] See Issa (2017) for a most recent account of Alevis in Britain.

In the late 1970s, number and variety of religious organizations within Turkish movers community started to expand (Küçükcan, 1999). Hence, they have become more visible and more influential in their representation of wider Turkish Muslim interests. The tendency therefore, has been for Turkish immigrants to address some of their religious problems through these organizations, while preserving their identities and the continuity of their communities (Çoştu and Ceyhan Çoştu, 2015).

In our research, ten (10) religious organizations established by Turkish communities were selected for further analysis (see Çoştu, 2013a; 2013b). Some of these organizations also provide opportunities for forming and maintaining a common identity and for a sense of belonging. Naturally they differ from other civil society and voluntary sector organizations in terms of objectives, service types and service areas. These organizations are often established nearby the mosques.

The Islamic discourses of these organizations established by Turkish movers in Britain can be classified into four main categories: a) Islamic discourses inspired by the Sufi movements in Turkey and North Cyprus[2], b) Islamic discourses inspired by the religious movements in Turkey[3], c) Islamic discourses inspired by the religious-political movements in Turkey[4], d) Mosques/mosque unions affiliated with the official religious discourse in Turkey[5].

It is understood that in formation of these religious organisations, migration motivations, residence statuses in the UK as well as religious, ethnic, cultural, and political discourses in Turkey and North Cyprus played an important role (Küçükcan, 1999; Çoştu, 2013a). A significant number of foundations and unions in Britain providing religious services for Turks are simply extensions of religious groups, sects and movements within Turkey and North Cyprus. The fact that Turkish Muslim movers do not have a single culture with single religious practice and belief is reflected in very heteregenous scene of these religious organizations. There is also a subtle competition between these organisations to offer religious services for movers from Turkey. Each organization aims to

---

[2] Sufi organizations; the followers of Sheikh M. Nazim Qibrisî, the followers of Mahmut Ustaosmanoglu, the followers of Muhammed Rasit Erol/Menzil Naqshbandiya Sufi Order (For further information see Çoştu, 2013a, 2013b).

[3] Religious movement organizations; the followers of Suleyman Hilmi Tunahan/Süleymanci group, the followers of Fetullah Gulen/Hizmet Movement, and Alevis (For further information see Çoştu, 2013a, 2013b).

[4] Religio-political movement organizations National Vision/MilliGörüş and Milliyetciler/Nationalists (For further information see Küçükcan, 1999; Çostu, 2013a, 2013b).

[5] Official religious organization; Turkish Religious Foundation of the UK/Diyanet (For further information see Çoştu, 2013a, 2013b).

attract more followers to become a leading organisation for the Turkish Muslim community of movers, both in terms of economic resources and in religious school of thought and practice. Similar to the religious groups within Turkish mover communities in continental Europe and particularly in Germany, these organisations in Britain also follow the agenda set in homeland, Turkey (See Persembe, 2005; Çelik 2008; Adıgüzel, 2011).

Like the population, religious organisations of Turkish movers are heavily concentrated in the Greater London region (DCLG, 2009). The field research on which this chapter draws upon was also conducted in London, interviewing heads and/or members of these organizations[6]. Now we describe each of the mainstream organisations in London:

Sheikh Nazim Al-Haqqani Derghai (1972)

'*Sheikh Nâzım Al-Haqqani Derghai*'[7] was established by the followers of Sheikh Nâzim Qibrisî[8] (1922-2014) (Nâzım Adil) under the guidance of Sheikh, who follows the Naqshbandiya Sufi tariqa / order. The Derghai / Dervish Lodge is one of the institutions which provide religious services to Turkish communities in London and considered as one of the pioneers in this area (Atay, 1994).

Sheikh Nâzim started his mission of spreading the message of Islam in London in the early 1970s (Atay, 1996; Küçükcan, 1999). In the beginning years of his visit, Sheikh was staying at homes which belong to Turks, and organising dhikr/recitation ceremonies. Later on, with the efforts of Sheikh, a synagogue (Shacklewell Mosque) and a church (Peckham Mosque) were purchased by Turkish movers (mostly Cypriot Turks) and turned into mosques. Sheikh Nâzim had continued spreading Sufi teachings and organising dhikr ceremonies in these places turned into mosques. In 1992, a monastery in North London was bought and restored, and had started to be used as the headquarters of derghai.

The organization has a predominantly Sufi religious structure, and its target audience is heterogeneous as there are Cypriot Turks and movers from Turkey, as well as Muslims from Britain, Pakistan, Indian and several European countries rank among the followers and sympathisers of the Sheikh. Atay (1994) shows ethnic and national diversity of community

---

[6] Field research done by the author from July 9, 2012 to September 9, 2012 in London.This field research included interviews and observations about these religious communities.

[7] According to the records of the Charity Commission of the UK, the registration of this foundation was held with the charity number 1030802 on December 22, 1993. See. www.charitycommission.gov.uk (accessed: 15/03/2014).

[8] Sheikh Nâzim is a religious personality who is mainly a follower of the Naqshbandiya Sufi Order, but also connected with the Mevlevi Order and Qadiriyya Order (see. Atay, 1994; 1996).

members of Sheikh Nâzim derghai in London: Accordingly, there were people from 56 different countries among the Sheikh followers (1994: 61).

Since 2000, Sheikh Nâzim's visits to London had become infrequent due to his advancing age and health issues, and it was observed that services of the derghai and the ethnic diversity of the followers have declined. After the Sheikh passed away in 2014, active services of the derghai declined significantly to a symbolic level. The headquarters of derghai in North London offers broad range of services including mosque services, religious and educational activities for children and youngsters.

Personality, charisma and the teachings of Sheikh Nâzim had played an important role in shaping the religious identity of followers among Turkish-Muslim movers in London and in maintaining traditional and cultural values among this community (Küçükcan, 1999). It is understood that the first serious steps towards religious based activities was offered by or under the guidance of Sheikh Nâzim. Despite the fact that it has a predominantly Sufi religious interpretation, in the first years of migration, activities of the group attracted a wider audience among Turkish movers seeking religious services and identity.

London Islamic Turkish Association (1976)

'*London Islamic Turkish Association*' was set up on December 15, 1976 mainly by Turkish Cypriot movers, and nowadays it is mostly run by Turkish movers from Turkey (Küçükcan, 1999). According to official data of the Charity Commission of the UK, the London Islamic Turkish Association is the first official/registered organization of Turkish Communities in London.

In 1976, the current centre of association in North London (16 Green Lanes) was purchased, under the guidance of Sheikh Nâzim Qibrisî and Cypriot businessman Ramazan Güney. During his visits, Sheikh Nâzim was occasionally staying and performing Sufi religious practices in this place. This pattern continued until the beginning of the 1980s (Atay, 1996: 79). As the audiences grew and Sufi practices of Sheikh Nâzim moved into bigger places such as Shacklewell Mosque and Peckham Mosque the dominance of Turkish Cypriots in management of the association weakened.

Until the 1990s, this association did not have any political-ideological connections. In a small mosque named Muradiye owned by the association, religious services were carried out and religious and cultural activities offered to immigrant communities. In the 1990s, Turkish nationalists (also known as *Ülkücüler*) became stronger in the association and this shaped the political discourse of the association. 1993, when the nationalists gained significant representation at the board meeting was a turning point for the association. After 1993, a nationalistic view based on a synthesis of Turkish and Islamic values started to dominate the socio-political discourse of the association. Soon after, London Islamic Turkish Association became a member of the 'Turkish Federation'[9] which is a nationalist umbrella organization with strong membership in Germany. Küçükcan (1999) argued that, due to this change in management and shift towards nationalism, some members of the association who disagree with the ideological and political discourse of the federation turned toother religious organizations run by Turkish movers in London.

Currently, it can be said that London Islamic Turkish Association is an organization with a religio-political mission running activities to preserve and maintain religious and national values among the movers from Turkey with an agenda mostly set along the lines of political-ideological debates in Turkey.

The UK Turkish Islamic Trust (1977)

'*The UK Turkish Islamic Trust*' registered on June 21, 1978 is another old religious organization in the Turkish community in London. The organization was established in Hackney, a borough of London with strong Turkish concentraion, around a mosque (Shacklewell Mosque), which was once a synagogue purchased in 1977 by Northern Cyprian businessman Ramazan Güney and later turned into a mosque (Atay, 1994). The mosque was organised with the efforts of Güney, who was a close follower of Sheikh Nâzım. This mosque is known among the community as 'The Mosque of Cypriots' (Atay, 1996). Shacklewell Mosque was named as the 'Ramazan-i Şerif Mosque' in November of 2008. The Trust also provides funeral services along with other religious services.[10]

As one of the first mosques of Turkish Communities in London, the Ramazan-i Şerif Mosque can be considered as one of the serious steps taken by the community towards organising a religious sphere. Similar to others, this mosque was also set up as an effort to protect and maintain religious and national identity in a "foreign land".

The United Kingdom Turkish Islamic Association (1979)

'*The United Kingdom Turkish Islamic Association*' was established on January 28, 1979 by the founders of today's Aziziye Mosque located in

---

[9] 'Europe Democratic Nationalist Turkish Unions Federation', which is shortly known as the 'Turkish Federation' was established in 1978, and is an organization that accepts and supports the nationalist ideology of the Nationalist Movement Party in Turkey (see. Perşembe, 2005; Adıgüzel, 2011; www.turkeyfederasyon.com -accessed: 08/09/2013).

[10] After the death of R. Güney his daughter took over the administration of the trust. His son is responsible for funeral services of the trust. See. www.brookwoodcemetary.com (accessed: 25/08/2012))

North-East London and offers both in religious services and socio-cultural activities (Küçükcan, 1999).

Turkish movers from Turkey had an important role in the formation of this organization. This organization can be seen as continuation of institutionalisation efforts started by Sheikh Nâzim Qibrisi in the 1970s. This was beginning of the decline Turkish Cypriot influence and growing Turkish influence in religious sphere in London's Turkish mover population.

With the efforts of Turks from Turkey, an old movie theatre in Stoke Newington High Road was purchased (1983) and turned into a mosque (i.e. Aziziye Mosque). After building extensions completed, in Aziziye Mosque, the association began its religious services and cultural activities including educational activities. Accordingly, the mosque and several service areas around it (a small school, an all-purpose meeting hall, restaurant, market etc.) serves to Turkish and other Muslim movers in London.

It is known that the board chairman and some members of the board of trustees of 'The United Kingdom Turkish Islamic Association' had close relationships with Mahmut Hoca (Ustaosmanoğlu) who is the sheikh of the Naqshbandiya Sufi Order that is also known as the 'Ismail Aga Movement' based in Çarşamba district of Fatih, Istanbul (Çakır, 2002; Atay, 1996; Küçükcan 1999). Atay (1996) stated that the connection of the administrators of the Aziziye Mosque with Mahmut Hoca did not interrupt the collaboration of the community with other Turkish Muslim communities and tariqahs. Aziziye mosque and community, overtime, became a meeting point for various Islamic communities with political roots in Turkey. However, with the rise of number of religious associations who set up their own mosques, the role of Aziziye mosque diminished since 2000. Thus religious fragmentation among the Turkish community of movers in London has become apparent.

'The United Kingdom Turkish Islamic Association', which tries to provide services with its mission of maintaining and flourishing religious and national values, is another concrete step towards building and identity and belonging to Turkish immigrants.

UK Turkish-Islamic Cultural Centre Trust (1984)

'*UK Turkish-Islamic Cultural Centre Trust*' officially registered on February 22, 1984 is one of the most institutionally developed among the religious organizations of the Turkish movers in London. Administration and members of this association are connected with a movement named the 'Süleymancı group'[11], who are followers and disciplines of Süleyman Hilmi Tunahan[12] (1888-1959) who was a Naqshbandiya Sufi leader. The main views of the association show parallelisms with those of the Süleymancı movement in Turkey (Küçükcan, 1999).

Organisation of the Süleymancı group in London begun in the mid-1980s under the name of the 'UK Turkish-Islamic Cultural Centre Trust' in 1984, and opened their first Mosque (Valide Sultan) in London in 1987. Similar to other religious organisations, the UK Turkish-Islamic Cultural Centre Trust offers religious services while also running educational[13] and cultural[14] activities in mosque centres[15] and affiliate branches of the Trust in and outside London.

The UK Turkish-Islamic Cultural Centre Trust has many mosques to provide religious services and offers various other services to Turkish communities and others. This makes the association the most active and institutionalised Islamic organization among the Turkish movers in Great Britain. The association is a member of Federation of Turkish Associations in the UK.

England Alevi Cultural Centre and Cemevi (1993)

The history of Alevi religious organisations in London dates back to the beginning of the 1990s. The majority of the Alevi population in London are of Kurdish origin who fled Turkey and arrived as refugees in Great Britain in large numbers at the beginning of the 1990s. There is no

---

[11] This group has several organizations in various European countries. The first systematically organised group which is connected with the movement is 'Islam Cultural Centres Union' and was established in 1973 in Cologne/Germany. The union acts as a higher frame and has 300 mosques in Germany, and 125 mosques in other European countries (see. Perşembe, 2005; Adıgüzel, 2011)

[12] He is the founder of this movement which is connected with the Naqshbandiya Sufi Order. Considering its Islamic teaching, organization and operation style, the Süleymancı group is a rather accepted religious movement than the tariqah/Sufi Order (see Aydın, 2004).

[13] The Marathon Science School opened in 2009. See. www.matarhonschool.com (accessed: 15/03/2013).

[14] They organise an annual 'Anatolian Culture Festival' since 2007 with the partnership of the Anatolian Community Association founded in 2006. See. www.anatolianfest.com (accessed: 15/03/2013).

[15] The mosques affiliated with the Trust are: Valide Sultan Mosque, Wood Green Fatih Mosque, Greenwich Mosque, Süleymaniye Mosque (this is the first Turkish mosque with minarets, and call of prayer is recited openly in midday and for afternoon prayers), Ilford Mosque, Edmonton Fazilet Mosque, Morden Mosque, UxbridgeEyup Mosque, Ponders End Mosque in London, and Selimiye Mosque in Manchester, Hamidiye Mosque in Leicester, Osmaniye Mosque in Stoke-on-Trend, and Northampton Mosque in Northampton (see. table 1). Also, see further information about these Mosques at www.suleymaniye.org (accessed: 15/08/2012).

accurate estimation of the number of the Alevis in the UK but as we have presented a detailed account of Turkish movers in London in earlier chapters, Alevis are a strong segment of the Turkish mover population in the UK.[16] Similar to Alevis in Turkey, Alevis in the UK as well as in continental Europe are fragmented and divided between different factions.

Alevi movers in London established *"England Alevi Cultural Centre and Cemevi"* was registered as a charity on September 12, in 1994 and was founded on March 14, 1993 in Hackney, London with the aim of preserving and maintaining and spreading the Alevi thought, identity, and practices (Cem, Semah, etc.) while offering religious services and educational and cultural activities. Alevi Cultural Centre and Cemevi is part of the Britain Alevi Federation, an umbrella organisation of fifthteen Alevi Cultural Centres and Cemevis based in London, Glasgow, Leicester, Croydon, Harrow, Northampton, York, Newcastle, Liverpool, Bournemouth, Nottingham, Doncaster, Hull, Sheffield and Edinburgh.

In its constitution, the Centre states that its aims are "give necessary services in order to protect our religious and cultural heritage and support other organizations which offer the same services; address the needs for religious services" (See www.alevinet.org).

The Britain Alevi Federation and the Alevi Cultural Centre and Cemevi have also encouraged and played a pivotal role in establishment of other Cemevis around the UK.[17] These associations and cemevis offer a wide range of acitivities including classes on mathematics, music, folk dances, football, and GSCE (exam) support classes for school children. Alevis have also a strong presence in local and national politics as they actively pursue Alevism to be officially recognised. As a result, there is now an All Party Parliamentary Group for Alevis led by Joan Ryan and Kate Osamor, Labour Party MPs with stated aim of "To promote in Parliament awareness, recognition and engagement of and with the Alevi community in Britain and internationally. To advance their development and recognise

---

[16] Although it is an overly exaggerated number, Britain Alevi Federation claims that it "is an umbrella organisation established by 14 Alevi Cultural Centres and Cemevis serving approximatelly 300,000 Alevis in UK". (See: http://www.alevinet.org/).

[17] According to the Charity Commission of the UK, by 2013, Cemevis established by Turkish and Kurdish Alevi immigrants were: 'South London Alevi Cultural Centre & Cemevi' (registered at: 15 July 2011, No: 1142427), 'Bournemouth Alevi Cultural Centre' (registered at: 14 May 2012, No: 1147244), 'Coventry Alevi Bektasi Cultural Centre and Cemevi' (registered at: 5 November 2010, No: 1138831), 'Croydon Alevi Cultural Centre' (registered at: 23 January 2012, No: 1145567) and 'Nottingham Alevi Cultural Centre' (registered at 7 February 2013, No: 1150736). See. www.charitycommission.gov.uk (accessed: 14/09/2013).

their legitimate socio-political aspirations".[18] Alevism has also been recognised as part of the religious education curriculum in some British primary schools.[19]

Islamic Community Milli Görüş UK (1994)

'*Islamic Community Milli Gorus UK*'[20] is another organization which operates with a religio-political mission. The organization was established in 1994 and is connected to the 'European Islamic Society Milli Görüş' (IGMG) which is based in Germany.

Political-ideology discourse of National Vision (Milli Görüş) organizations which were first organised in Germany as an extension to the original political movement in Turkey (Perşembe, 2005). National Vision organizations in Europe[21] are closely linked to the Milli Görüş political view gathered around the leadership of Necmettin Erbakan, also a former prime minister in Turkey (Adıgüzel, 2011). This organization was originally established by Turkish immigrants in Europe and has a religio-political discourse which prioritises a distinctive Islamic identity (see www.igmg.org/tr)

The mission of the Milli Görüş organization in London shares religious and political discourses of the main movement in Europe and Turkey (Küçükcan, 1999). The organization aims to provide educational and cultural services in a small place purchased in North London. With support of the European Milli Görüş organization some religious services including funeral services, hajj and umrah organization are also provided.

London Milli Görüş organization, compared to other Turkish community religious organizations in London, was established more recently and its religio-political discourse is rather unpopular among the community and not yet institutionalised.

---

[18] Register of All Party Parliamentary Group for Alevis in the UK Parliament: http://www.publications.parliament.uk/pa/cm/cmallparty/151223/alevis.htm.

[19] See Prince of Wales Primary School in London: http://www.princeofwales.enfield.sch.uk/school-curriculum/re/

[20] I could not detect any registration information about this organization on the Charity Commission of the UK website.

[21] Branches operate in connection with regional organizations. IGMG has a total of 30 regional organizations across Europe, 15 of them are in Germany. IGMG has 514 mosques in Europe (323 of them are in Germany), and with women and youth branches, sports, culture and education unions there are 1833 local branches and 87.000 members. See. www.igmg.org.tr (accessed: 16/09/2013).

The Menzil Trust (1999)

'*The Menzil Trust*'[22] was established in London by immigrants who were members of the Naqshbandiya Sufi Order based in Menzil district of Adıyaman, an eastern province in Turkey[23] (Çoştu, 2013a).

Similar to other religious organisations, socio-religious structure of contemporary Menzil Naqshbandiya Sufi Order in Turkey can also be seen among Turkish movers who are followers of the center in London. For example, during our field research it was observed that the branches of the Sheikh Seyyid Abdulbaki and Sheikh Seyyid Fevziddin were separated and operating in different places.

Followers of the Sheikh Seyyid Fevziddin branch of the Menzil Naqshbandiya Sufi Order in London have a small place (which they call "home") in Green Lane, Newington Green. Sufi followers of the Sheikh Seyyid Fevziddin perform Sufi ceremonies such as dhikr and hatme at this centre.

The administration of the London Menzil Trust was controlled by the Sufis who are followers of the Sheikh Seyyid Abdulbaki. The Menzil Trust purchased a large building in Leyton, North-East London at the beginning of 2012. Volunteers carry out activities in this derghai. There were 300 Sufi members of the derghai in Central London at the time of our field research. Most of the Sufis are Turkish, but there are also a small number of others. Sufis share the derghai chores among themselves and the works of the trust and the derghai are carried out by volunteers, which is similar to most other religious community organisations we have observed in London's Turkish, Kurdish and Turkish Cypriot communities.

Turkish Religious Foundation of the UK (2001)

The *Presidency of Religious Affairs (DIB)* is the official institution providing public religious services in Turkey. As the international extension of the official *Religious Affairs Presidency* aims to meet societal

---

[22] According to the records of the Charity Commission of the UK, the registration of this foundation was held with the charity number 1074978 on April 1, 1999. See. www.charitycommission.gov.uk

[23] The founder of the Menzil Naqshbandiya Sufi Order is Sheikh Abdulhakim El-Huseyni. His son Muhammed Raşit Erol took over his place after his death in 1973 (see. Usta, 1997). Nowadays Menzil (Adıyaman/Menzil (Durak) Village) is known with Muhammet Raşit Erol's name and is being visited as a centre (see. Çakır, 2002). After the death of Muhammet Raşit Erol in 1993, his brother SeyyidAbdülbaki took his place. Seyyid Abdülbaki still operates the derghai. However, due to the reason some Sufis think that rather than Sheikh Seyyid Abdülbaki, son of Muhammed Raşit Erol, SeyyidFevziddinErol should took over the derghai, some separations had occurred. Nowadays, Menzil Naqshbandiya operates from two separate branches, one by Sheikh Seyyid Fevziddin Erol, based in Ankara and Afyon, the other by Sheikh Seyyid Abdulbaki, based in Adıyaman/Menzil and Istanbul (see. Usta, 1997).

needs and requirements through domestic and international service networks. The international remit of the DIB is concentrated in countries where Turkish citizens live, and are served by the Counsellors of Religious Services stationed at Turkish Consulates (Çoştu & Ceyhan Çoştu 2015).

DIB's overseas organization is named ''Office of the Counsellor for Religious Services'' affiliated with the Turkish consulates in some European countries. Also, there are semi-official religious foundations linked to these offices and named "Turkish Religious Foundations".

Office of the Counsellor for Religious Services within the Turkey's General Consulate in London was founded in 1998. '*Turkish Religious Foundation of the UK* (ITDV) was registered as a charity on April 30, 2001 and is affiliated with the Religious Services Office was established in North London in 2001, to provide religious services and organise cultural activities.

This foundation started its activities in a small residence at Wood Green in 2004. Then, ITDV purchased a sizable estate that has administration offices, a mosque, meeting rooms, classrooms and a cafeteria in Hornsey, London. The previous location was converted into a guest house for girls.

ITDV operates with the support of official representatives from their offices in the Turkish Consulate in London through the Office of Religious Affairs Counsellor, and benefiting from a supply of well experienced and educated imams and other support staff. It offers religious services, runs a mosque in Hornsey, North London but also offers Islamic services targeting children and young people, elderly, and people with disabilities. IDTV works in three main service areas: (a) religious services at its five mosques[24], Hajj and Umrah organizations, funeral services, services of al-adha, religious counselling and guidance; (b) educational activities for Turkish children and adults and (c) socio-cultural activities through women's organisation, family information and guidance office, events and services during religious holidays and holy nights, print publications, and a student house for girls.

Anatolian Muslim Society (2004)

'*Anatolian Muslim Society*' registered as a charity on November 17, 1996 and was operational in North London since 2004. It is known that the

---

[24] There are five mosques belonging to the IDTV, named as North London Diyanet Mosque, Luton Turkish Islamic Centre and Mosque, Bristol Somuncu Baba Mosque, Edinburgh Cultural Centre and Mosque, Newcastle Kotku Mosque (see Table 1). Also, the foundation's religious officials take charge in Aziziye Mosque in North London. See for further information www.diyanet.org (accessed: 15/03/2014).

administration of the organization is connected with the Gülen Movement / Hizmet[25] in Turkey (Çoştu, 2013a).

Turkish movers who are sympathisers or followers of the Gülen movement have set up many organisations with educational purposes in various European countries (Perşembe, 2005). In Great Britain, institutional activities of the Gülen movement and their supporters started in the mid-1990s. Until 2004, the Gülen movement had focused on educational, social and cultural services. For example, they opened up a school called Wisdom School mainly targeting immigrant community in North London[26]. They have also focused on "religious dialogue" and set up such associations to propagate their religious world views and strengthening the movement.[27] Supporters of the Gülen movement provide religious, educational and cultural services via trusts, research centres and associations under different names in London and beyond (Çoştu, 2013a).

Regarding religious services, the groups' activities were rather confined to organising sermons and study groups, and classes to teach reading the Quran in the houses of members/followers until 2004. In 2009, this movement purchased a Sikh temple in North London in 2009 in the name of the 'Anatolian Muslim Society' and restored it as a mosque. It is named 'Mevlana Rumi Mosque'[28] with facilities for educational and cultural activities as well as religious services.

Turkish Mosques and Cemevis in Britain

Mosques and Cemevis play an important role within diaspora communities. They offer religious services but also serve to communities in preserving the heritage cultures as well as offering various social and public support services including education and advice on public services. In this sense, places of worship function as a demonstration of cultural, religious and ethnic aspects of heritage identity.

In a society that Muslims are majority, generally the mosque or cemevi is only a place of worship and religious service, however in a society that Muslims are a minority or immigrant minority, the mosque also has the role of a place of refuge which has social, cultural, educational and political functions and roles. Turkish and Kurdish Muslim movers living in various European countries have established mosques and cemevis. These places have many different functions besides being houses of worship.

---

[25] The Gülen or Hizmet Movement is a socio-religious movement developed by Fetullah Gülen, a Turkish cleric currently lives in the USA. This movement has been in a political conflict with the current government and president Erdogan in Turkey since 2013.

[26] See wisdomschool.org.uk (accessed: 15/11/2009).

[27] See www.dialoguesociety.org (accessed: 15/11/2009).

[28] See www.rumicentre.org.uk (accessed: 15/11/2009).

These religious organisations represent a space where culture and values from the homeland are shared, where courses and educational activities are carried out, possible problems that are experienced in the host countries can be solved and religious and cultural values are preserved and presented to the host countries.

According to our research, there are a total of 40 active religious prayer places (mosque, prayer room, cemevi) across Great Britain (Table 8.1.). It was clear that these places of worship have differentiated from those one would find in Turkey. Organisations in Britain often offer more than just a religious service and goes beyond being a mere place of worship as they offer a wide range of services and support for Turkish movers who settle in a foreign country. These services include educational activities for children, young adults and adult movers (supplementary school programmes, teaching Islam and the Quran, etc.), social and cultural activities concerning health, sports, and wider community support services such as accommodation services, legal and economic support, and even assistance and mediation in conflict situations.

Table 8.1. Turkish places of worship in Great Britain

Places of worship (Mosque/Cemevi/Sufi Centre)	Opening Date	Location
Muradiye Mosque	1976	London
Ramazan-i Serif Mosque	1977	London
Peckham Mosque	1980	London
Aziziye Mosque	1984	London
Valide Sultan Mosque	1987	London
Sheikh Nazim Dergahi (Masjid)	1992	London
England Alevi Cultrual Center and Cemevi	1993	London
Süleymaniye Mosque	1998	London
Wood-Green Fatih Mosque	2000	London
Hamidiye Mosque	2001	Leicester
Osmaniye Mosque	2002	Stoke
Luton Mosque	2004	Luton
Selimiye Mosque	2004	Manchester
Greenwich Mosque	2005	London
Bristol Mosque	2006	Bristol
Glasgow Alevi Cultural Centre and Cemevi	2008	Glasgow
Mevlana Rumi Mosque	2008	London
Edinburgh Mosque	2009	Edinburgh
Newcastle Kotku Mosque	2009	Newcastle
Northampton Mosque	2010	Northampton
Ilford Mosque	2011	London

Table 8.1. continued.

Edmonton Fazilet Mosque	2011	London
Uxbridge Eyup Mosque	2011	Uxbridge
Ponders End Mosque	2011	London
Said-i Nursi Mosque	2011	London
England Habes Alevi Cultural Centre and Solidarity Association	2011	London
North London Diyanet Mosque	2012	London
Morden Mosque	2012	London
Menzil Derghai (Masjid)	2012	London
Croydon Alevi Cultural Centre and Cemevi	2012	London
Nottingham Alevi Cultural Centre and Cemevi	2012	Nottingham
Sheffield Alevi Cultural Centre and Cemevi	2013	Sheffield
Bournemouth Alevi Cultural Centre and Cemevi	2013	Bournemouth
Doncaster Alevi Cultural Centre and Cemevi	2014	Doncaster
Edinburgh Pir Sultan Abdal Cultural Centre and Cemevi	2014	Edinburgh
East Midlands Alevi-Bektaşi Cultural Centre and Cemevi	2015	Leicester
Coventry Alevi Cultural Centre and Cemevi	2015	Coventry
Hull Alevi Cultural Centre and Solidarity Association	2015	Hull

Preserving national identity and cultural heritage is important for movers away from their homeland and religion plays an important role in this process. Faith-based organizations can play a central role as community centers and venues for cultural activities. The Turkish, Kurdish, and Turkish Cypriot movers have organised themselves around various faith organisations over a period of five decades. The variety and number of faith-based organisations increased as the size of the population of mvoers from Turkey grew in Britain. These organisations, naturally, also offer an important religious service to the community in providing places of worship, funeral and wedding services, and services for other religious ceremonies and rituals. In this chapter we have presented an inventory of these organisations with brief descriptions of origins and services offered.

Chapter 9. Diasporic identities and ethnic football in London

Different diaspora groups with origins in Turkey, living in close proximity and doing business with one another have been divided by religious, cultural, and political differences from the very beginning. Like in Germany and elsewhere, these diaspora groups from Turkey often carry their conflicts from homeland to destinations (Baser, 2014; Sirkeci, 2003). However, one common passion has long stood out among others as a useful instrument for communal mobilisation: football! The first Turkish community league was established as early as in 1976 when the Cyprus conflict was at its peak. Football has ever since provided a prolific transnational social space in which identities are represented and contested, political statements are made, and communal bonds are re-negotiated.

For the Turkish-Cypriot, Turkish and Kurdish communities in London, football has become one of the biggest, most effective, most dynamic and most inclusive arenas for the diverse Turkish-speaking community nearly four decades later. There are two football federations (the Turkish Community Football Federation established in 1976 and the Turkish and Kurdish Football Federation established in 1992); over 65 football clubs many of which are formed by community associations, including mosques and *Cemevi*. These associations own and manage clubs which represent their respective identities in regular competitions which attracts significant local and transnational media attention as well as some sponsorships from businesses from the Turkish-speaking community.

The Turkish and Kurdish Football Federation (TKFF-hereafter the Kurdish League) was established in 1992 following in the footsteps of some other successful ethnic community leagues such as the Cypriot Football Federation (KOPA-hereafter the Greek-Cypriot League) and Turkish Community Football Federation (TCFF-hereafter the Turkish League) which were established in 1975 and 1976, respectively. The stated main purposes of establishment and continued existence of all these ethnic community leagues are mainly related to giving the younger generations of each respective community a safe and secure space for sporting activities, thereby protecting them from joining street gangs or doing drugs and so on. However, a closer investigation on each of these community leagues in a historical context apparently shows that the meaning and functions of these leagues have always gone beyond these concerns about the youth. The ethnic community leagues in London have long been hubs for communal mobilization for mutual help and solidarity as well as socio-political spaces wherein collective identities have been negotiated, reproduced, transmitted to the younger generations and represented in the public space in diaspora. It is also argued that, besides the fact that football is a common passion particularly amongst men of all ages, the very nature of this social field with respect to its position has made it particularly useful. This social space effectively defies a separation between public and private sphere thereby providing a convenient social field in which diverse and hybrid diasporic identities are reproduced, represented, and negotiated. This space is both public and private, or it is a publicly-owned-private space creating unique opportunities for various identity projects to be adopted and implemented.

The findings and analysis presented in this chapter are derived from Onur Unutulmaz's doctoral research project on Turkish-speaking community in London and their football leagues in between 2010 and 2012 in Haringey, London (See Unutulmaz, 2014a). The material we focus on here mainly comes from participant observations and 72 tape-recorded in-depth interviews as well as reviews of media and archives. Complying with the regulations of research ethics, pseudonyms are used in most cases to protect participants' privacy although informed consent was given.

First, we will look into the Turkish and Kurdish football leagues in London with reference to the historic context in which they are embedded. The Kurdish league needs a separate treatment here as it appears to have been established as a reaction to the previous experiences in the Turkish league as well as an instrument for ethnopolitics reflecting the big Turkish Kurdish divide imported from Turkey. In the following section, specific position of these two leagues as both public and private spaces for the ethnic communities is discussed. We conclude with a discussion of the implications of this specific position of these leagues in terms of reproduction, negotiation, and representation of ethnic identities as well as for immigrant integration.

Emergence of ethnic community leagues in London

As Turkish-Cypriot football league has something to do with the Greek-Cypriot league which was established a little earlier, the emergence of the Kurdish league is also somehow linked to the Turkish league. These contesting establishments reflect the conflicts in the respective countries of origin of the involved communities. Hence the former was a reflection of the Cyprus conflict whereas the establishment of the Kurdish league was referring to the conflict in Turkey as well as growing size of the Kurdish population in London which transformed the composition of the Turkish-speaking community in London. With reference to the Cyprus conflict, while Turkey and Greece constantly trying to justify and propagate their respective positions, Greek-Cypriot and Turkish-Cypriot diasporic communities in London are also mobilised to ensure their ethnic representation in the public political space. The establishment of the Greek-Cypriot Football Federation (KOPA) in 1975, the year following Turkish military intervention in Cyprus, can be seen as part of such mobilisation. The official logo of Greek-Cypriot league in London has a flag of Republic of Cyprus which depicts a picture of the island representing the refusal of partition and the claim of the whole island being under a single legitimate rule (see Figure 9.1). Establishment of the Turkish Community Football Federation (originally named 'England Turkish Sports Federation') in 1976 is also not a coincidence.

Figure 9.1. The official logo of the KOPA and The flag of Cyprus

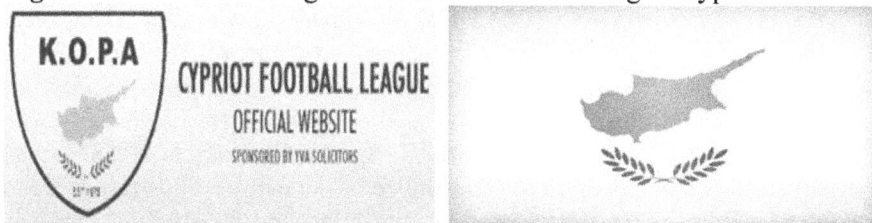

Source: http://www.kopaleague.com   and   http://en.wikipedia.org/wiki/ Flag_of_Cyprus

Arguably the most important reason for the establishment of Turkish league in 1976 was a desire to declare the existence of the Turkish-Cypriot community and to claim a place in London's public space. Turkish-Cypriots had been a minority community back in Cyprus and they were still a minority community in London. Thus being small in numbers, to make a strong case was depended heavily on their ability to get mobilised and speak with a unified voice:

> *It was July, 1976. It all started then. Why? We wanted to let everybody know that Turks lived and were still living in Cyprus. Because for a long time, when someone talks about Cyprus, people only thought Greeks lived there. We wanted everybody in London to know we were also there. And football seemed to be the only medium around which all of us could unite and make that statement" (Interview with Zico1)*

---

[1] All respondents are given pseudonyms to protect their privacy. Exception to this is the names of public figures who consented for disclosure. Zico is a 65-year-old Turkish-Cypriot who was a member of the TCFF Executive Committee at the time of the interview and involved in Turkish community football leagues as a former player, Federation President, and club administrator.

Another reason for establishing the club was a common concern for the youth. In his book, Atay (2006: 117) says "the members of the Turkish-speaking community, divided in ethnic, political, ideological and religious lines, are united in the fear of 'losing their children'!" In fact, this concern was there even in the 1960s. Minutes from the TCA meetings show that then everyone in the community seemed to desire returning to the homeland, partly because there was this concern about youth getting out of hand by acquiring bad habits and losing their cultural identity. Therefore, there was an urge to be united as a community and protect children from assimilation by teaching them their heritage language and culture while also 'taking them back from the streets':

So my idea was to establish an institution which could attract people, which could save the youth from drugs, gangs and losing their identity, which could help them learn and speak Turkish... So we decided to establish a football team! (Interview with Yaşar İsmailoğlu)

As a result, the England Turkish Sports Federation (ETSF) was established in September 1976. The choice of the name is illustrative of the political nature of the whole process. While around 90% of the Turkish-speaking community was Turkish-Cypriot at the time, the newly founded Federation was called 'Turkish', instead of Cypriot or Turkish-Cypriot. This way, the community leaders' choice to emphasise the ethnic or national aspect of their identity (defined in a certain way), over their country of origin. This was partly because they did not wish to exclude the small number of Turkish immigrants from Turkey, but also because, in the political climate of the time, they felt the need to emphasise their Turkish identity over their Cypriot identity. They might have also anticipated the growing size of Turkish immigrant population as well as hoping to attract support from the Turkish government and its diplomatic mission in London. In the founding bylaws of the Federation, the *raison d'etre* of this organisation was spelled as follows: *"Our purpose is to make our existence, unity and sportsmanship known in a manner best fit to our nation"*.

In this climate, following the suit as the Greek-Cypriot league having done the same in 1975, the new federation's concerns about the identity and national representation were reflected in the design of the Turkish league's logo. The basic design and the elements involved in the logo include the 'twin olive branches' that come from the flag of Cyprus and represent the Turkish-Cypriot community. A crescent and star come from the national flags of Turkey and the TRNC. Lastly, there is a football around the star symbolising the central place of the sport for the nation and the community (see Figure 9.2). Here, it is also significant that the founders and administrators of the TCFF sought to accommodate symbols from both the Turkish-Cypriot and the Turkish identities.

Figure 9.2. The official logo of the TCFF and the Turkish flag.

Source: TCFF Yearbook, 2012 and http://en.wikipedia.org/ wiki/Flag_of_Turkey.

Establishment of Kurdish leagues

Formation of the Kurdish community in the UK is different in terms of the conflict on which their migration trajectory is built. Long history of conflict over Kurdish regions and Kurdish identity in Turkey characterised not only by assimilationist policies, denial of ethnicity, socio-economic and political pressures has been the obvious major driver for Turkish Kurds' emigration, a typical case for "conflict model of migration" (Sirkeci, 2000, 2003). As we have documented and explained in the earlier chapters of this book, majority of the Kurds from Turkey arrived in the UK as asylum seekers similar to over a million Turkish citizens who sought refuge in Europe since the 1980 military intervention (Sirkeci & Esipova, 2013, pp.3-6). As the late-comers (off Turkey) in London and mostly being asylum-seekers, the Kurds have experienced a hard time in settling and building a collective identity. Turkish Kurds were the first from the Turkish-speaking community to establish their own ethnic league and those Kurdish clubs and players stayed with the Turkish leagues very often complain about anti-Kurdish discrimination, or 'racism'.

The Kurdish league was setup by the individuals who quit the Turkish league in 1992. This was the last step of a rather gradual process and should be seen in its wider context. The ever-present ethnic dynamics in the Turkish-speaking football field were transformed with the arrival of large number of Kurds from the mid-1980s onwards. The major ethnic contest was between the Turkish-Cypriots and Turks from Turkey up until the mid-1980s. Then it has suddenly gained a third dimension with Kurds entering the scene. Many Kurds have been playing in the TCFF leagues

155

since the 1980s along with some clubs, such as *Anadolu* FC known as Kurdish clubs. By the time the new millennium has arrived, the number of Kurds from Turkey has become much more sizeable in London. Eusebio, a former *Anadolu* FC player and a founding member of the Kurdish Federation which he currently chairs, explains the reason for establishing a second league in such logistic terms:

"when we considered the problems of the community here, the problems of the youth, the need of the youth to have better sporting opportunities and more time to be together; we thought that a second league was necessary."

Bozcader football team (*Photo by Telgraf.co.uk*)

When probed, he goes on to explain that the point of the league was to create a social gathering place for the community where "racism could be prevented" and where "different cultures and identities could meet each other and prejudices and stereotypes were destroyed". Although Eusebio does not directly spell out the feeling of discrimination in the TCFF leagues, he alludes to that all along. What he clearly spells out is the feeling that the Kurds were discriminated against and they faced racism back in Turkey, just as well as they face it today in London. Hence in response to such discrimination, the Kurdish federation was established and this rather political project incorporates a discourse of resistance together with representation and reproduction of identity as is the case for the Turkish league.

Notably, this federation describes itself as Turkish-Kurdish representing both Turks and Kurds in London. While the organisation and administration of the federation is in the hands of politically active pro-Kurdish community association, Day-Mer, which aims at "reconstructing a Kurdish-identity that has been under siege by the assimilationist policies of Turkey" (Pattison & Tavsanoglu, 2002, p. 7), the league itself does not seem to pursue such political purposes directly. Instead, it aims to give a message in protest against what they consider to be the discriminatory and exclusionary nature of the Turkish leagues by imposing an inclusive approach.

Figure 9.3. Official logos of the TKFF and Kurdish Community organisation Day-Mer

Source: http://www.daymer.org

This is, we would definitely argue, a carefully calculated self-declaration. The name of the federation is 'Turkish and Kurdish Football Federation' emphasizing Turkey as their country of origin. Both Day-Mer and the Kurdish league have chosen to emphasise Turkey as their country-of-origin, while offering a reconciliatory message by using "shaking of hands" in the logo referring to the potential of football for bringing people together.

Diaspora politics through football: Actors, agents, agendas

Many researchers have suggested that sport is a particularly useful sociological site for the study of identities "as it articulates the complex interplay of 'race', nation, culture and identity in very public and direct ways" (Carrington & McDonald, 2001, p.3). In the same way, Back et al. (2001, p.270) show through their fieldwork on English football teams that football "provides one of the few spheres in which ideas about identity, ethnicity and race can be expressed, embodied and performed". Gilchrist (2005, p.119) suggests that those who are actively involved in sports teams act as "corporeal representatives of broader collectivities", even nations.

After all, the identity of a nation of unnamed millions "seems more real as a team of eleven named people" (Hobsbawm, 1990, p.43).

The establishment of these ethnic community leagues need to be considered in a larger and different political context of 'ethnopolitics'. This term is used to describe the process of 'mobilizing ethnicity from a psychological or cultural or social datum into political leverage for the purpose of altering or reinforcing ... systems of structured inequality between and among ethnic categories' (Rothschild, 1981, p.2). Both the establishment process of the Turkish and Kurdish leagues included an effort of communal mobilisation and representation of ethnic identities in the public space. Furthermore, the establishment process of the Kurdish league is part of a different ethnopoloitical project of defining the terms of ethnic/cultural identity all along. In this process, ethnopolitics 'stresses, ideologizes, reifies, modifies, and sometimes virtually re-creates the putatively distinctive and unique cultural heritages of the ethnic group that it mobilizes' (Rothschild 1981, p.3). How exactly does ethnic community football do all these? We have collected many examples through which ethnic community leagues and individual football clubs within these leagues have served as mechanisms through which identities are transmitted to younger generations through a process of actively and dynamically defining the very terms of them. The example of *Anadolu* FC, a Kurdish club to play first in the Kurdish and then in the Turkish league is among the most illustrative.

Zidane, who is at his mid-40s, is a small cafe owner in North London and a Kurdish refugee from Southeast Turkey. He had played amateur football back in Turkey before he moved to London in the aftermath of violent clashes between Turkish troops and Kurdish separatist groups. He was very active in politics up until he got married. A member of the Turkish Communist Workers' Party (*Türkiye Komünist İşçi Partisi*), he was seriously involved in the activities of this party's youth organisation. As a passionate football player, it was around this time that he started his attempts to form a football team. With a few friends from his political group, he established *Aydınlık FC* in late 1990s. Name he chose refers to the Maoist Marxist *Aydınlık Movement* in Turkey. Made up of a group of Kurdish *Alevis* footballers, *Aydınlık* joined the Kurdish league in 1992. In their first year, according to Zidane, they "won everything, like an unstoppable hurricane".

He wanted to establish an amateur football club instead of just joining an existing team or playing with friends regularly because there was a 'culture shock' amongst the Kurdish immigrant youth back then: "the kids were getting the English culture outside and the Turkey culture at home. They were not able to cope easily. We thought we could reach more youngsters through football as this was a common passion among all the people, no matter what political ideology they would have". He says the football team was not only about playing football. It was more about unity, being together, and solidarity. The team was also a way to 'help the youth learn some things' that they would not otherwise have been interested in, but he insists there was no 'political agenda':

We would gather up at the association in the morning on the match days. We would gather all our money to buy food for breakfast. No one of us was rich back then, we would eat what we could buy; cheese, jam, bread, whatever. They would come to the association building at other times to hang out and socialise with teammates. Of course, as we spent that much time in the association, we would talk about political matters. The kids would show great interest and they would become aware of many issues of the time. But we never imposed anything on anyone. We didn't even force them to read our own journal, you know. The journals would just sit on the tables, if the kids wanted to read, they could. Otherwise, no one would say anything. Once, we took them to Cardiff for a preparation camp for a few days. There were some political meetings, and conversations, if you will, there too. But no one ever forced anyone to take part.

Although they were in the Kurdish league, he says there was never an issue of ethnicity or faith in his club. "I consider a boy as a football player; he is either a good player or a mediocre one" he explains. Yet they started at the Kurdish league because the majority of the founders were Kurdish and because they had more contacts in the wider Kurdish community abroad. The glorious days of *Aydınlık* FC at the Kurdish league, however, did not last very long. In their second year, *Aydınlık* FC was kicked out of the Kurdish league after a fight broke up in one of their important games. Zidane thinks that was extremely unfair and, in fact, a biased decision with political motives:

This is what happened back then; our opponent belonged to another political fraction. And the referee was with them as well. Of course, whatever the reason, fighting is wrong. But he was so biased, so provocative, I was not able to hold the boys down anymore. And then after the fight, the (Kurdish) Federation imposed big penalties on us; many of my players were banned for six weeks, and they kicked us out of the league. After that, we went to the league of the Cypriots [the Turkish league].

With this move to the Turkish league, or as it had been referred by him, the Cypriots' league, they also decided to change the name of the club to a politically neutral one, hence becoming *Anadolu* FC (Anatolia). When they made their application to join the league at the General Annual Meeting, all 23 existing clubs in the league but three have welcomed them.

Anatolia FC before their game against East Goscote (14 Feb. 2016) (*Photo by Atatolia FC website*)

Zidane's adventure with ethnic community football ended some 15 years ago when he decided to move away from London to Oxford to open up a little cafe. However, the adventure of *Anadolu* FC is still going on today where they compete in the Turkish league. Today, the club is managed by *Cemevi*[2] in London. The Chairman of the '*England Alevi Cultural Centre and Cemevi*', Figo, who is a former player of the team a decade ago, explains why they are competing in the Turkish league:

As far as I can see, football is one of the common denominators we different Turkish communities can unite under a Türkiyeli identity. For instance, two groups who confront each other as Turkish and Kurdish outside, can unite at a Galatasaray match against the rival club from another country. In other words, although we create arbitrary divisions, we fall in love with the same girls, like the same sort of food, come from the same culture. The Turkish league has a mission here. We have a team there, the associations with a leftist ideology has teams

---

[2] *Cemevi* is the Alevi religious centre in North London (see previous chapter).

there, and those who identify themselves as Kurdish have teams there. All these can unite under the same roof. They do not go to play to the Yugoslavian or Bosnian league. So it has this mission and ability to play a unifying and peaceful role.

The *Anadolu* FC deliberately puts a lot of emphasis on the youth and attracting them to *Cemevi*; they have four different teams for boys under the age of 16, 14, 12, and 10. This already implies a political agenda, but further into our conversation he spells this out much more explicitly:

Of course, our real purpose here is to bring our children together. We are looking for a way to attract them to the Cemevi and to our culture. The kids in our teams get in contact with the Cemevi in one way or another. They meet here before and after the matches, for example. This is so that we can protect the child from losing himself, falling into that gear we call assimilation, so that he can both protect who he is and learn what is out there and become a proper and competent individual to cope with everything out there. Of course, keeping these two on a balance is not very easy. I mean to protect one's traditions and culture is difficult even in Turkey, in our own country. To protect them here is much more difficult. Football, or another sport, is a medium around which to organise. It is difficult for us to put the Alevi philosophy into the head of the kid. That requires a process. So it is easier for us to bring the kid closer to us through football.

Reproduction and negotiation of identities in a 'publicly-owned-private-space'

The field of ethnic football constitutes a particularly useful platform for the construction and embodiment of identities. The space appears to be ideally situated in between the private sphere and the public sphere. Although these leagues have to be registered with and sanctioned by the London Football Association (LFA), they have a significant degree of freedom in how they govern the leagues. In my interview with the Chairman of the LFA, David Hawkes, explains this in the following way:

if the rules say Christmas can be in July, it is not for us to say it's got to be in December. If the rules say it can be in July, then... It is their rules and it's their Christmas.

In fact, different ethnic community leagues do enjoy their autonomy to a large extent. For example, each league can and does decide on how many 'foreign' players can play for each team. In the Turkish league, the rules state that "[t]he number of non-Turkish players should not exceed 4", with no further clarification about who would be considered Turkish and who would be considered non-Turkish. This has been used as a tool of actively defining who is Turkish and who is not and as such it has been subject to much contention. One specific example concerning the Bulgarian Turks I witnessed during a Turkish Union of Clubs' meeting was striking:

> *"The Cyprus Turks are Turkish, the Turkey Turks are Turkish, the London Turks are Turkish... Why aren't the Bulgarian Turks Turkish? Why is there this double standard just because in their passport there is a foreign name? Let me remind you that those names were forced on them by the oppressive Bulgarian governments in the 70s and 80s. In reality, they are much more Turkish than most of the London-borns who cannot even speak any Turkish!" (Maldini from a TCFF Union of Clubs meeting)*

The same process of actively defining who would be called a 'Cypriot' has been apparent in the Greek-Cypriot league as well where the rule states that only 3 'non-Cypriots' could be registered by each time. Here is how they came up with their definition as recounted by the President of the Greek-Cypriot league:

> *We have a limitation of 3 non-Cypriots, non-Cypriots [strongly emphasised]. People want to see everything in black and white: you either are or you are not. But that is not the picture, is it? In reality, you are not anything. There's been an issue of trying to identify what constitutes a Cypriot and what doesn't. Now, the issue is if you adopt a too narrow classification, you are then lumbered with lots of problems. Because, the narrow view suggests that it would exclude automatically, say, 3rd generation youngsters born here. Right? You have to prove if you had a grandparent who is a Cypriot. Obviously it applies to your parents and yourself. You have to be born in Cyprus or up to your grandparent, someone. But that is almost impossible to do. Particularly when you got people spread all over the world, which you have with Cypriots.*
>
> *The other issue is Turkish Cypriots. Since 74 [date of Turkey's military intervention in Cyprus], you have an all new influx of people [to Cyprus] from Turkey. How could you say if they are Cypriots or not? Does the political description apply? if you're born there, you are Cypriot, even though your parents came from Turkey. So we adopted, if you're born in Cyprus, it doesn't matter where you come from, it could be an Italian born in Cyprus, then you are Cypriot. But prior to that we have a slightly looser classification. This has been in force only 3-4 years. Prior to that, the looser classification was anyone with a Greek or Turkish name basically was eligible as a Cypriot. That included*

anyone from Greece, Turkey, all the people born in wherever in the globe, as long as they appear to be Greek or Turkish.

We changed that because it got to a point where in the junior division, we had a Kurdish junior team, which was entirely Kurdish. Then you can argue, well they are not really Cypriot. So the question came up, if you take anybody who speaks Turkish or has a Turkish name, how can you exclude a Kurdish team? To me it makes no difference. But to the community, it was like that doesn't sound right. Let's make the description a bit narrower. But we are more or less where we were even though we said 'even though you have a Turkish name, you still have to prove that you have some sort of a Cypriot connection.' (Interview with Markos Chrysostomou, KOPA President)

It is obvious that what is at stake is not a matter of procedural discussion on who can play and who cannot. At every level what is being discussed is the meaning and boundaries of ethnic identities; effectively defining who is 'one of us' and who is not. More importantly, this is a dynamic and ongoing process of defining and redefining identities. Undoubtedly, this is always a process of social and political construction; the identity of the community is being reflected on and defined in the game:

You are doing this only because you want to keep the cultural identity through communal organization. It is really not professional football, it has not really to do with the game. It's to do with the cultural activity as a community. The game is just a reflection of the community. It is not the community being a reflection of the game. (Interview with Markos Chrysostomou, KOPA President)

The case with the Kurdish league, however, is once again quite different in this respect. The Kurdish league has chosen to put no restrictions or regulations concerning the ethnic, cultural, political, or legal identities of the players or the clubs to participate in its competitions. The current president of the Kurdish league suggests that their rationale is for everyone to get involved, get to know each other, and shatter all their prejudices. The Kurdish leagues, expectedly, display the greatest degree of diversity with respect to ethnic and cultural identities compared to other ethnic community leagues. There are teams that identify themselves to be from different ethnic communities. The Kurdish league was founded under a politically-active Turkish-Kurdish community organisation which declares its purposes to be to promote Turkish and Kurdish people's cultural, economic, social, and democratic rights; to strengthen solidarity among themselves as well as local people; and to help their integration into the society. As seen in the cases of *Day-Mer* and the Kurdish league, there seems to be a greater emphasis on interaction and integration as opposed to holding onto the community's roots.

Reproduction of diasporic identities in the football pitch

In the fieldwork, it was often heard that people talk about a 'culture shock' that the young people were supposedly suffering from because of the differences between and the incompatibility of the 'Turkish-speaking home' and the 'English/British outside'. The field of Turkish-speaking football constitutes a peculiar space which defies this duality. The sentiment of the community seems to view the field as belonging to 'us' but placed in the public and sanctioned by 'them', which makes it possible to call this field a 'publicly-owned-private-space'.

The private sphere seems to be associated with the Turkish-speaking ethnic and cultural identities, the Turkish (and Kurdish) language, the authentic ethnic cuisines, Turkish satellite TV, a firm patriarchal leadership, and the strongest sense of belonging and acceptance. From the perspective of the individual immigrant, in other words, the private sphere is that which belongs to him/her, where he/she can be 'him/ herself' most safely and easily. The public sphere, on the other hand, is quite different in the diaspora. Even in the absence of open and explicit discrimination, racism, and xenophobia, the public sphere never belongs to the immigrant in the same way that his/her home does. This may look like a dull point which is the same for everyone, whether they are an immigrant or not, but in truth it is not the same at all. The degree to which one feels safe and at ease on the street or in the park depends significantly on the strength of his or her sense of belonging. The more closely regulated and strictly structured the public space is, the more likely it is that the immigrant will feel less 'at home', or more 'insecure'. With added impact of exclusion and discrimination, the situation can become much more adverse for an immigrant.

The field of Turkish-speaking football is public in the sense that it is open to anyone and everyone (albeit with the some stated restrictions on numbers); most of the time you spend your time with a large number of diverse people in the parks; you play in a league that is registered to and operates under the authority of the London Football Association; you are involved in an activity which is a common passion for you, for other migrants, and for wider British society; you are at a place where you are not in close proximity to the members of your family; and you enjoy a significant degree of freedom.

However, it is also private in the sense that it is called the 'Turkish Community Football League' (or the 'Turkish and Kurdish Football League') and that you are a member of this community; you can speak, joke around, and swear in Turkish; you talk about similar issues and problems with your mates; when you win a match, you can dance the traditional dance of your town; everybody around you knows who you are; people accept and value you for who you are; although there is great diversity, you are sure that you are surrounded by a lot of people who have experienced a lot of what you have experienced; and so, you enjoy a significant degree of security.

There are many significant implications of this unique position of the field of ethnic community football simultaneously in between and out of the 'Turkish/Kurdish private v. British/Londoner public' duality. Especially for the younger players but also for the more senior members of this field, the ethnic community leagues are the most conveniently hybrid social spaces to form, experiment with, and express all the hybrid diasporic identities. The freedom and safety simultaneously enjoyed in the field of Turkish-speaking football, combined with the joys and lure of actually playing the 'beautiful game' makes it one of the most dynamic places to observe and experience diasporic identities.

Another significant implication of this specific positioning of the field of ethnic community football concerns different 'identity projects'. It is suggested that a common fear of 'losing the youth' has been a major factor in the creation of these leagues and still keeps motivating large numbers of adult members of the communities to get involved in order to protect youth, save them from assimilation, and keep them from degradation. The structure and position of the field of ethnic community football leagues, which are conveniently situated in the Turkish/Kurdish private and the British/Londoner public, has been an essential factor accounting for the effectiveness of this field for (re)producing, maintaining, transmitting, and representing the hybrid masculine ethnic identities. This has been documented particularly in relation to the representation of identities in the London public space since the establishment of these leagues. One important general conclusion of my fieldwork would be that while the clubs, leagues, social events, role models, and so on have been extremely successful in (re)producing, embodying, and representing collective identities in the sense that they do create an identification on the part of those who get involved in the field, the substantive content of that identity is inevitably and infinitely diverse and hybrid. In other words, the Turkish-speaking football leagues have definitely managed to make many kids who were born and bred in London, never having been in Cyprus, to consider themselves as *Boğaziçi köyünden* (from Boğaziçi village).

We would also argue that it is a particularly open social space for third parties to become involved to reach out to the Turkish and Kurdish communities. There is great potential in terms of reaching out to these groups, particularly youth through these leagues and public-private-spaces they create. There are implications for integration policies ethnic community football can easily and effectively be part of integration effort (Unutulmaz, 2014b & 2015).

Conclusion

Following the 2nd World War, several West European countries turned their faces towards less developed countries in order to find workers to work in the reconstruction of their economies. Through the postwar guest worker arrangements, millions of workers moved to countries like France, Germany, and Switzerland (Martin et al. 2006; Martin & Miller, 1980). Turkey was one of the source countries signing its first bilateral agreement with [Federal Republic of] Germany in 1961. These government-run schemes were expecting movers not to settle and eventually return home, hence the term "guest" worker. Nevertheless, like guests from other countries, many of those "guests" from Turkey did not return and they formed large diasporas (Sirkeci, Cohen, Yazgan, 2012; Sirkeci, 2005). 55 years on from the first bilateral labour agreement, the number of immigrants from Turkey is estimated to be between 4 to 6 million with large presence in certain countries such as Germany, France, Switzerland and Austria (Sirkeci & Yucesahin, 2014). Britain was not a main destination and migrants from Turkey have been a small portion of the whole immigrant population which is dominated by South Asians, Irish, Polish and others. Nevertheless, as we have clearly shown in the opening chapter, Turkish, Kurdish and Turkish Cypriot population in the United Kingdom is not negligible, and particularly visible in London.

The settlement of Cypriot Turks as well as Turks and Kurds from mainland Turkey in the UK occured without any bilateral agreements; they arrived in periodical waves and triggered by various conflicts. Starting with migration of Cypriot Turks in the 1920s, 1950s, 1960s and onwards, flourishing with Turkish immigrants migrated from Turkey in 1970s, and Kurdish immigrants from Turkey in 1990s, nowadays the UK has a sizeable communities of Turkish Cypriots, Turks and Kurds. These communities are not homogeneous but differ in their lifestyles, experiences, ideas, emotions, hopes and expectations. These communities are also divided along various ethnic, ideological, cultural and religious differences.

It is known that a majority of immigrant Cypriot Turks and Turkish Turks and Kurds reside in London (approximately 75%). Settlement patterns of these immigrant communities are quite similar to other immigrant communities (Indian, Pakistani, Bangladeshi, Chinese, Japanese, Russian, Polish, etc.). Minority groups in London often live in ethnic enclaves. Reasons for this enclave structure include that these minorities like to live with people with whom they share the same culture, language, and religion; and solidarity overbeing a minority in a foreign land as well as being a stranger to the host country's main language, culture and habits. Thus it is a way to ensure relative security in a foreign environment. Early immigrants created social spheres, employment opportunities, businesses, became able to provide accommodation, as well as setting up non-governmental organisations helping new comers. Newcomers benefited from the presence of these early movers as well as all the institutions and space they had created. These were crucially important after arrival and in the transition period for new migrants. Settlement patterns of newcomers, who migrated as a result of sequential migration waves helped by means of families, friends and "*hemşehrilik*" ties (originally being from same country, same city, or same town/village), show similarities with settlement patterns of early immigrants. Similarities in the settlement patterns of Turkish Cypriots, Turks and Kurds offer evidence for this argument. These similarities guide them to work in almost identical places as well as to perform almost identical social, cultural and economic activities.

Integration process of Turkish immigrants whose possibilities and hopes to return had vanished was quite painful. Impact of the dominant culture in the UK and rapid social change, and conflict over the values from home country and host country have affected the identities of movers. In fact, cultural shock and identity search as they struggle to settle in and adapt to the new environment and new culture in the destination might stress movers and even cause depression. Although acquisition of British citizenship brings some legal advantages to Turkish movers in Britain, they face many identity problems around national, ethnic and religious identities and this might be behind the emphasis on preservation of culture and identity by religious organisations for example.

In this book, Little Turkey in Great Britain, we have attempted to offer a comprehensive account of Turkish, Kurdish and Cypriot movers looking into challenges and strategies to overcome in the process of integration, political participation, employment, identity, beliefs, culture, and struggles.

From an economics perspective, employment and economic activities of immigrants from Turkey are largely shaped by the structure of ethnic enclave economy and their position in the labour market. While majority is concentrated in the service sector, self-employed owner workers of doner-kebab take away shops, Turkish restaurants, cafes, bars, and supermarkets and corner shops are the dominant features in the economics of *Little Turkey in Great Britain*. Most of these businesses are small family businesses where either family members or other people from the ethnic enclave work at low wages and for longer hours. Small business owners often work even longer than their employees. These small businesses are unlikely to survive without this kind of a cheap labour supply due to tough competition. On the other hand, this pool of workers who are ok with lower wages does exist to be exploited due to complicated immigration laws, tightening admission rules and loads of other reasons for people around the world to move to London despite high costs, relatively low wages and tough working conditions in such sectors.

Women's invisible work in the ethnic economy is seemingly very important for ethnic business and in success of movers settling in economically. There was a shift in women's visibility and recognition in the community from factory work while the textile sector was around towards more private domestic work and unpaid family work becoming dominant. The expansion of the Turkish ethnic economy, thus confined women into the domestic sphere and pushed them towards domestic roles as wives, mothers, sisters, and daughters.

Religion is a key element in identity politics in diasporas and Turkish, Kurdish and Cypriot movers have put a significant effort in organising their places of worship with varying tones of political conviction and differences in practice but focusing on preserving the cultural heritage they believe they have brought from Turkey. As it was briefly presented earlier, the movers we have interviewed and surveyed were not a homogeneous mix and included a much larger portion of Alevis and non-believers along with a large Sunni group unlike the profile one may find in Turkey.

Thus, there is clear evidence for the selectivity of migration processes. Similarly, Kurds are overrepresented within the Turkish movers population in the UK. These are reflections of various conflicts registered in Turkey's recent history. Turkey is unfortunately full of contests and more conflicts are likely to emerge and result in many more voting by the feet. This is evident in high numbers of asylum applications lodged by Turkish citizens abroad in the last three decades or so.

As underlined in the opening chapter, idea of such a book was born out of a need felt for a comprehensive account of movers who left Turkey for Britain. We have drawn upon eight different and current research projects carried out by competent teams and independent researchers investigating different aspects of this diaspora community. We do hope this volume will serve as a starting point for future researchers while also remaining as a reference book for those who want to understand Turkish, Kurdish and Cypriot community in the UK.

References

Abu-Rayya, M. H., & Abu-Rayya, H. M. (2009). Ethnic identification, religious identity, and psychological well-being among Muslim and Christian Palestinians in Israel. *Mental Health, Religion and Culture, 12*(2), 147-155.

Adigüzel, Y. (2011). Yeni Vatanda Dini İdeolojik Yapılanma Almanya'daki Türk Kuruluşları. (Religious and Ideological Situations in the New Homeland; Turkish Organizations in Germany). İstanbul: ŞehirYayınları. (in Turkish).

Aksiyon, (2015). İlticanın Yerine Ankara Anlaşması Aldı, http://www.aksiyon.com.tr/roportaj/ilticanin-yerini-ankara-anlasmasi-aldi_551203. Accessed: 8 June 2015.

Aksoy, A. (2006). Transnational virtues and cool loyalties: Responses of Turkish-speaking migrants in London to September 11. *Journal of Ethnic and Migration Studies, 32*(6), 923-946. doi: 10.1080/13691830600761487

Aldrich, H. (1977). Testing the Middleman Minority Model of Asian Entrepreneurial Behaviour: Preliminary Results from Wandsworth, England. Chicago: Paper presented at *the Annual Meetings of American Sociology Association*.

Alexander, C., Edwards, R., Temple, B., (2007). Contesting Cultural Communities: Language, Ethnicity and Citizenship in Britain, *Journal of Ethnic and Migration Studies, 33*(5), pp.783-800.

Almond, G.A. and Verba, S. (1963). *The Civic Culture: Political Attitudes and Democracy in Five Nations*, Princeton: Princeton University Press.

Ansala, L. (2012). Motives, channels and migration for remittances: Evidence from Uganda, Senegal and Nigeria, Master Thesis, Aalto University, Department of Economics, Finland.

Anthias, F. (1992). *Ethnicity, Class, Gender, and Migration: Greek Cypriots in Britain.* Aldershot: Ashgate.

Arat, Y. (2013). Violence, Resistance, and Gezi Park. *International Journal of Middle East Studies, 45*(04), 807-809.

Atay, T. (1994). *Naqshbandi Sufis in a Western Setting.* Unpublished Ph.D. dissertation, School of Oriental and African Studies, University of London, London.

Atay, T. (1996). *Batı'da Bir Nakşi Cemaati Şeyh Nâzım Örneği.* İstanbul: İletişimYayınları.

Atay, T. (2006). *Turkler, Kurtler, Kibrislilar: Ingiltere'de Turkce Yasamak.* Ankara: Dipnot Yayinlari.

Atay, T. (2010). Ethnicity within Ethnicity among the Turkish-Speaking Immigrants in London. *Insight Turkey, 12*(1), 123-138.

Austin, R. & Tjernström, M. (2003). *Funding of Political Parties and Election Campaigns*, Trydells Tryckeri AB.

Aydin, M. (2004). Süleymancılık. In: Aktay, Y. (ed.) *Modern Türkiye'de Siyasi Düşünce; İslamcılık.* Volume: 6, İstanbul: İletişimYayınları, (pp.308-322).

Back, L., Crabbe, T. & Solomos, J. (2001). *The Changing Face of Football: Racism, Identity and Multiculture in the English Game.* Oxford: Berg.

Bakewell, O. (2010). Some Reflections on Structure and Agency in Migration Theory, *Journal of Ethnic and Migration Studies, 36*(10), 1689-1708.

Bank of Uganda (2010). *Inward Remittances 2009. Uganda: Workers' Remittances Report.*

Barber, B. (1995). *Güçlü Demokrasi*, Tra. Mehmet Beşikçi, İstanbul: Ayrıntı Yayınları.

Baser, B. (2014). The awakening of a latent diaspora: The political mobilization of first and second generation Turkish migrants in Sweden. *Ethnopolitics, 13*(4), 355-376.

Bastina, T. (2007). From mining to garment workshops: Bolivian migrants in Buenos Aires, *Journal of Ethnic and Migration Studies, 33*(4), 655–669.

Bauman, Z. (2000). *Siyaset Arayışı*, Tra. Tuncay Birkan, İstanbul: Metis Yayınları.

BBC (2015). Election 2015, http://www.bbc.co.uk/news/ politics/constituencies, Accessed: 13 August 2015.

Berry J. W. (1997). Immigration, acculturation and adaptation. *Applied Psychology: An International Review, 46*(1), 5-34.

Berry, J. W., Phinney, J. S., Sam, D. L., & Vedder, P. (2006). Immigrant youth: Acculturation, identity, and adaptation. *Applied psychology, 55*(3), 303-332.

Bilecen T. & Araz M. (2015a). Influence of Ethnic and Sectarian Origins On Political Choices of the Immigrants from Turkey in London, *Logic of Our Age: The Individual and Society in the Market's Grasp*, Ijocep publication, pp.133-152.

Bilecen T. & Araz M. (2015b). Londra'da Yaşayan Türkiyeli Göçmenlerin Etnik ve Mezhepsel Aidiyetlerinin Siyasal Tutum ve Davranışlarına Etkisi, *Göç Dergisi*, 2: 2, pp.189-207.

Blackwell, M. & Seddon, D. (2004) *Informal Remittances from the UK - Values, Flows and Mechanisms*, A report to DfID by the Overseas Development Group. Norwich, March.

Bosch, G. & Lehndorff, S. (2001). Working-time reduction and employment: experiences in Europe and economic policy recommendations. *Cambridge Journal of Economics*, 25, 209-243.

Buencamino, L., S. Gorbunov (2002). Informal Money Transfer Systems: Opportunities and Challenges for Development Finance, *UN, Economic and Social Affairs, DESA Discussion Paper* No. 26

Çağlar, A. & Onay, A. (2015). Entegrasyon/ Uyum: 'Kavramsal ve Yapısal Bir Analiz', In: Seker et al. (eds.) *Göç ve Uyum*, London: Transnational Press London, pp.39-76.

Çakir, R. (2002). *Ayet ve Slogan; Türkiye'de Islami Oluşumlar*. İstanbul: Metis Yayınları.

Çakir, S. G. (2014). Ego identity status and psychological well-being among Turkish emerging adults. *Identity, 14*(3), 230-239.

Carrington, B., & McDonald, I. (Eds.). (2001). *'Race', Sport and British Society*. London: Routledge.

Çelik, C. (2008). Almanya'da Türkler: Sürekli Yabancılık, Kültürel Çatışma ve Din, *Milel ve Nihal*, 5(3): 105-142.

Chin, M. (2005). *Sewing Women: Immigrants and the New York City Garment Industry*. New York: Columbia University Press.

Chrysostome, E. & Lin, X. (2010). Immigrant entrepreneurship: Scrutinizing a promising type of business venture. *Thunderbird International Business Review*, 52(2), 77-83. Doi: 10.1002/tie.20315

Cleveland, M., & Chang, W. (2009). Migration and materialism: The roles of ethnic identity, religiosity, and generation. *Journal of Business Research,62*(10), 963-971.

Cohen, J. H., & Sirkeci, I. (2011). *Cultures of migration: the global nature of contemporary mobility*. Austin: University of Texas Press.

Cohen, J. H., & Sirkeci, I. (2016). Migration and insecurity: rethinking mobility in the neoliberal age. In: Carrier, J.G (ed.) *After the Crisis: Anthropological Thought, Neoliberalism and the Aftermath*, London &New York: Routledge, pp. 96-113.

Çolak, Y. (2005). *Din Hizmetleri Baglamında İngiltere Dosyası*. (Religious Services in England). London. www.diyanet.org.uk/yazilar/ ingiltere dosyasi.pdf (available on: 15/02/2008) (in Turkish).

Comini, D. (2009). *Migration and Remittances: A Challenge for Statistics*. EFMA Conference: *Growth Opportunities on the Migrants' Market*, Paris, 10–11 February 2009. Paris: Eurostat.

Commonwealth Contractors (2010). Turkish ECAA Deadline Approaching, http://www.commonwealthcontractors.com/tag/ immigration/page/20/. Accessed: 10 June 2015.

Constant, A., Shachmurove, Y. & Zimmermann, K. (2007). What makes an entrepreneur and does it pay? Native men, Turks, and other migrants in Germany, *International Migration*, 45(4), 71-100.

Çoştu Y. and F. Ceyhan Çoştu (2015). An Investigation on the Turkish Religious Foundation of the UK (Diyanet)", In: Sirkeci, I. et al., (eds.) *Turkish Migration, Identity and Integration*. London: Transnational Press London, 2015. pp. 149-157.

Çoştu. Y. (2013a). *İngiltere'deki Türk-Müslüman Gocmenler; Dini Organizasyonlar*. Çorum: Lider Matbaası.

Çoştu. Y. (2013b). Turkish Muslim Immigrants in Britain; Religious Life and Religious Organizations, *Sociology Study* Volume: 3, Number: 7, pp. 493-501.

Cumhuriyet (2015). İngiltere'den flaş cemevi kararı, http://www.cumhuriyet.com.tr/ haber/turkiye/382079/ingiltere_den_flas_cemevi_karari.html, Accessed: 6/10/2015.

Dahl, R. A. (2001). *Demokrasi Üstüne*, tra. Betül Kadıoğlu, Ankara: Phoenix Yayınları.

DCLG (Department of Communities and Local Government). (2009). The Turkish and Turkish Cypriot Muslim Community in England, Understanding Muslim Ethnic Communities, London: Queen's Printer and Controller of Her Majesty's Stationery Office. www.communities.gov.uk/documents/ communities/pdf/1203710.pdf, accessed: March, 03, 2011.

Dedeoğlu, S. (2014). *Migrants, Work and Social Integration / Women's Labour in Turkish Ethnic Economy*, London: Palgrave-Macmillan.

Demireva, N. (2011). New Migrants in the UK: Employment Patterns and Occupational Attainment, *Journal of Ethnic and Migration Studies*, Vol. 37, No. 4, April 2011, pp. 637-655.

Department for Business Innovation & Skills. (2013). *Zero Hours Employment Contract*, www.gov.uk/government/uploads/system/uploads/attachment _data/file/267634/bis-13-1275-zero-hours-employment-contracts-FINAL.pdf, Accessed: 14/06/2015.

Dimitrova, R., Bender, M., Chasiotis, A., & van de Vijver, F. J. (2013). Ethnic identity and acculturation of Turkish-Bulgarian adolescents. *International Journal of Intercultural Relations*, 37(1), 1-10.

Dumont, W. (2003). Immigrant religiosity in a pluri-ethnic and pluri-religious metropolis: An initial impetus for a typology. *Journal of Contemporary Religion, 18*(3), 369-384.

El-Qorchi, M., Maimbo, S. M., and Wilson, J. W. (2003). Informal Funds Transfer Systems: An Analysis of the Informal Hawala System. A Joint IMF- World Bank Paper. *Occassional Paper* No. 222. International Monetary Fund, Washington, D.C.

Endo, I., J. Namaaji and A. Kulathunga (2011). Uganda's Remittance Corridors from United Kingdom, United States, and South Africa *Challenges to Linking Remittances to the Use of Formal Services,* Worl Bank Working Paper No: 201.

Enfield Council (2015). "Your Councillors", https://governance.enfield.gov.uk/ mgMemberIndex.aspx?bcr=1&_ga=1.114420485.384373349.1438020821, Accessed: 13 August 2015.

Ersanilli, E. & Koopmans, R. (2011). Do Immigrant Integration Policies Matter? A Three-Country Comparison among Turkish Immigrants, *West European Politics*, 34, 2, Pp208-234.

Fennema, M. & Tillie, J. (2010). Political Participation and Political Trust in Amsterdam: Civic Communities and Ethnic Networks, *Journal of Ethnic and Migration Studies*, 25:4, pp.703-726.

Ferrari, L., Ranieri, S., Barni, D., & Rosnati, R. (2015). Transracial adoptees bridging heritage and national cultures: Parental socialisation, ethnic identity and self-esteem. *International Journal of Psychology*, 50(6), 413-421.

Gilchrist, P. (2005). Local heroes and global stars. In: Allison, L. (ed.) *The Global Politics of Sport: The Role of Global Institutions in Sport*. London: Routledge.

Gilliat-Ray. S. (2010). *Muslims in Britain.* Cambridge: Cambridge University Press.

Giugni, M., Noémi M., Gianni M. (2014). Associational Involvement, Social Capital and the Political Participation of Ethno-Religious Minorities: The Case of Muslims in Switzerland, *Journal of Ethnic and Migration Studies*, 40:10, pp. 1593-1613.

Gov.uk. (2011). "Turkish ECAA business EC applications – flowchart", https://www.gov.uk/government/uploads/system/uploads/attachment _data/file/265790/Turkish-EEA-business-chart.pdf. Accessed: 10 June 2015.

Gov.uk. (2015). *Working, jobs and pensions*, https://www.gov.uk/browse/ working/contract-working-hours, Accessed: 15/06/2015.

Gov.Uk. (2014). Trade Union Membership Statistical Bulletin 2013. (Erişim adresi: https://www.gov.uk/government/uploads/system/uploads/ attachment_data/file/313768/bis-14-p77-trade-union-membership-statistical-bulletin-2013.pdf, Accessed: 10 June 2015.

Gül, M., Dee, J., & Nur Cünük, C. (2014). Istanbul's Taksim Square and Gezi Park: the place of protest and the ideology of place. *Journal of Architecture and Urbanism*, 38(1), 63-72.

Güngör, D., Fleischmann, F., & Phalet, K. (2011). Religious identification, beliefs, and practices among Turkish Belgian and Moroccan Belgian Muslims intergenerational continuity and acculturative change. *Journal of Cross-Cultural Psychology*, 42(8), 1356-1374.

Gürcan, E. C., & Peker, E. (2014). Turkey's Gezi Park demonstrations of 2013: A Marxian analysis of the political moment. *Socialism and Democracy*, 28(1), 70-89.

Gupta, C., S. Pattillo and Wagh S. (2007). Making Remittances Work for Africa, *Finance and Development*, 44(2), 1-8.

Hariharan, A. (2012). Hawala's Charm: What Banks Can Learn from Informal Funds Transfer Systems. *William & Mary Business Law Review*, 3(1), 273-308. http://scholarship.law.wm.edu/cgi/viewcontent.cgi?article =1036&context=wmblr

Haringey Council (2015). "Your Councillors by Party", http://www.minutes.haringey. gov.uk/mgMemberIndex.aspx?FN=PARTY&VW=LIST&PIC=0&J=2 , Accessed: 13 August 2015.

Hillmann, F. (1999). A look at the "hidden side": Turkish women in Berlin's ethnic labour market', *International Journal of Urban and Regional Research*, 23(2), pp. 267–282.

Hobsbawm, E. (1990). *Nations and Nationalism since 1780: Programme, Myth, Reality*, Cambridge, Cambridge University Press.

Holgate, J., Keles, J., Pollert, A., and Kumarappen, L. (2012). "Workplace Problems Among Kurdish Workers in London: Experiences of an 'Invisible' Community and the Role of Community Organisations as Support Networks", *Journal of Ethnic and Migration Studies*, 38(4), pp.595-612.

Home Office (2015a). UK Visas and Imigration Costumer Service Depertmant 16, TURKEEL - Turkish Employed ECAA - LTR NB, Application number: 35837.

Home Office (2015b). ECAA Turkish employed applications, https://www.gov.uk/ government/uploads/system/uploads/attachment_data/file/421115/Turkish_ECAA_V9_ 0.pdf. Accessed: 12 June 2015).

Home Office (2015c). Turkish Businessperson visa, https://www. gov.uk/turkish-business-person/overview. Accessed: 10 June 2015.

Hugo, G. (2014). Migrants in society: diversity and cohesion, In: Vertovec, S. (ed) *Migration and Diversity,* London: E. Elgar, pp.243-294.

IFAD (2015). *Sending money home: European flows and markets*. Rome: International Fund for Agricultural Development.

Islington Council (2015). "Your Councillors", http://democracy.islington.gov.uk/ mgMemberIndex.aspx?utm_content=google|organic&utm_term=(not%20provided), Date accessed: 13 August 2015).

Issa, T. (2005). *Talking Turkey: The Language, Culture and Identity of Turkish Speaking Children in Britain*. Staffordshire: Trentham Books.

Issa, T. (Ed.). (2017). *Alevis in Europe: Voices of Migration, Culture and Identity*. London, New York: Routledge.

Jacobs, D. & Tillie, J. (2004). Introduction: social capital and political integration of migrants. *Journal of Ethnic and Migration Studies*, 30(3), 419-427.

Jacobs, D. & Phalet, K. (2007). Political Participation and Associational Life of Turkish Residents in the Capital of Europe, *Turkish Studies*, 7:1, Pp.145-161.

Jensen, L.A. (2008). Immigrants' Cultural Identities as Sources of Civic Engagement, *Applied Development Science*, 12 (2), pp.74-83.

Johnson, G.E. & W.E. Whitelaw (1974). "Urban-Rural Income Transfers in Kenya: An Estimated-Remittances Function", *Economic Development and Cultural Change*, 22(3), 473-479.

Johnston, R., Sirkeci, I., Khattab, N., & Modood, T. (2010). Ethno-religious categories and measuring occupational attainment in relation to education in England and Wales: a multilevel analysis. *Environment and Planning A*, 42(3), 578-591.

Kastoryano, R. (2002). *Negotiating identities: States and immigrants in France and Germany*. Princeton University Press.

Kaya, A. (2000). *Berlin'deki Küçük İstanbul: Diyasporada Kimliğin Oluşumu*. İstanbul: Büke Yayıncılık.

Khattab, N., Johnston, R., Sirkeci, I., & Modood, T. (2010). The impact of spatial segregation on the employment outcomes amongst Bangladeshi men and women in England and Wales. *Sociological Research Online*, 15(1), 3.

Khattab, N., Sirkeci, I., Johnston, R., & Modood, T. (2011). Ethnicity, religion, residential segregation and life chances. In: Modood, T. and Salt, J. (eds.) *Global migration, ethnicity and Britishness* (pp. 153-176). Palgrave Macmillan UK.

King, R., Thomson, M., Mai, N., Keles, Y. (2008). 'Turks' in the UK: Problems of Definition and the Partial Relevance of Policy, *Journal of Immigrant & Refugee Studies*, 6:3, pp.423-434.

Kosse, A., and Vermeulen, R. (2014). Migrant's choice of remittance channel: Do general payment habits play a role? *World Development*, 62, p. 213-227.

Küçükcan, T. (1999). *Politics of Ethnicity, Identity and Religion Turkish Muslims in Britain*. Aldershot: Ashgate.

Küçükcan, T. (2006). The Making of Turkish Muslim Diaspora in Britain. *Journal of Muslim Minority Affairs*, 24:2, pp.243-258.

Kulu-Glasgow, I. & Leerkes A. (2013). Restricting Turkish marriage migration? National policy, couples' coping strategies and international obligations, *Migration Letters*, 10(3), 369-382.

Ladbury, S. (1977). The Turkish Cypriots: Ethnic Relations in London and Cyprus. In: Watson, J. L. (ed.), *Between Two Cultures: Migrants and Minorities in Britain*. Oxford: Blackwell, pp. 301-331.

Laurence, J. (2011). The Effect of Ethnic Diversity and Community Disadvantage on Social Cohesion: A Multi-Level Analysis of Social Capital and Interethnic Relations in UK Communities, *European Sociological Review*, 27(1):70-89.

Lee, S., McCann, D. & Messenger, J. C. (2007). *Working Time around the World: Trends in Working Hours, Laws and Policies in a Global Comparative Perspective*. Geneva and New York: ILO and Rutledge.

Londra Gazetesi (2014, September 4). Ankara Anlaşması'na İlgi Azalıyor mu? http://www.londragazete.com/2014/09/04/ankara-anlasmasina-ilgimiz-azaliyor-mu/ Accessed: 8 June 2015.

Long, J., Hylton, K. & Spracklen, K. (2014). Whiteness, Blackness and Settlement: Leisure and the Integration of New Migrants, *Journal of Ethnic and Migration Studies*, 40(11), 1779–1797.

Lytra, V. & Baraç, T. (2009). Multilingual practices and identity negotiations among Turkish-speaking young people in a diasporic context. In A.-B. Stenstörm & A. M. Jorgensen (Eds.), *Youngspeak in a Multilingual Perspective* (pp. 55-80). Amsterdam: John Benjamins Publishing Company

Mahmutoglu, V. (2015). Constructing multicultural society on web: minorities on information society. In: Merviö, M.M. (ed.) *Management and Participation in the Public Sphere*. IGI Global, pp.323-336.

Maliepaard, M. & Phalet, K. (2012). Social Integration and Religious Identity Expression among Dutch Muslims, the Role of Minority and Majority Group Contact. *Social Psychology Quarterly*, 75(2), 131-148.

Maphosa, F. (2007). Remittances and development: the impact of migration to South Africa on rural livelihoods in southern Zimbabwe. *Development Southern Africa*, 24(1), 123-136.

Martin, P. L. & Miller, M. J. (1980). Guestworkers: Lessons from Western Europe. *Industrial & Labor Relations Review*, 33(3), 315-330.

Martin, P.L., Abella, M., Kuptsch, C. (2006). *Managing Labour Migration in the 21st Century*. New Haven & London: Yale University Press.

Martinez, J. de Luna (2005). Workers' Remittances to Developing Countries: A Survey with Central Banks on Selected Public Policy Issues. *Policy Research Working Paper* 3638. Washington, DC: World Bank.

Martinovic, B., & Verkuyten, M. (2012). Host national and religious identification among Turkish Muslims in Western Europe: The role of ingroup norms, perceived discrimination and value incompatibility. *European Journal of Social Psychology*, 42(7), 893-903.

Massey, D. S. (2015). A Missing Element in Migration Theories. *Migration Letters*, 12(3), 279-299.

Mehmet Ali, A. (2001). *Turkish Speaking Communities and Education-No Delight*. London: Fatal Publication.

Mehran, F. (2005). *Measuring excessive hours of work, low hourly pay, and informal employment through a Labour Force Survey: a pilot survey in the Philippines*, Geneva: UNECE/ILO/Eurostat Seminar on the Quality of Work.

Messenger, J. C. (2011). Working time trends and developments in Europe. *Cambridge Journal of Economics*, 35, 295-316.

Modood, T., Berthoud, R., Lakey, J., Nazroo, J. Y., Smith, P., Virdee, S. ve Beishon, S. (1997). *Ethnic minorities in Britain: Diversity and disadvantage*. London: Policy Studies Institute.

OECD (2014). Education Database: Foreign / international students enrolled, *OECD Education Statistics (database)*. DOI: http://dx.doi.org/10.1787/data-00205-en (Accessed on 27 April 2015).

Ojo, S., Nwankwo, S. and Gbadamosi, A. (2013). Ethnic entrepreneurship: the myths of informal and illegal enterprises in the UK, *Entrepreneurship & Regional Development*, 25(7-8), 587-611. http://dx.doi.org/10.1080/08985626.2013.814717

Olay Gazetesi, (2013). "Ankara Anlaşması'na En Çok Öğrenciler Başvuruyor", http://olaygazetesi.co.uk/turk-toplumu/ankara-anlasmasina-en-cok-ogrenciler-basvuruyor.html , Accessed: 10 June 2015.

ONS (The Office for National Statistics). (2013). *2011 Census: Key Statistics and Quick Statistics for local authorities in the United Kingdom.* http://www.ons.gov.uk/ons/guide-method/census/2011/census-data/2011-census-user-guide/quality-and-methods/index.html

ONS (The Office for National Statistics). (2015). *Unemployment Rate, Region,* http://data.london.gov.uk/dataset/unemployment-rate-region

Orozco, M. (2002). Worker remittances: the human face of globalization, Working Paper commissioned by the Multilateral Investment Fund of the Inter-American Development Bank.

Orozco, M. (2003). Worker remittances: an international comparison, Working Paper commissioned by the Inter-American Development Bank.

Panayiotopoulos, P. (2010). *Ethnicity, Migration and Enterprise*, London: Palgrave-Macmillan.

Panayiotopoulos, P.I. (1996). Challenging orthodoxies: Cypriot entrepreneurs in the London Garment industry, *Journal of Ethnic and Migration Studies*, 22(3), pp. 437–60.

Parent-Thirion, A., et al. (2007). *European Foundation for the Improvement of Living and Working Conditions 'Fourth European Working Conditions Survey 2005'*, Luxembourg: Office for Official Publications of the European Communities.

Passas, N. (2005). *Informal Value Transfer Systems, Terrorism and Money Laundering*, A report to the National Institute of Justice, United States of America.

Pattison, G. & Tavsanoglu, S. (2002). Ethnicity, Identity, Cultural Change: Kurdish, Turkish and Turkish Cypriot Communities in North London *Everyday Cultures Working Papers* [Online], No 1.

Pendleton, W. et al. (2006). Migration, remittances and development in Southern Africa. The Southern African Migration Project (SAMP), *Migration Policy Series* No.44. Available at: www.queensu.ca/samp

Perşembe, E. (2005). *Almanya'da Türk Kimliği Din ve Entegrasyon*, Ankara: Araştırma Yayınları.

Phalet, K. & Güngör, D. (2004). *Moslim in Nederland: Religieuze dimensies, etnische relaties en burgerschap: Turken en Marokkanen in Rotterdam [Muslim in the Netherlands. Religious dimensions, ethnic relations and citizenship: Turks and Moroccans].* The Hague: Sociaal Cultureel Planbureau.

Phinney, J. S. & Ong, A. D. (2007). Conceptualization and measurement of ethnic identity: Current status and future directions. *Journal of Counseling Psychology*,54(3), 271.

Phizacklea, A. (1988). Entrepreneurship, ethnicity and gender, In: S. Westwood and S. Bhachu (eds), *Enterprising Women: Ethnicity, Economy and Gender Relations*, pp. 20–33. London: Routledge.

Puri, S. & T. Ritzema (1999). Migrant Worker Remittances, Micro-Finance and the Informal Economy: Prospects and Issues. *Working Paper 21. Social Finance Unit*, International Labour Organization, Geneva.

Putnam, R. D. (1993). *Making Democracy Work: Civic Traditions in Modern Italy*, NJ: Princeton University Press.

Rath, J., & Kloosterman, R. (2000). Outsiders Business, Research of Immigrant Entrepreneurship in the Netherlands. *International Migration Review*, 34 (3), 656–680.

Ratha, D. (2003). Workers' remittances: An Important and Stable Source of External Finance, *Global Development Finance*, Washington DC.: World Bank.

Ratha, D., & Sirkeci, I. (2010). Remittances and the global financial crisis. *Migration Letters*, 7(2), 125-131.

Resmi Gazete (2008). Seçimlerin Temel Hükümleri ve Seçmen Kütükleri Hakkında Kanuda Değişiklik Yapılmasına Dair Kanun, http://www.resmigazete.gov.tr/eskiler/ 2008/03/20080322M1-3.htm, Accessed: 13 August 2015.

Rizvi, F., (2005). Rethinking 'Brain Drain' in the Era of Globalisation. *Asia Pasific Journal of Education*, 25: 2, Pp.175-192.

Robins, K. & A. Aksoy. (2001). From Spaces of Identity to Mental Spaces: Lessons from Turkish-Cypriot Cultural Experience in Britain. *Journal of Ethnic and Migration Studies*. 27(4), pp. 685-711.

Rothschild, J. (1981). *Ethnopolitics: A Conceptual Framework*. New York, Columbia University Press.

Salomoni, F. (2015). Göçmenlerin İtalya'da Entegrasyonu, In: Seker, Sirkeci, Yucesahin (eds.) *Göç ve Uyum*, London: Transnational Press London, pp.165-186.

Sander, C. (2004). Capturing a market share? Migrant remittance transfers & commercialisation of microfinance in Africa, *Small Enterprise Development*, 15(1), 20-34.

Sevimli, K. & A. S. Reçber (2014). Avrupa Birliği'nde İşçilerin Serbest Dolaşımı ve Türk İşçilerinin Serbest Dolaşım Hakkı, *İstanbul Üniversitesi Hukuk Fakültesi Mecmuası*, 76(2), pp. 391-440.

Sharma, U. (1986). *Women's Work, Class, and the Urban Household: A Study of Shimla, North India*. London: Tavistock.

Shaw, W. (2007). *Migration in Africa: A Review of the Economic Literature on International Migration in 10 Countries*. Development Prospects Group. Washington, DC: World Bank.

Sirkeci, I. (2000). Exploring the Kurdish Population in the Turkish Context, *Genus*, 56 (1-2/2000), pp. 149-175.

Sirkeci, I. (2002). *The Ethnic environment of insecurity as a facilitating factor in asylum migration: the Turkish case*, paper presented at UNU-WIDER Conference on Poverty, International Migration and Asylum, 27-28 September, 2002, Helsinki, Finland. Received from http://www.mmo.gr/pdf/library/Balkans/Turkey%20and%20ethnic%20insecurity.pdf available on: 10.03.2014.

Sirkeci, I. (2003). *Migration, Ethnicity and Conflict.The Environment of Insecurity and Turkish Kurdish International Migration*, Doctoral dissertation, University of Sheffield.

Sirkeci, I. (2005). Diaspora: Turkish. In: M.J. Gibney & R. Hansen (eds) *Immigration and Asylum from 1900 to Present, Volume II*. California: ABC Clio, pp.607-610.

Sirkeci, I. (2006). *The Environment of Insecurity in Turkey and The Emigration of Turkish Kurds to Germany*. Lewiston, Queenston, Lampeter: The Edwin Mellen Press.

Sirkeci, I. (2009). Transnational mobility and conflict. *Migration Letters*, 6(1), 3-14.

Sirkeci, I. (2012). Transnasyonal Mobilite ve Çatışma, *Migration Letters*, 9(4), pp.353-363.

Sirkeci, I. (2016). Transnational Doner Kebab Taking over the UK. *Transnational Marketing Journal*, 4(2)

Sirkeci, I. (2017). Turkey's Refugees, Syrians and Refugees from Turkey: A country of insecurity, *Migration Letters*, 14(1).

Sirkeci, I. & Açık, N. (2015). İngiltere'de Göçmenlerin Ekonomik Uyumu ve İşgücü Piyasasında Azınlıklar. In: Şeker, B., Sirkeci, İ. & Yüceşahin, M. M. (eds). *Göç ve Uyum, 2nd Edition*, London: Transnational Press, 113-130.

Sirkeci, I. & Cohen, J.H. (2016). Cultures of migration and conflict in contemporary human mobility in Turkey. *European Review*, 24(3), 381-396.

Sirkeci, I. & Esipova, N. (2013). Turkish migration in Europe and desire to migrate to and from Turkey. *Border Crossing*, 2013(1), 1-13.

Sirkeci, I. & Martin, P. (2014). Sources of Irregularity and Managing Migration: The Case of Turkey. *Border Crossing*, 4(1-2), 1-16. Retrieved from http://www.tplondon.com/journal/index.php/bc/article/view/373

Sirkeci, I. & Yüceşahin, M. M. (2014). Editörden: Türkiye'de göç çalışmaları. *Göç Dergisi*, 1(1), 1-10.

Sirkeci, I. & Zeyneloglu, S. (2014). Abwanderung aus Deutschland in die Türkei: Eine Trendwende im Migrationsgeschehen? In: Alscher, S. & Krienbriek, A. (eds.) *Abwanderung von Türkeistämmigen: Werverlässt Deutschland und warum?* Germany: BAMF, pp. 30-85.

Sirkeci, I. Acik, N. & Saunders, B. (2014). Discriminatory labour market experiences of A8 national high skilled workers in the UK. *Border Crossing,* 4(1-2), 17-31. Retrieved from http://www.tplondon.com/journal/index.php/ bc/article/view/400

Sirkeci, I. Cohen, J. H. & Ratha, D. (Eds.). (2012). *Migration and Remittances during the Global Financial Crisis and Beyond.* Washington, D.C.: The World Bank.

Sirkeci, I. Cohen, J.H. & Yazgan, P. (2012). Turkish culture of migration: Flows between Turkey and Germany, socio-economic development and conflict. *Migration Letters,* 9(1), 33-46. http://www.tplondon.com/journal/index.php/ml/article/view/105

Sirkeci, I., Şeker, B. D. & Çağlar, A. (2015). *Turkish Migration, Identity and Integration.* London: Transnational Press London.

Sönmez Efe, S. (2015). To What Extent Are Migrant Workers' Rights Positioned within the Discourse of Human Rights? In: Sirkeci, I., G. Seker, D. Elcin (eds.) *Politics and Law in Turkish Migration,* London: Transnational Press London, pp. 53-70.

Strüder, I. (2003). Self-employed Turkish-speaking women in London: opportunities and constraints within and beyond the ethnic economy. *International journal of entrepreneurship and innovation,* 4(3), 185-195.

Şeker, B. D. & Sirkeci, I. (2014). Birleşik Krallık'daki Türkiye Kökenli Kadınlarda Yaşam Doyumu: Kimlik, Kültürleşme ve Ayrımcılık. *Türk Psikoloji Yazıları,* 17 (34), 69-81,

Şeker, B.D. (2015). Göç ve Uyum Süreci: Sosyal Psikolojik Bir Değerlendirme. In: Seker, B.D., I. Sirkeci, M. Yucesahin (eds.) *Göç ve Uyum.* London: Transnational Press London, pp.11-26.

Tansel A. & Yaşar P. (2012). Türkiye'de İşçi Dövizlerinin Toplam Üretim Büyümesine Makroekonomik Etkisi, *Migration Letters,* 9(4): 337-351.

Tanyas, B. (2012). Making sense of migration: young Turks' experiences in the UK, *Journal of Youth Studies,* 15(6), 693-710.

Tatar, T. (2003). Malatya'da Siyasi Katılım: Karşılaştırmalı Bir Analiz, *Fırat Üniversitesi Sosyal Bilimler Dergisi,* 13(1), 331-350.

Terry, D. J., Pelly, R. N., Lalonde, R. N. & Smith, J. R. (2006). Predictors of cultural adjustment: Intergroup status relations and boundary permeability. *Group Processes & Intergroup Relations,* 9(2), 249-264.

Ting-Toomey, S., Yee-Jung, K. K., Shapiro, R. B., Garcia, W., Wright, T. J. & Oetzel, J. G. (2000). Ethnic/cultural identity salience and conflict styles in four US ethnic groups. *International Journal of Intercultural Relations,* 24(1), 47-81.

Toksöz, G. (2008). *Decent Work Country Report – Turkey.* ILO EUROPE Regional Office.

Truen, S. et al. (2005). *Supporting remittances in Southern Africa. Estimating market potential and assessing regulatory obstacles.* Genesis Analytics report prepared for CGAP and the Finmark Trust. Available at: www.finmark.org.za.

UNHCR (United Nations High Commissioner for Refugees). (2013). *A New Beginning Refugee Integration in Europe,* (http://www.unhcr.org/52403d389.html, 13/06/2015).

Unutulmaz, K. O. (2014a). *Football and immigrant communities: transnational diaspora politics, Identities, and integration in Turkish-speaking ethnic football in London.* D.Phil Doctoral Thesis, University of Oxford.

Unutulmaz, K. O. (2014b). Integration of Immigrants through Football: the Case of Turkish-Speaking Communities in London. In: Icduygu, A. & Goker, Z. G. (eds.) *Rethinking Migration and Incorporation in the Context of Transnationalism and Neoliberalism.* Istanbul: ISIS Press.

Unutulmaz, K. O. (2015). Ethnic Community Football in Integration Policy: Case of Turkish Football Leagues in London. In: M. A. Icbay, H. Arslan, & S. M. Stanciu (Eds.), *Contemporary Studies in Humanities*. Mannheim: Ehrmanm Verlag.

Usta, N. (1997). *Menzil Nakşiliği: Sosyolojik Bir Araştırma*. Ankara: Töre Yayınları.

Verkuyten, M. & Martinovic, B. (2012). Immigrants' national identification: Meanings, determinants, and consequences. *Social Issues and Policy Review*, 6(1), 82-112.

Voicu, B. & Comşa, M. (2014). "Immigrants' Participation in Voting: Exposure, Resilience, and Transferability", *Journal of Ethnic and Migration Studies*, Vol.40, No. 10, pp. 1572-192.

White, J.B. (1994). *Money Makes Us Relatives: Women's Labor in Urban Turkey*. Austin: University of Texas Press.

World Bank (2013). Migration and Remittance Flows: Recent Trends and Outlook, 2013-2016, *Migration and Development Brief* 21, October 2013,

World Bank (2015). *Migration and Remittances Factbook 2015*. Washington DC, US: The World Bank (Available at: http://www.worldbank.org/prospects/migrationandremittances).

World Bank and IFC-International Finance Corporation (2009). *Remittance Prices Worldwide, Making Markets more Transparent*. Home page.

World Bank and International Bank for Reconstruction and Development (2006). *Global Economic Prospects: Economic Implications of Remittances and Migration*. Washington, DC: World Bank and International Bank for Reconstruction and Development.

World Bank (2014). Bilateral Remittance Matrix 2014, 2013, 2012, 2011, 2010 http://www.worldbank.org/en/topic/migrationremittancesdiasporaissues/brief/migration -remittances-data Accessed: 03.03.2016.

Wright, S. & Kurtoglu-Hooton, N. (2006). Language maintenance: the case of a Turkish-speaking community in Birmingham. *International journal of the sociology of language* (181), 43-56.

Yazgan, P. (2010). Danimarka'daki Türkiye kökenli göçmenlerin aidiyet ve kimlikleri. PhD Dissertation, Sakarya University, Turkey. http://dspace.sozlutarih.org.tr/bitstream/handle/20.500.11834/188/265886.pdf

Yazgan, P. (2016). Hareketlilikte Kimlik İnşasına Yönelik Analitik Bir Çerçeve. *Göç Dergisi*, 3(2), 282-296. http://www.tplondon.com/dergi/index.php/ gd/ article/view/100 Accessed: 10/12/2016.

Yazgan, P. & Sirkeci, I. (2012). Financial Crisis and Remittances from Denmark to Turkey. In: Sirkeci, I., Cohen, J. H., & Ratha, D. (Eds.). (2012). *Migration and remittances during the global financial crisis and beyond*. Washington DC: World Bank Publications, pp.301-307.

Yazgan, P., Utku, D. E., & Sirkeci, I. (2015). Syrian crisis and migration. *Migration Letters*, 12(3), 181-192.

Yiadom, L. B. (2008). *Rural-Urban Linkages and Welfare: The Case of Ghana's Migration and Remittance Flows*. Bath: University of Bath.

YSK (Yüksek Seçim Kurulu) (2015). 25. Dönem Milletvekili Genel Seçimi Sandık Sonuçları, https://sonuc.ysk.gov.tr/module/ssps.jsf, accessed: 13 August 2015.

Zeyneloğlu, S. & Sirkeci, I. (2015). Türkiye'de Almanlar ve Almancılar. In: Seker, B.D., I. Sirkeci, M. Yucesahin (eds.) *Göç ve Uyum*. London: Transnational Press London, pp.217-266.

Zeyneloğlu, S., Sirkeci, I., & Civelek, Y. (2016). Language shift among Kurds in Turkey: A spatial and demographic analysis. *Kurdish Studies*, 4(1), 25-50.

Index

www.ingramcontent.com/pod-product-compliance
Lightning Source LLC
Chambersburg PA
CBHW020245290326
41930CB00038B/355